THE LURKING HYDRA

South Asia's Terror Travail

THE LURKING HYDRA

SOUTH ASIA'S TERROR TRAVAIL

Lt Gen (Dr) Subroto Mitra
PVSM, AVSM, SM, VSM

PENTAGON PRESS LLP

THE LURKING HYDRA: South Asia's Terror Travail
by Lt Gen (Dr) Subroto Mitra PVSM, AVSM, SM, VSM

First Published in 2022

ISBN 978-93-90095-55-1

Disclaimer: The views and opinions expressed in the book are the individual assertion of the Author in his personal capacity and do not have any official endorsement. Moreover the Publisher does not take any responsibility for the same in any manner whatsoever. Attributability of the contents lies purely with the Author.

Published by
PENTAGON PRESS LLP
206, Peacock Lane, Shahpur Jat
New Delhi-110049
Phones: 011-64706243, 26491568
Telefax: 011-26490600
email: rajan@pentagonpress.in
website: www.pentagonpress.in

Printed at Aegean Offset Printers, Greater Noida, U.P.

CONTENTS

FOREWORD

Lt Gen Subroto Mitra, the author of this book, was a colleague and a great friend. So, when his wife Mrs Pushpita Mitra asked me to write the Foreword for his book, I was elated at the honour accorded to me. Gen Mitra and I attended the Higher Command Course (HCC) together and developed great affinity with each other. I found him extremely well read and possessing a wonderful sense of humour which he expressed only with people he was very familiar with. People with a sense of humour invariably have a sharp mind and that was so with him too. Not a very expressive person by nature, Gen Mitra never held back from those with whom he felt he had similar ideas and beliefs. There were long journeys during the HCC-27 and we often teamed up to sit together and discuss the world. We were both deeply interested in geopolitics and international security issues. He had a good knowledge of history, a subject with which I have been associated for many years. That is what gave him the power to discuss wider issues with relative ease. 1998-99 were the years when international terror had not reached its peak but was slowly emerging as one of the major post Cold War threats for the world. Its only when 9/11 occurred and the Global War on Terror commenced that terrorism and counter terrorism became the subjects of focus. South Asia, on which Gen Mitra has focused this book is a region hugely affected by terror threats. That is primarily because many of the ingredients of terror situations exist here. Poverty, wide disparity in income and standards of living, non-realization of aspirations, poor standards of education and many times questionable standards of governance, characterised by high levels of corruption makes for such situations.

Infused into this, radical ideology harping on faith, came like a dose of poison and the lethality increased by many levels. These are all issues prevailing within nations in South Asia but the very nature of the subcontinent being Indo-centric in nature provides the avenues for transnational links which is extremely helpful for terror organisations and demands greater cooperation among South Asian nations.

Gen Mitra served in the North East with his unit but his tenures as a Brigade Commander and a General Officer Commanding (GOC) of a division were in J&K. He commanded the 87 Infantry Brigade in the Rajouri sector and later 28 Infantry Division in Kashmir. Both were very challenging assignments where the hard core practical aspects of terrorism and asymmetric warfare were experienced on an everyday basis. Such experience in Flag rank adds much to the knowledge of warfare at strategic, operational and tactical level. The proxy war that has been going on in J&K for the last 33 years needs a high degree of application of kinetics to eliminate terrorists who form a part of the human resource elements of proxy war. What most people do not realize is the fact that kinetics and hard power are just subsets of proxy war. Terrorism is known to have systems which network human resources, material resources, finance conduits, over ground workers (OGWs), street turbulence, media and information systems, ideology and culture, and a whole gamut of domains which keep springing up from time to time. Its not just the terrorist who with his weapons and skewed thinking, is the one conducting acts of mindless terror. Behind him there are networks that strategize and manage so that terrorism continues to aim at achieving the objectives that have been laid out. The system of Counter Terrorism is therefore far beyond the common public understanding that concentrates on eliminating terrorists and hoping that terror will simply disappear. For neutralizing proxy war, which uses terrorism as one of its subsets, a comprehensive understanding of all the other sub-parts is an absolute necessity. While much has been written on this, the Indian context of counter terrorism has been missing detailed research based literature especially that which is also based upon ground experience. Theoretical expertise exists in fair quantum but there has been a dearth of synchronised research which reflects both the depth of theory, concept, practice and experience.

Gen Mitra was one senior Indian Army officer who had the right understanding based on experience and wide study of trans-national terrorism. He wished to pursue an academic course to crown his military career and rightly chose terrorism and counter terrorism as the themes for his research. He read widely for this and the effect of that makes itself evident in the layout, content and arguments in this book which has been aptly titled – 'The Lurking Hydra: South Asia's Terror Travail'.

Lt Gen Subroto Mitra did not live long enough to see his thesis getting approved for publication. It is his wife Mrs Pushpita Mitra who pursued the project and ensured its fruition. A work of this nature may just have disappeared into oblivion if this effort had not been put in by Mrs Pushpita Mitra. I feel privileged to have assisted in a small way to bring the hard work put in by Gen Mitra to public knowledge. I am sure the good General will remain proud of his work which actually gives an in-depth insight into the various facets of terrorism and counter terrorism in South Asia. It is immensely readable and the fact that the mind of an experienced Indian Army General Officer has analysed the entire theme minutely and presented it here makes it a virtual authority.

Noida
09 Mar 2022

Lt Gen Syed Ata Hasnain
PVSM, UYSM, AVSM, SM, VSM & BAR (Retd)

FOREWORD

An Officer and a Gentleman, that is how I remember General Subroto Mitra. An able leader but also an unassuming kind-hearted individual whose dedication to scholarship was all the more appreciable, given the huge task bestowed upon him as GOC ATNK&K Area and later as GOC Delhi Area. He was ever willing to help whoever sought assistance in whatever manner possible.

In a climate where doctoral thesis writing was deemed onerous by many due to lack of focus, rigour or discipline, General Mitra completed the dissertation in a relatively short time. Never using his official duties as excuse to evade academic process, he was determined to follow all dictates of the institution in letter and spirit.

General Mitra used to frequently interact with younger co-researchers at the department. He also addressed other students whenever he could find time. He was open to suggestions and inputs from much younger students as well as faculty while he was ready to offer his valuable wisdom to them.

In his choice of terrorism as the field of enquiry for his thesis, there was a deep sense of anguish and humanitarian concern for the havoc wrecked by this scourge on the entire region. He was particularly disturbed by the effect terror had on innocent civilians including women and children of South Asia as a whole. As an experienced soldier who had first-hand dealt with the issue during many of his assignments, he brought clarity and in-depth analysis to the subject of study.

The book, though being published posthumously has remained literally intact and unchanged filled with General Mitra's insights. He has commented extensively on the Afghan situation and he clearly brought out the difficulty in handling a Taliban-controlled country and rightly pointed the need for continuation of humanitarian help for the people of the war-torn and terror-plagued nation. The recent Indian government despatch of relief materials to the people of Afghanistan is an illustration of his suggestion. His analysis of the impact of terror in Pakistan as a nation and particularly on its people is very incisive. Expressing faith in the regional multilateral mechanisms like SAARC, he suggests ways it could be strengthened to counter terrorism. Another interesting idea is the creation of an ICJ-like SAARC court to address terror issues.

In the words, "Nimbleness of thought and action is generally not associated with governments, but that is the precise requirement of the day to deal with rapidly emergent situations, worldwide", General Mitra reflects a wider understanding of word and deed beyond the confines of the subject in question. His futuristic vision of raising an air national guard to effectively deal with emerging aerial threats is especially relevant given the growing number of drone-capture incidents along the sensitive Indo-Pak border in recent times.

In enabling India to face terror in the future he dwells upon capacity-building among youth in a big way. Volunteer National Development Service that equips civil service aspirants as well as technically-skilled youth in contributing to rural environment is a sample of his holistic approach to handling this vexing problem of terror and addressing its roots.

Each and every suggestion he has offered in his conclusion can be taken up for further examination and research by students of security and strategic studies. Though the book talks extensively on the South Asian region, it offers immense scope for interpretation for other terror-affected areas of the world. This book thus would certainly serve as a guide to not only researchers but civil and military practitioners as well.

I wish to congratulate Mrs Pushpita Mitra and the Pentagon Press LLP for taking the initiative to bring out this insightful work for wider dissemination.

Dr S. Utham Kumar Jamadhagni
Professor & Head, Dept of Defence and Strategic Studies
University of Madras

PROLOGUE

Soon after India attained its independence, it had become clear to the Western nations that the rich bounty of natural resources/raw material to feed their burgeoning economies like petroleum and natural gas, would no longer be freely available as the growing sentiment for independence among the subjugated Asian nations was becoming stronger day by day.

India commands an important strategic position on the globe with respect to trade as well as social and cultural interaction. These geographical features provide India a significant edge in international trade as it is favourably located on the world's highway of trade and commerce, both to the east and the west.

It was India's status as the principal entry point in a highly profitable oceanic trade structure that has been attracting the West Asian Muslims and the European colonial powers towards India. It has been a fulcrum upon which the power and commercial system in Asia was balanced.

Consequently, the West found it in their best interest to keep these newly-independent nations weak and off balance. All this was to continue exploiting the wealth of the land of Asia!

While India and a few of the other littoral states appear to be on a path of sustained economic progress, most of the region is characterised by high levels of poverty, and international and internal conflict, making it a key venue for international piracy. For these reasons and others, the region has given rise to an "insecurity community" which has played into the hands of local and international terrorists, thus becoming a broad incubator of terrorism and posing additional challenges of violence, terrorism, and instability across the entire Indian Ocean region.

With trade volumes increasing by the day due to booming production, land routes are no longer able to manage the large bulk of trade. The sea routes are the new commercial highways. As a result, the littoral states of the Indian Ocean will come under heavy pressure.

However, they would have to gear up their defences to meet the threats of impending terrorism. India therefore will need to give full support for the defence of its territorial waters, emerging as the principle nation to thwart the designs of predatory powers. India and these littoral states would be better placed to meet these challenges.

Col Shanti Swaroop
1st Commanding Officer of 28 Madras

PREFACE

This work is the result of having witnessed the havoc wrought by terrorism, insurgencies, and other violent upheavals in our country and in neighbouring nations. SAARC member-states, all of which were once part of the British Empire or allied to it, formed the association for geopolitical and economic reasons in December 1985 in pursuance of commonality. Political and social factors and developments led to steady and sometimes rapid decline of governance in most of these nations, consequent to which internal turmoil surfaced and boiled over, predictably aided and abetted, overtly or covertly, by foreign powers keen on destabilising weak states. For any student of history and the geopolitics of SAARC nations, comprehending the background and arriving at solutions to deal with the fallout of such turmoil leading to increasing terror-related activities mandates that greater attention be paid to India's expanding areas of interest and influence in the light of the Global War on Terror (GWOT). GWOT has emerged, consequent to the invasion of Afghanistan by the Soviets and subsequently as a follow up to the First Gulf War, leading to an increase in terror-related strikes worldwide. The growth of terrorism-induced instability in large parts of North Africa, West Asia, the SAARC nations, and the Indian Ocean Region (IOR) can be attributed to the spectacular rise of Islamic fundamentalism over the past two decades.

It has often been said that the 21st century is destined to be Asia's century, and in this, the principal claimants for becoming dominant world powers, India and China, are also the oldest civilisations in the world. Both have seen rapid growth, urbanisation, religion/politics-based self-righteousness, burgeoning populations, as well as recent economic booms having emerged from self-imposed economic shackles, bound by Nehruvian Socialism on the one hand and Mao's Communism in the case of the other. Market-driven economies and aspirations clash with realities and give vent to anger directed towards the State. Consequently, turbulence gives way to radicalisation (religion or ideal-based) of vast segments of population, leading ultimately to terrorism-driven activities and movements. Interestingly enough, intra-Islamic religious conflicts are taking place in the West Asian Region with spill-overs into Africa. The recent mass migration of refugees from the Levant and North Africa into Europe, due to turbulence in these regions, has brought into focus the emerging contours of conflict in the coming times, with a potential clash of civilisations—Christian/Hindu/Sinic—arrayed against a strident Islam in the offing.

The South Asian Region, which forms the sub-Himalayan rim nations, essentially encompassing SAARC countries besides Myanmar and Iran and, to an extent, China, on the periphery is a region in ferment. Essentially, the problem is terrorism in its various avatars—be it internationally-sponsored, domestic, or political. It runs the risk of manifesting the full bandwidth of bio, cyber, economic, nuclear, narco, neo, environmental and nano or state terrorism. It has been practised by states, non-state actors, fundamentalists, fringe groups and allied organisations out to weaken the democratic and secular fabric of our nation and cripple its economic development.

Sir Halford J. Mackinder's oft-quoted dictum, *"Who rules East Europe commands the Heartland; Who rules the Heartland commands the World island; Who rules the World Island commands the World"* predicted that the future led to a large extent in the monsoon lands of India and China. Nicholas Spykman famously quoted, *"Who controls the Rimland rules Eurasia, who rules Eurasia controls the destinies of the world"*. The Rimland has great importance coming from its demographic weight, natural resources, and industrial development. Spykman sees this importance as the reason that the Rimland will be crucial to containing the Heartland. The geo-political dynamics of the Rimland has acquired the dimension of New Great Game of the 21st century. As the USA and China become great power rivals, the Indian sub-continental mass looms as the ultimate pivot in the Rimland. K.M. Pannikar had forecast that were Pakistan and Hindustan (India) integrated conditionally; there would be no problems of peace being disrupted in South East Asia.

Political fallouts notwithstanding, the Indian subcontinent, which spans all of erstwhile British protectorates or were part of the Empire and now members of SAARC or having observer status, have a common thread. Most of them were created out of artificially induced boundaries and the wounds still show. Trade, development and the need to progress have, however, broken most barriers and interdependence exists through the medium of various alliances—South Asian Association of Regional Cooperation (SAARC), Bay of Bengal Initiative for Multi-Sectoral Technical and Economic Cooperation (BIMSTEC), Mekong–Ganga Cooperation (MGC), Association of South East Asian Nations (ASEAN), Shanghai Cooperation Organisation (SCO), and Economic Cooperation Organisation (ECO). The region, however, is in constant ferment as the Global Peace Index 2015 shows it to be the second-most conflict ridden area in the world with Afghanistan (160), Pakistan (154), India (143) and Myanmar (130) ranked out of 160 countries assessed, with only Bhutan ranked as the 18th most peaceful nation. The costs of direct containments of violence as a percentage of GDP ranges from a high for Afghanistan (21%), Myanmar (8.1%), and Pakistan (6.9%) to a lower 2.4% for Nepal, Bangladesh at 1.9% and Bhutan only 0.5%. This effectively puts into perspective the allocation of funding for development issues.

The wounds of the partition to form India and Pakistan fester for a variety of reasons—religion and the baggage of history being prime drivers in the sub-continent. Musharraf let the cat out of the bag when he termed South Asia as the most dangerous place on Earth, carefully omitting to mention whose culpability it derived from. India has suffered enormous losses due to its tolerance, restraint and poor legislative practices in dealing with terrorism—internal or imported. For example, the Mumbai terror strike of 2008, when 10 terrorists held the nation to ransom for four days, cost insurance agencies an estimated INR 1,400 crore, not including other losses, besides *man days* lost, in a shutdown of virtually the entire megapolis.

'Terrorism & Insurgency' moved to the third position of risk ranking by corporate India in 2015, up from 10th in 2014, highlighting the need to re-align security standards and measures, if India is to emerge economically stronger than before. Emerging trends in the sub-continent and amongst SAARC nations, on the contours of terrorist actions and activities in the light of the prevailing security scenario indicate that the unstable states forming the Islamic Crescent, exacerbated by the emerging ISIS and instability in most of the Rimland and SAARC nations, presages continued vulnerability to nation-states in this region. Also, jihadist violence will increasingly spillover from the ISIS and Afghanistan into the Rimland and SAARC nations in the coming decade(s) leading to greater fragility of the security situation post the US withdrawal from Afghanistan. Religious fundamentalism is becoming stronger than before. The increased vulnerability of the civilian populace as well as industrial/economic assets and their preference by terrorists over traditional government and military targets has been observed. The emergence of a growing band of well-educated, cyber and media-savvy, highly motivated manpower in the ranks of terrorists is another worrisome factor. Information and cyber security issues are now ranked second in terms of threats to the Indian economy. Organised crime, i.e., illegal drug trade and arms trafficking, both of which are adjuncts to terrorism, is on the increase and these crimes, per se, are rated the fifth-most important threat to the nation's economy.

It is important that India recalibrates its foreign and economic policy backed by adequate and appropriate military power and includes in its area of interest, the whole of the Indian Ocean Region up to Indonesia, Malaysia, the erstwhile Indo-China region, Thailand, Myanmar, Tibet the Xinjiang provinces of China, Afghanistan, the energy-rich *Sthans*, Iran, the Middle East, West Asia, North Africa and the East African coast in addition to the SAARC nations forming an area of influence to form a bulwark against any threats that may emerge. The phenomenal Indian Diaspora, residing in most of these nations, approximately 18 million PIOs and NRIs out of a total of 28 million, are a rich resource force multiplier—both in terms of financial as well as physical assets, and needs to be tapped in order to secure our frontiers even better.

Lt Gen (Dr) Subroto Mitra PVSM AVSM SM VSM

CHAPTER 1

SOUTH ASIA'S TERROR TOPOGRAPHY

Background

The security challenges to India and its neighbouring countries is a pointer to the importance of the geographical location of the Indian subcontinent and its neighbourhood. Termed as Monsoon Asia, and located demographically and strategically at the crossroads of the Pacific and Indian Oceans, India, and its neighbouring countries are ideally poised to be the hub of this century.[1] In proximity to the storehouse of Africa on its west, with the energy-rich Gulf states and Central Asian Republics (CAR) to its northwest, Tibet, China and the vast Russian heartland to its north and with teeming East and South East Asia, all of which are part of what Mackinder referred to as the 'World Island', it is ideally located to dominate events of the 21st century. The rimland of Eurasia[2] with India as its core, commands the Indian Ocean seaplanes, through which transits annually, two-thirds of the world's seaborne trade in oil, 50 per cent of the world's seaborne container traffic, one-third of the world's seaborne bulk cargo and the world's highest tonnage in the seaborne transportation of goods, reportedly involving some 100,000 ships that transit the Indian Ocean and its adjacent waterways.[3] Piracy, at one time rampant in the Horn of Africa, is no longer a threat in being, due to coordinated anti-piracy measures.

The rise of Islamic fundamentalism in the swathe extending

eastwards from North Africa encompassing Saudi Arabia, Syria, Iraq, Iran, Afghanistan and Pakistan, has been witness to the Arab Spring and the rise of the Islamic States of Iraq and Syria (ISIS) and is the epicentre of what some call an 'Arc of Crisis'[4] stretching from the Horn of Africa to the Indian subcontinent.

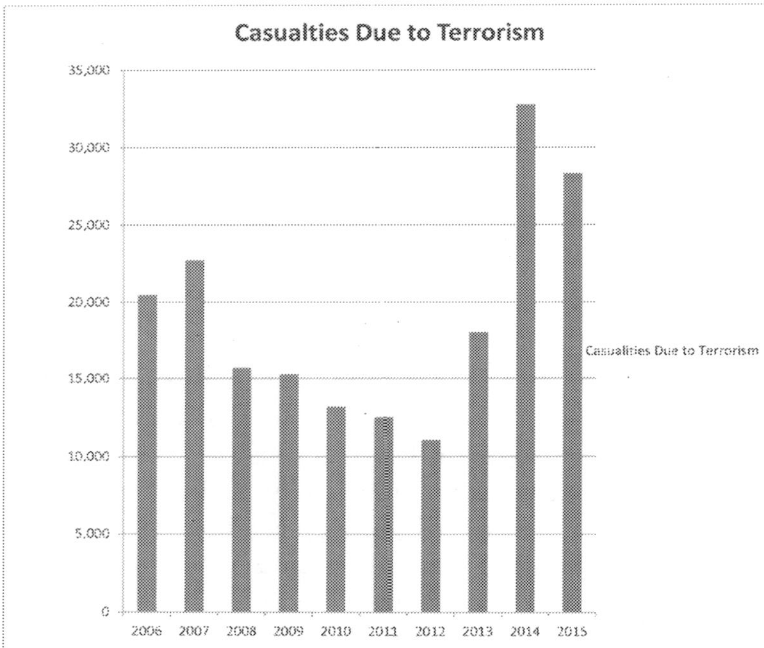

Source: U.S. Department of State & The Statistics Portal

The root causes that give rise to terrorism have been deliberated upon in a large number of studies. It is generally agreed that a lack of good governance and democracy, civil liberties and the rule of law are preconditions for many forms of domestic terrorism.[5] To that, we can add the factor of religious fundamentalism as evidenced from the spurt of such a sustained phenomenon worldwide and especially in the Indian subcontinent.[6]

Origins of Terrorism and its Spread in the Subcontinent

Terrorism is not a recent phenomenon; it has been described differently by Kautilya in his treatise on statecraft in the third century BCE. The Sicarii are recorded as having carried out extremist activities as part of Jewish resistance to Roman rule in the region, in the first century BCE. The Hashhashin, from whose name is derived the English word 'assassin', were a secretive Islamic sect that was known to be active in Iran and Syria from the 11th to the 13th centuries and were responsible for the killings of key functionaries of the Abbasid Caliphate and the Seljuk Empire. The freedom fighters in the Indian sub-continent, post 1857, dubbed as terrorists by the British, were dealt with summarily—either executed or sent off to political exile to the Andamans. Terrorism, post-independence, took on the form of violent insurgencies in the Naga, Mizo, and Cachar hills, but these rarely transcended the confines of state boundaries, notwithstanding active support by China and the former East Pakistan. Khalistani separatists during the 1980s, and later Kashmiri separatists, trained and actively supported by Pakistan, began their first forays into India and carried out bomb blasts and targeted innocent people in different states and cities.

The global epicentres of terrorism happen to be located in India's backyard—Pakistan, the nursery; Afghanistan, the training ground—and from where jihadists are sent to battle 'infidels' in and around the region. There has been an increase in foreign 'recruits' in almost all terrorist-affected spots around the globe, so much so that the United Nations (UN) Security Council plans to press countries to update their laws to make travelling abroad to join a terrorist group a serious criminal offence, in the hope of stemming the flow of fresh foreign recruits into the ISIS.[7] Some 12,000 fighters from 74 nations have travelled to Syria and Iraq to fight with extremist groups, as stated by Peter Neumann, a professor at the International Centre for the Study of Radicalisation and Political Violence at King's College, London, as reported by Reuters.[8] It is clear that participation in terrorism has acquired ominous overtones and transcended transnational boundaries—the Pakistani military operation in North Waziristan, called 'Zarb-e-Azb', is focused exclusively on foreign fighters from the Islamic Movement of Uzbekistan and the Turkistan Islamic Party, as well as the Taliban in Pakistan.[9]

Utterances ascribed to Al Zawahiri of a new Al Qaeda franchise—Al Qaeda in the Indian subcontinent,[10] to announce the revival of the

Al Qaeda in Afghanistan has been taken note of. Consequent to the death of Bin Laden, and with the rise of the ISIS and its establishment of a caliphate in captured territory in Iraq and Syria, the Al Qaeda had been on the wane. However, with this new franchise of the Al Qaeda, the focus will switch to India and its South Asian neighbours, in particular to Buddhist Myanmar and Sri Lanka, both of which have Muslim minorities, that were recently targeted by local religious zealots; Bangladesh with an overwhelming Muslim population, seemingly tolerant of its minorities and India, where tensions simmer between dominant Hindus and a sizeable Muslim population. Considering the slow return to normalcy in Hindu Nepal (now constitutionally defined as 'secular'), with a stable but militarily weak Buddhist Bhutan, predominantly Islamic Maldives and an embattled Islamic Pakistan, the entry of the Al Qaeda into this huge swathe, affects the lives of millions and seriously challenges existing security and stability amongst the South Asian Association for Regional Cooperation (SAARC) nations.

SAARC

SAARC, a regional, geopolitical, and economic organisation, was set up by a charter on 8 December 1985 at Dhaka and with the exception of The Maldives, an archipelago in the Indian Ocean, all other member-countries—Bangladesh, Bhutan, India, Nepal, Pakistan, and Sri Lanka—are located in the Indian subcontinent. Afghanistan became a member only in April 2007. SAARC has five observer countries—China, Japan, South Korea, the European Union and the USA. Of the eight-member states, India occupies the pre-eminent position in terms of location, size, and population, and economic and military strength. Commonalities run deep between member-nations, with the bulk of the nations having been part or protectorates of the British Empire. Bhutan has been guided by India in matters of external affairs since 1949 and The Maldives has historical linkages with the Indian subcontinent.

The SAARC nations together constitute an economic powerhouse with the World Bank expecting growth in the region to exceed 7.6 per cent in 2016.[11] The short- and medium-term outlook for SAARC points towards continued macro-economic stability and relatively strong growth, with potential downside risks concentrated on the fiscal side. It is home to more than 1.7 billion people in the world with approximately a third of the populace being urban dwellers. Nearly 55 per cent of the population is in the age group of 15-65, the annual GDP increase has been a steady 8 per cent,[12] and unemployment is high at an average of 25.61 per cent (2010). South Asia has experienced a long period of robust economic growth and has been among the fastest growing in the world. This strong growth has translated into declining poverty and impressive improvements in human development. However, poverty in the region remains high. About 399 million people, 40 per cent of the world's poor, live on less than $ 1.25 a day. More than 200 million people live in slums, and half a billion people go without electricity. Many countries in the region suffer from extreme forms of social exclusion and huge infrastructure gaps, and the larger countries are experiencing increases in inequality. Development in the region will be the key to meeting global poverty and prosperity goals.

SAARC will play an important role in the global development story as it takes its place in the Asian century. It has the world's largest working-age population, a quarter of the world's middle-class consumers, the largest number of poor and undernourished in the world, and several fragile states of global geopolitical importance. With inclusive growth, South Asia has the potential to change global poverty.[13] The World Bank has averred that to unlock the SAARC region's development potential, the countries must focus on regional economic integration considering that its intra-regional trade accounts for just 5 per cent of the total trade, compared to 25 per cent[14] in the Association of Southeast Asian Nations (ASEAN). Given the commonalities of historical and cultural ties that bind the nations, there exists considerable scope to enhance growth whilst addressing the issues of social inclusion, and climate and environmental management, besides bringing in good governance.

However, as an entity, this region which earlier had the dubious distinction of being the most unsafe in the world, SAARC fared slightly better in the Global Peace Index (GPI) 2015 rankings than the

Middle East and North Africa (MENA), with a regional average of 2.352 for the former and 2.385 for the latter, which is now considered as the most volatile region in the world.[15] Not surprisingly, terrorism, political instability and militarisation has taken its toll with the state of peace rated 'Very Low' in Pakistan and Afghanistan, with only Bhutan and Mauritius ranking 'Very High', Nepal at 'High', Bangladesh and Sri Lanka at 'Medium', and India ranked 'Low'.[16] The direct violence containment costs are very high for Afghanistan at 31 per cent of the GDP, Bhutan 9 per cent, Pakistan 8 per cent, Sri Lanka and India 5 per cent, Mauritius 4 per cent, and Nepal and Bangladesh at 3 per cent each.[17] These costs stem primarily from expenditures on internal security, losses from conflicts, terrorism, lost production from refugees who are no longer part of the economy, and incremental expenditures for national police and private security presence. It also represents both direct and indirect costs, which, had there been a reduction in violence, would be utilised in other areas of economic, health and educational activities and for making the environment safer and more productive. By understanding and addressing the social and economic drivers of violence, policymakers and business leaders can better understand the costs and benefits of particular social and economic investment programs. Furthermore, by directing resources towards addressing the root causes of violence, society can begin to make long-term investments in the creation of a virtuous cycle of peace and economic prosperity.[18] For example, a study looking at the effect of terrorism in Spain estimated that each transnational terrorism incident in the years 1970-91 was estimated to dissuade 140,000 tourists. This had the effect of decreasing large amounts of revenue from tourist expenditure and flow-on effects within the local economy. Consequently, with greater levels of violence, it is likely that we would expect lower levels of employment and economic productivity over the long-term, as the incentives faced discourage new employment creation and longer-term investment.[19]

In terms of parameters for the Human Development Index, formulated by the UNDP, the SAARC nations fare poorly. This annual composite statistics of life expectancy, education, and income per capita indicators encapsulate the progressive improvements in qualities of life, and ranks inequality in income, health, and education.

The report says that inequality has declined in health access, remained constant in education, but increased by two percentage points with respect to income. India is ranked at 130, among the 'medium development' countries with Bhutan (132) and Bangladesh (142) too figuring in this category —Sri Lanka (73) and The Maldives (104), are pegged as High Development Nations. Nepal (ranked 145), Pakistan (147), and Afghanistan (171) are in the 'low development' category.[20] There is an intrinsic relationship between work and human development—work bonds people and serves as a foundation for social cohesion and stable societies. SAARC nations have high population and unemployment rates, a fertile combination for unrest and an available captive audience for radicalisation of its foot soldiers.

Geographic Extent of Conflict induced by Non-State Actors in South Asia

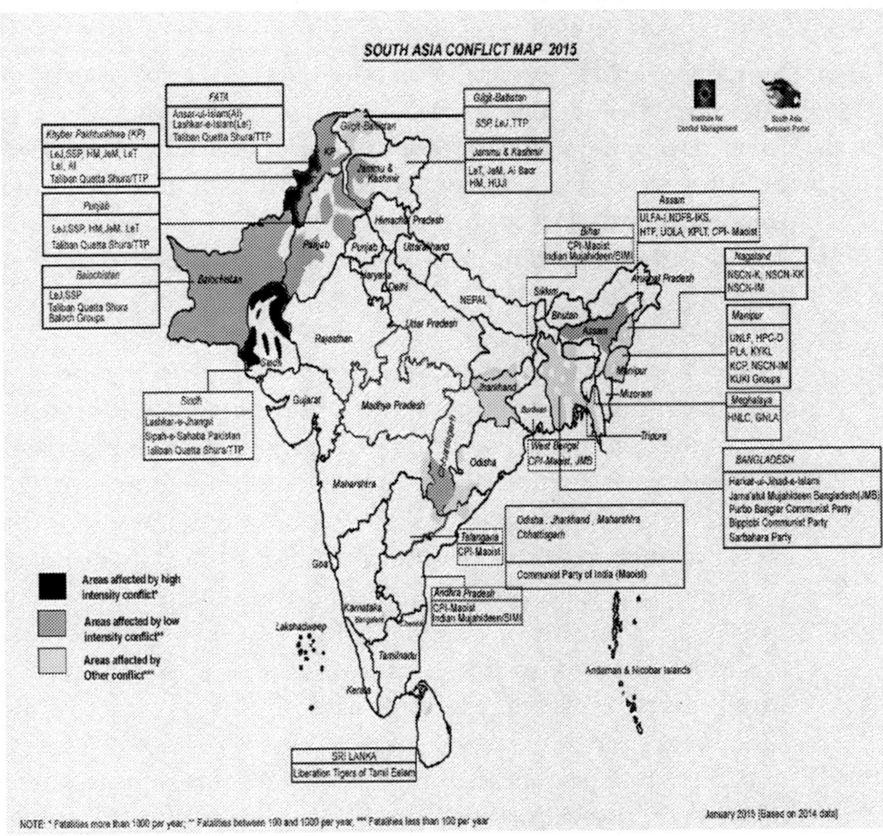

Source: http://www.satp.org/satporgtp/southasia/images/conflict_map.html

Definitions

The United Nations has yet to arrive at a consensus[21] on an acceptable definition of terrorism[22] because of a divergence of views over issues concerning self-determination and liberation struggles. It is interesting to note that the League of Nations, in its 1937 Convention for the Prevention and Punishment of Terrorism, defined Acts of Terrorism as "Criminal acts directed against a State and intended or calculated to create a state of terror in the minds of particular persons or a group of persons or the general public".[23]

India, for long a victim of terrorism, defines a terrorist act thus, "Whoever does any act with intent to threaten or likely to threaten the unity, integrity, security or sovereignty of India or with intent to strike terror or likely to strike terror in the people or any section of the people in India or in any foreign country,

(a) by using bombs, dynamite or other explosive substances or inflammable substances, or

(b) firearms or other lethal weapons or poisonous or noxious gases or other chemicals or by any other substances (whether biological, radioactive, nuclear or otherwise) of a hazardous nature or by any other means of whatever nature to cause or likely to cause:

  (i) death of, or injuries to, any person or persons; or

  (ii) loss of, or damage to, or destruction of, property; or

  (iii) disruption of any supplies or services essential for the life of the community in India or in any foreign country; or

(c) damage or destruction of any property in India or in a foreign country used or intended to be used for the defence of India or in connection with any other purposes of the Government of India, any State Government or any of their agencies; or overawes by means of criminal force or the show of criminal force or attempts to do so or causes death of any public functionary or attempts to cause death of any public functionary; or

(d) detains kidnaps or abducts any person and threatens to kill or injure such person or does any other act in order to compel the Government of India, any State Government or the government of a foreign country or any other person to do or abstain from doing any act, commits a terrorist act."[24]

India's Second Administrative Reforms Committee in its 8th Report specifies the different Types of terrorism[25] as under:

Ethno-Nationalist Terrorism: Defined, as deliberate violence by a sub-national ethnic group to advance its cause. Tamil nationalist groups in Sri Lanka and insurgent groups in North-East India are prime examples.

Religious Terrorism: Its practitioners being motivated either in whole or in part by a religious imperative and consider violence as a divine duty or a sacramental act. The Islamic State of Iraq and Syria (ISIS) and the Lashkar-e-Taiba (LeT) are the best examples.

Ideology-Oriented Terrorism: Ideology used to support the use of violence and terrorism, divided into Right- and Left-wing terrorism.

Left-wing Terrorism: Violence against the ruling elite, mostly by the peasant class, motivated by what are called Leftist ideologies. Maoist groups in India and Nepal are classified thus.

Right-wing Terrorism: Violence to maintain the status quo or to return to some past situation that the group feels should have been conserved, examples being the Nazis in Germany, Fascists in Italy and white supremacist groups in Europe and the USA.

Narco-Terrorism: Violence by narcotics traffickers to influence government policies, for example, Al Qaeda, Islamic Movement of Uzbekistan, Islamic Jihad in Palestine, Hezbollah in Lebanon.

State-sponsored Terrorism: State-sponsored terrorism or warfare by proxy, initiated to obtain certain clearly defined foreign policy objectives. Pakistan, Iran, Sudan, and North Korea have been active sponsors of such political violence against their enemies.

India has been a victim of state-sponsored terrorism from the dawn of Independence, which saw Pakistan unleash tribal raiders[26] backed by disguised regular army troops to seize the Kashmir Valley on the Maharaja's domain, a campaign that persists till today, with former Pakistan President Pervez Musharraf admitting that Islamabad supported and trained groups like the Lashkar-e-Taiba (LeT) to carry out militancy in Kashmir.[27] The insurgency in the North-East was actively supported and sponsored by China and also by Pakistan through its then eastern wing.[28] Trans-national affinities have allowed safe sanctuaries to develop in the lesser-administered regions abounding India in Burma (now Myanmar), Bhutan, and Nepal for terror groups that sought and received external patronage.[29] The left wing extremism (LWE) manifesting in the central and eastern parts of India owes its origins to peasant uprisings and the Naxalite movement of the 1960s.[30] LWE or Maoists have reported linkages with Maoist guerrillas of Nepal and with the Liberation Tigers of Tamil Eelam (LTTE).[31] The support of China to the Maoists of Nepal is well documented, being a stepping stone to its security interests.[32] Sanctuaries in Bangladesh for India's North-Eastern insurgent groups were provided for by the Director-General of Forces Intelligence in connivance with Pakistan's ISI.[33]

India has been blamed, rightly or wrongly, by its neighbouring countries, for its support, tacit or otherwise, to terror groups. Pakistan has always blamed India for the problems in Baluchistan and Karachi,[34] ignoring its own home grown terror groups, likened by Hillary Clinton as having "snakes in its backyard".[35] Nepal has also indirectly blamed India for not doing enough to contain Nepalese Maoist activities in the Indian border states of Uttar Pradesh, Bihar, and Bengal.[36] India had directly intervened in Sri Lanka in the arming of the LTTE, and its training and financing,[37] and with the deployment of the ill-fated Indian Peace Keeping Force, consequent to the 1987 Indo-Sri Lankan Agreement; the mission ended in failure in 1990.[38]

Notwithstanding the definitions mentioned above, the same Administrative Reforms Committee has opined that "A comprehensive and effective legal framework to deal with all aspects of terrorism needs to be enacted. The law should have adequate safeguards to prevent its misuse".[39] Ironically, no clear-cut definition of what constituted terrorism emerged, despite a plethora of various enactments including The Unlawful Activities (Prevention) Act, 1967 [as amended by the Unlawful Activities (Prevention) Amendment Act, 2004]; The National Security Act, 1980; Terrorist and Disruptive Activities (Prevention) Act, 1985 and 1987 (allowed to lapse in 1995) and The Prevention of Terrorism Act, 2002 (repealed in 2004). It has also been recommended that there was a requirement to define more clearly those criminal acts that could be construed as being terrorist in nature.[40] Due to political expediencies, dilution and repeals, existing laws to fight terrorism, have proved ineffective in the case involving the assassination of Rajiv Gandhi, the former Prime Minister.[41]

The main counter-terror arm of the USA, the Federal Bureau of Investigation (FBI), describes terrorism as either domestic or international, depending on the origin, base, and objectives of the terrorist organisation. It is amplified as:

> **Domestic Terrorism** as the unlawful use, or threatened use, of force or violence by a group or an individual based and operating entirely within the USA or Puerto Rico without foreign direction, committed against persons or property to intimidate or coerce a government, the civilian population, or any segment thereof in furtherance of political or social objectives. **International Terrorism** involves violent acts or acts dangerous to human life that are a violation of the criminal laws of the USA and occur outside the USA or transcend national boundaries in terms of the means by which they are accomplished, the persons they are intended to coerce or intimidate, or the locale in which their perpetrators operate or seek asylum.[42]

The **US Homeland Security Act, 2002** defines "Terrorism" to mean any activity that

(A) involves an act that:
  (i) is dangerous to human life or potentially destructive of critical infrastructure or key resources; and
  (ii) is a violation of the criminal laws of the USA or of any State or other subdivision of the USA; and

(B) Appears to be intended:
  (i) to intimidate or coerce a civilian population;
  (ii) to influence the policy of a government by intimidation or coercion;
  (iii) to affect the conduct of a government by mass destruction, assassination, or kidnapping.[43]

Pakistan's Anti-Terrorism (Amendment) Ordinance, 1999, defines actions that strike terror or create a sense of fear and insecurity in the people, causes destruction of, property on a large scale, or a widespread disruption of supplies of services essential for the life of the community, or threatens, with the use of force, public servants in order to prevent them from discharging their lawful duties and includes gangrape, child molestation, or robbery coupled with rape as constituents of terror. [44] The subsequent and stringent Anti-Terrorism (Amendment) Ordinance, 2002, introduced by Pervez Musharraf on 16 November 2002 as well as the Constitution (Twenty-first Amendment) Act, 2015, were brought in to curb terror activities, especially in the restive North-West, but leaving out the domestic grown terror groups meant for 'export', and nurtured by the State[45] through the Inter Service Intelligence agency (ISI).

Terrorism being a global phenomenon, several countries, including our smaller neighbours have passed comprehensive, stringent and effective laws to deal with various facets of terrorist activities including terror funding. Bangladesh passed the Suppression of Terrorist Offences Act, 1992, and the Suppression of Terrorist Offences (Special Provisions) Act, 1994, followed by the Anti-Terrorism Act, 2009[46] and the Anti-Terrorism Rules, 2013, (mainly dealing with financial transactions).[47] Sri Lanka dealt the separatist LTTE a fatal blow by implementing Emergency Regulations No. 1 of 1989 in conjunction with the Prevention of Terrorism (Temporary Provisions) Act No. 48 of 1979. Nepal promulgated the Terrorist and Destructive Activities (Control and Punishment) Ordinance on November 26, 2001, to deal with the Maoists. The Bhutan Citizenship Act, 1985, brought to the fore the simmering discontentment of the Nepalese living in Bhutan and their consequent expulsion and exodus. The Maldives passed an Anti-Terror Bill on 27 October 2015, which opposition members termed 'draconian'; and that it did not deal with terror financing or the aspect of Maldivians joining foreign militant organisations.[48] Myanmar, faced with continued unrest and strident calls for democratic reforms, passed the Anti-Money Laundering Law in conjunction with an Anti-Terrorism Law, in June 2014.[49]

The USA armed itself with the Uniting and Strengthening America by Providing Appropriate Tools for Interpreting and Obstructing Terrorism Act (USA PATRIOT ACT), 2001[50] that was further amended in March, 2006 by integrating the Financial Anti-Terrorism Act. The British Parliament passed a Terrorism Act in March, 2006.[51] The Acts and Legislations of most countries are periodically updated and upgraded to keep in sync with the ever-changing dynamics of terror organisations and threats. In India, lack of consensus between Central and State governments and the politics of populism has severely diluted the counter-terror campaign.[52] Delays in investigations, trials, court hearings, and the inevitable charges of Human Rights abuses have reduced the efficacy of anti-terror laws and the counter-terror campaign. It took 22 years for one of the key plotters of the Mumbai bomb blasts of March 1993, in which 257 people were killed and more than 700 injured, Yakub Memon, to be executed, but the main perpetrators are still at large.[53] Ironically, the wife of a former prime minister pleaded for mercy of her husband's killers,[54] forgetting that there were many other victims of the same tragedy. Lord Denning, the celebrated British judge, had said, "The freedom of the individual must take second place to the security of the state".

Means of Terrorism

Terror can be inflicted by various means—these can be direct or indirect and manifest in the immediate, mid or long term. The impact of terror in the immediate term has a profound shock effect, but the implications of terror over the mid or long term can have a long term and serious effect, imperilling lives and national security. Some of the major deliverables of terrorism could take on various *avatars* as outlined below.

Bio-Terrorism: A bio-terrorism attack is the deliberate release of viruses, bacteria, or other germs (agents) to cause illness or death in people, animals, or plants. These agents are typically found in Nature, but it is possible that they could be changed to increase their ability to cause disease, make them resistant to current medicines, or to increase their ability to be spread in the environment. Biological agents can be spread through the air, through water, or in food. Terrorists may use biological agents because they can be extremely difficult to detect and do not cause illness for several hours or several days.[55] The earliest recorded example of bio-terror was in 600 BC when Solon used the purgative herb Hellebore during the siege of Krissa.[56] However, the most well-known example is the attempted use of anthrax bacteria to inflict casualties by various terrorist groups including the Al Qaeda in the aftermath of 9/11.

Chemical Terrorism: In World War I, liberal use of poisonous gases was made of by the Germans and the British. In the Persian Gulf War of 1980–1988, Iraq used mustard gas, Sarin and Tabun against Iran and ethnic groups inside Iraq. In 1995, the terror cult group Aum Shinrikyo used Sarin gas in a Tokyo subway system.[57]

Nuclear Terrorism: It has been defined as acts of violence and destruction performed by non-state actors where the means applied are nuclear explosive devices—or threats of such actions—with the purpose of inflicting destruction, creating a condition of fear, getting attention, blackmailing, instilling instability, and to affect an audience beyond the victim(s) directly targeted.[58] The growing reach of the Taliban and domestic terror groups in Pakistan make the threat of nuclear terrorism a grim reality in the Indian subcontinent, considering the vulnerability of Pakistan in safeguarding its nuclear weapons and other Weapons of Mass Destruction (WMD).

Cyber Terrorism. The FBI defined cyber terrorism as "the premeditated, politically motivated attack against information, computer systems, computer programs, and data which results in violence against non-combatant targets by sub-national groups or clandestine agents". James Lewis from the Centre for Strategic and International Studies and an internationally acknowledged expert on cyber security expanded the scope of cyber terrorism to be, "The use of computer network tools to shut down critical national infrastructure (such as energy, transportation, government operations) or to coerce or intimidate a government or civilian population". Dorothy Denning put it across brilliantly as, cyber terrorism to be the convergence of terrorism and cyberspace.[59] It is acknowledged to be extremely difficult to either ascertain the identities of these attackers in cyberspace or know whether they are private or government-backed. Examples of these are the hacking of the US Office of Personnel Management in June 2015 resulting in the theft of Social Security numbers and other personal information for former and current 22 million US government employees. China is also being blamed for a major cyber-attack on the computers at the Australian Bureau of Meteorology, which has compromised sensitive systems across its federal government.[60] Malware Stuxnet pushed back the Iranian enrichment programme by many years and was acknowledged by Iran to have retarded its nuclear ambitions.[61] Over 700 attempts by cyber criminals to hack Government of India websites including Department of Atomic Energy sites have been reported since 2012.[62]

Environment/Ecological Terrorism

The FBI defines ecological (Eco)-terrorism as the use or threatened use of violence of a criminal nature against innocent victims or property by an environmentally-oriented, sub-national group for environmental-political reasons, or aimed at an audience beyond the target, often of a symbolic nature.[63] In the 1960s and 1970s, the US military used the defoliant Agent Orange to destroy forest cover in Vietnam and, in 1991, Iraqi military forces retreating during the Persian Gulf War set fire to Kuwaiti oil wells, causing significant environmental damage.[64] According to Dr. Amy Zalman, eco terrorism describes violence in the interests of environmentalism when environmental extremists sabotage property to inflict economic damage on industries or actors they see as harming animals or the natural environment. Nitin Gadkari had stated that an aggressive green stand was also eco-terrorism, when development works were stalled under the garb of environmental protection.[65]

Economic Terrorism

The Geneva Centre for Security Policy defined economic terrorism as contrary to 'economic warfare' that is undertaken by states against other states; Economic terrorism would be undertaken by transnational or non-state actors. This could entail varied, coordinated and sophisticated or massive destabilising actions in order to disrupt the economic and financial stability of a state, a group of states or a society (such as market oriented Western societies) for ideological or religious motives. Economic targeting has been identified as a terrorist group's intent to inflict economic costs on a targeted state by doing one or both of two things: threatening to destroy or damage property or harm people or actually destroying or damaging property to harm people.[66]

Narco Terrorism

The term 'Narco Terrorism' was coined in the early 1980s when President Fernando Belaunde Terry of Peru gave it to the attacks his police forces were facing from drug traffickers. The term refers to one of two types of terrorism; international drug dealers who use terrorist tactics to maximise their profits or terrorists who use drugs to fund their organisation and operations. Latin America is the birthplace of narco terrorism and the region has become synonymous with the term.[67] The United States Drug Enforcement Agency (DEA) defines narco terrorism as the "participation of groups or associated individuals in taxing, providing security, or otherwise aiding or abetting drug trafficking endeavours in an effort to further, or fund, terrorist activities". UNODC reports aver that the major source of heroin is the region comprising Iran–Afghanistan–Pakistan–Myanmar–Lao DPR. With India being a major transit route as well as a destination for drug trafficking, emphasis to secure its borders by preventing easy ingress and egress of drug traffickers and their consignments through the borders as well as the sea coast and airports is essential to check the threat posed by the financing of terror through the narcotics route. Narco terrorism is motivated mainly by economic reasons as it helps terrorist organisations raise huge sums of money with minimum cost for their activities. Thus, the political, ideological, religious, and ethno-nationalist motives generally associated with terrorism are secondary to the economic gains associated with it.[68]

Suicide Terrorism

The current trend of suicide bombings began in Lebanon in the early 1980s. The practice soon spread to civil conflicts in Sri Lanka, Turkey, and Chechnya. Palestinian attacks on Israeli civilians in the 1990s and during the Al Aqsa Intifada further highlighted the threat. The World Trade Centre and the simultaneous attacks of September 2001 engineered by Al Qaeda saw a spike in the casualties and complexities of such terror acts. The Iraq and Afghanistan wars have seen daily suicide attacks of varying intensities and casualties and it has spread around the world to countries such as Saudi Arabia, Morocco, Tunisia, Kenya, Indonesia, Turkey, Pakistan, India, Afghanistan, Egypt, Jordan, Bangladesh, and Britain.[69]

State of the Field

While terrorism as a subject matter has been dealt with at length, this book is necessitated by the scarcity of South Asian regional-level works especially in the resolution aspect. The use of terrorism as a tool of modern foreign policy began in the European heartland, particularly the Balkans. *Balkan Ghosts*, by Robert D. Kaplan, (1993) succinctly brings out the pan-regional effect of ethnic, religious, and cultural tensions through a tracing of the ethnic wars in Serbia, Bosnia and Croatia and lessons derived from them. Understanding how the current world climate, in terms of major trends like globalisation and technological revolution, have impacted the mechanics of terrorism is extremely important to contextualise terrorism in the South Asian neighbourhood.

Globalization, Democracy and Terrorism by Eric Hobsbawn (2007) traces the defining moments that have shaped the past tumultuous century into the present-day period of rapid changes and turbidity and explains how the use of terror as a political tool is part of barbarisation post World War I. Identifying George Bush's policy including the Global War on Terror as one of the factors aiding the increase in political violence, he cautions that the new worry is the involvement of disparate groups or even individuals, often internet inspired too, in terror attacks.

Thomas Friedman in his book *The World is Flat* (2006) opines that globalisation has led to a "flattening of the world" as seamless connectivity within terror groups across the globe is now a reality. Radicalisation has been made easier by the world wide web. In his earlier book, *The Lexus and The Olive Tree*, published in 2000, he explained the effect of globalisation on cultures, geographies and traditions the world over as well as on approaching and managing conflicts in a region like West Asia.

In *Without Hesitation,* General (Retd.) Hugh Shelton (2010) provides an insider's account of the joint chiefs of staff under two presidents. He opines that the decisions have had disturbing and continued effects on the state. *The Utility of Force* by General Rupert Smith (2007) examines how the instrument of war has brought about a greater disturbance to terror-affected countries. Case studies of regions and terror groups also abound like *Zone of Crisis: Afghanistan, Pakistan, Iraq and Iran* by Amin Saikal (2014) covering the West Asian states of Iraq and Iran and its more volatile neighbours—Afghanistan and, Pakistan. This Southwest Asian region is looked at through the prism of domestic characteristics of recalcitrant political elites, fragile economies and policies, and constant ideological struggles between the forces of totalitarianism and democratisation as well as religious pluralism. The cascading effect of interventions and counter-terror efforts on the region has been negative for the most part.

Journalist Carlotta Gall's 2004 work. *Wrong Enemy,* offers an incisive account of the raison d'être for American involvement in Afghanistan, namely Pakistan. She also states that this was the USA's biggest mistake that resulted in a costly war resulting in the loss of American soldiers' lives.

Inside Terrorism by Bruce Hoffman (2006) offers an insight into the new threats that emerged post 9/11 and the modus operand of the Al Qaeda, post the Gulf War. Hoffman also addresses the issue of domestic terrorism in the USA including that of the rise of the white supremacist groups. Aspects of state-sponsored terror as well as religious and suicide terror are also covered.

Detailed accounts of the rise and operational aspects of terror groups, especially the Taliban and Al Qaeda, has piqued research interest. In *Soldiers of God,* Robert D. Kaplan, (1990) paints a vivid account of the emergence of the Taliban and its fighting techniques. Gretchen Peters (2009) work, *Seeds of Terror,* tackles a very important aspect of terror outfits like the Taliban, Al Qaeda and the ISI, namely, opium supply. With information gathered from hundreds of interviews with Taliban leaders and agents, Peters is convinced that the only way to truly defeat terrorists is to target drug money. He concludes that the war on terrorism is not just a war on radical and religious ideologies, but also on drug trafficking.

There have also been works that attempt to understand specific terror issues related to various South Asian countries.

The focus on Pakistan, often termed as a 'fountainhead' of terror, offers some interesting reading. In analyzing the nexus between radical Islamists and the military, Husain Haqqani's 2005 book titled *Pakistan: Between Mosque and Military* underlines the triad of Islam, anti-India stance and American aid dependence that have aided this nexus to endure and reap benefits. While Haqqani's work dwells on the Pakistani context, John Schmidt's 2011 book, *The Unravelling: Pakistan in the Age of Jihad* pinpoints the factor that has led to the country to the brink of disaster. He talks of the continuing state support, both, overt and covert, to Islamic fundamentalists that persists even in a climate of pursuing some groups due to the pressure of the USA and its allies while helping others ostensibly in pursuance of the nation's interests.

In the two works on Sri Lanka's brush with terror, Asoka Bandaranaike (2009) in *The Separatist Conflict in Sri Lanka: Terrorism, Ethnicity, Political Economy* elaborates on the causes of the political conflict that arose between the Sri Lankan government and the LTTE (Liberation Tigers of Tamil Eelam). Offering a unique perspective of the suppression of the Diaspora and its consequences, the author looks at the issue not as a typical good versus evil context but rather as a cause of several geopolitical, economic, religious and cultural clashes. Similarly, *Paradise Poisoned: Learning About Conflict, Terrorism and Development from Sri Lanka's Civil Wars* by John Richardson (2005) points to ten "developmental failures" and policies aimed at tackling such failures. This is prescriptive for any and all states facing threats from terrorist infractions. One of the very few books that addresses the question of problem resolution is *Talking To Terrorists* by Jonathan Powell (2014) in which he opines that parallel to a force-based counter-terror (CT) campaign, "talking to armed groups" is essential, especially those with a significant political base. However, he cites the dangers of third party involvement with reference to the Indian attempt in Sri Lanka from 1987 to 1990. The strategy of terror groups like the Al Qaeda, Taliban and now the ISIS, in the context of Powell's strategy that "we should be willing to talk even if they are not"—carries no weight, considering the uncompromising global and religious ambitions of these groups, at least so far.

In the case study on Bangladesh in his book, *Bangladesh: The Next Afghanistan?* Hiranmay Karlekar (2005) traces the birth, consolidation and growth of terrorist factions in Bangladesh, a country born out of linguistic nationalism. He holds that linguistic nationalism has given way to religious extremism in politics and governance. Karlekar ponders whether progression into radical Islamist fundamentalism will be inevitable for this neighbour of ours. In a comparative study of Nepal and Northern Ireland, Priya Dixit in her work, *The State and 'Terrorists' in Nepal and Northern Ireland: The social construction of state terrorism* (2015) tries to understand how the state categorises and labels groups and factions whose ideologies differ from its own, as 'terrorists'. Comparing the official representations of the Irish Republic Army and the Maoists of Nepal as 'terrorists' by the state and government, the book offers an interesting insight into critical terrorism studies as well as into the process of identity formation in small countries like Nepal and Ireland in the international political system.

As for India, the geo-strategic position of the subcontinent has been under repeated analysis be it Robert Kaplan's *Monsoon* (2010) which posits that the geography of the Indian subcontinent is a principal factor in the unveiling of the new great game or how, in another of his works, *The Revenge of Geography* (2012), he underscores how geography has made India the ultimate pivot state in the race between the USA and China. Kaplan traces the history of the world's hot spots (Kashmir being one) by examining their climates, topographies, and proximities to the other embattled lands.

India's War on Terror, edited by Gurmeet Kanwal and N. Manoharan (2012), gives a comprehensive picture of India's attempt to counter terrorism in all its facets. In *The Siege,* Adrian Levy and Cathy Scott

(2013) provide a vivid account of the attack on the Taj hotel in Mumbai, its perpetrators and the plot with reference to state-sponsored terror.

Through four terror cases, *The Politics of Counter Terrorism in India* by Prem Mahadevan (2012) gauges the performance of Indian Intelligence agencies in counter terrorism and propagates the idea of operational preparedness coupled with political will as an answer to prevent and neutralise terrorist attacks.

India's Military Conflicts and Diplomacy by General V. P. Malik (2013) provides an insight into the role of higher defence management before and during a military conflict. Aspects of Sri Lanka and The Maldives (1988) operations, nuclear tests as well as the Kargil operations are dwelt with partly. As a former member of the National Security Advisory Board, he provides a futuristic perspective on India's higher defence management.

Indian Mujahideen, the enemy within by Shishir Gupta (2011) attempts to trace the origins of the various jihadist groups that emerged in India and links them to terrorist cells operating abroad. Gupta, through in-depth research, brings out how the misinterpretation of religions is being used by a few to justify violence and terrorism in the country.

The focus of several works on India trains on the policy response to terror. *India at Risk* by Jaswant Singh (2013) examines the role of fault lines or fractures and governance in the inadequate response to Indian security, while A. S. Dulat's memoir, *Kashmir, The Vajpayee Years* with Aditya Sinha (2015), which is an insider's account of the strategies and politics involved in bringing Kashmir back from the brink of breaking away from India is on the policy response to terror. The trials and tribulations that Kashmir went through in the 1990s is an adequate launch pad for further enquiry.

However, the literature on India's general political, economic and internal security sets the contexts, challenges and approaches the country has experienced in handling terrorism. An examination of India's history like John Keay's works, *India: A History* (2010) and *The Honourable Company* (1991), offer the backdrop for the sources of discontent and disparity that have prepared a perfect ground for terrorism.

In the first book, John Keay traces the richest and longest history of civilisations that rose and fell in India. It offers an in-depth social, economic and cultural analysis of India, from the rise of ancient dynasties to the Islamic invasions; from colonial imperialism to the post-partition economic growth and present-day information and technology generation. Aspects of jihad, Kashmir and separatist activities are covered in passing in the light of political processes. In the next, he provides an insight into the history of the British East India Company, its commercial successes, failures, battles and politics in the Indian subcontinent and the world.

Caste and Race in India by G. S. Ghurye (1969) brings out the history of the caste system in India and how it has affected societal workings over the years. *India's Foreign Policy since Independence* by V. P. Dutt (2012) examines India's foreign policies under different prime ministers and how several dramatic instances changed and shaped the way India conducts its foreign policies. A must read for an in-depth and comprehensive understanding of the history, present and future, of India's foreign policies. *Rogue Elephant, Harnessing the Power of Democracy in the new India* by Simon Denyer (2014) traces the struggle faced by those fighting to create a better future for India in the twenty-first century, following a decade of scandals, violence, terrorism and slow economic growth. Denyer provides a balanced perspective on India's failures as a democracy as well as the aspirations of the people, which propelled them to vote in record numbers to bring about a positive change in India's future.

India grows at Night by Gurcharan Das (2012) captures India's struggle for growth as aspiring, innovating and flourishing companies are constantly being stumped at each turn by archaic government policies and outdated economic laws. Das rightly identifies India's need for a strong, liberal, and supportive state in order for it to grow economically, politically and diplomatically in today's global race for power and revenue.

Why India is not a Great Power (yet) by Bharat Karnad (2015) is a strategic critique on India's consistent underperformance in arenas of economics, diplomatic relations, military preparedness, and internal politics and the various strategies that can be employed to propel India's standing in the international environment as an emerging super power.

A Better India, A Better World by N. R. Narayana Murthy (2009) presents an argument on how focusing on two things, values and good leadership, can help change the world and bridge the divide between the rich and poor. The need for an accountable and responsive governance is essential to transform lives and the values imbibed in running enterprises are essential for meeting democratic ideals for the poor. This book presents an insight into how, by building a better India, one can set an example for the rest of the world to follow in order to leave for future generations, a better environment to live in and flourish.

India's internal security environment is another oft-written area.

Great Game East by Bertil Winter (2012) marks the North-East of India and continuing armed strife in that region as the key to understanding the true complexity of the hostilities and political ambitions that Asia's two giants harbour. *Internal Armed Conflict in India* by R. Nanavaty (2013) is based in the premise that internal armed conflicts are here to stay and that the armed forces shall continue to play a significant role in its management and resolution. The tabled analysis of the current internal armed conflicts is perhaps the best analysis of the Indian experience that has come out recently.

Internal Conflicts, Military Perspective edited by V. R. Raghavan (2012) provides a strategic overview on the effect that internal conflicts has on the doctrines, structure, civil-military relations, socio-political as well as psychological well-being of the defence forces of India and Nepal. It is an insightful read into the important issues faced by contemporary peninsular India.

Security Dimensions of Peninsular India (2005) edited by Dr. Gopalji Malviya is a collection of essays from leading Indian policy makers and subject specialists on various aspects of national security including the various avatars of terrorism. This study narrates how the changing perspectives of what constitutes a threat to national security—a combination of political, social, psychological, economic and personal safety of individuals—has brought out the need to change one's approach to tacking the threats more effectively.

Here the focus is essentially on the security challenges posed by state-sponsored terrorism that has exposed the vulnerabilities of India and SAARC nations and suggest comprehensive responses and strategies, through individual and collective, political, military and other measures to respond effectively to eliminate terrorism. The subcontinent is "home" to twelve of the US State Department's proscribed terror groups[70] of which eight are based in Pakistan and the remaining four operate under its sponsorship. India has proscribed a total of 38 terror groups,[71] whilst there are a total of 45 'organisations banned' in Pakistan.[72] Ironically, the most virulent terror groups—the Haqqani Network and the Jamaat-ud-Dawa (JuD)—were placed *under observation* since they were *charity organisations* only.[73] Notwithstanding regional and combined aspirations seeking economic growth, development, prosperity, peace and stability [74], terrorism, especially state sponsored, has retarded economic cooperation and stability in this region. The SAARC region also runs the risk of manifesting the full bandwidth—bio, cyber, economic, nuclear, narco, neo, environmental and nano or state terrorism. It is in this volatile and turbulent region that terrorism has been advocated and practised by states, non-state actors, fundamentalists, fringe groups and allied organisations out to weaken the democratic and social fabric of the SAARC nations and cripple their economic development. It has seriously impacted one of its principal creators, Pakistan, and has now spun well out of control. Our neighbours, wracked as they are by poverty, illiteracy, burgeoning population and absence of resources, fundamentalist fervour, and poor governance comprise the region where the seeds of terrorism have been sown and have reaped the grim consequences that have perpetuated conflicts even further. The SAARC states are thus living in an enviable neighbourhood. There, is thus an urgent need to evolve a mechanism for an effective regional response.

A look at the South Asian region in the context of India and its neighbours reveals that regardless of the scenario the future unfolds, the relevance of India as a bridge will remain central in the 21st century—be it to Africa as a repository of abundant mineral and economic wealth, to South West and Central Asia with its unmatched energy wealth, to Russia with virtually unlimited land, mineral and energy wealth concomitant to its sparse population, and to China with its aspirations and ambitions. Notwithstanding all this, India has to set its 'house in order' and 'make and mend its fences' with its neighbours to ensure prosperity, peace and stability in the region.

Despite the internal disequilibrium amongst SAARC nations,[75] the challenge is also to develop effective counter-terrorist (CT) strategies at this regional level to deal effectively with the scourge of terrorism whilst transcending boundaries and peoples. It is widely accepted that political violence and terrorism fall in a 'grey area' that involves threats to state security, both domestic and foreign. It is also established that support to the inimical forces of an unfriendly neighbour or perceived regional bully, be it tacit, implicit or implied, is to be found as a cornerstone in some national policies, stated or averred.[76] Whilst national CT strategies mostly focus on heavy-handed military or police responses and overlook the prospects of continued political and social measures and reforms, especially in the nascent stages, it is quintessential to formulate proactive mechanisms, political or military, supplemented by diplomatic and economic overtures to be adjusted and altered, as exigencies and expediency demand as part of policies in dealing with rogue nations/non-state actors and to protect national interests at home and abroad.

SAARC is a powerful and emerging option to carry forward the combined efforts of its member-nations towards an effective and cogent counter-terrorist policy in the form of the SAARC Terrorist Offences Monitoring Desk (STOMD) and the SAARC Regional Convention on Suppression of Terrorism and its Additional Protocol, but with periodic reviews.[77]

As far as India is concerned, whilst the *'Revolution in Military Affairs'* has led to modernisation of defence forces in our country, a culture of *'Revolutionary Strategic Thought and Action Processes'* is yet to emerge. We depend on outdated dogmas, plan, prepare, equip and train for the conventional threats of yesterday, in all its entirety, whilst the non-conventional, also known as 'Hybrid Warfare' has taken over the realms of undefined, unstructured and sometimes unknown 'battle spaces', with attendant consequences of impacting the security and stability of the country and its neighbourhood. This threat of hybrid circumstances and hybrid adversaries in future conflicts will fundamentally involve a competition for people—for their loyalty, support and security.[78]

This book thus aims to narrate the terror scenario in the Indian subcontinent post independence until the departure of the International Security Force in Afghanistan. It also seeks to examine the proliferation of state-sponsored terror and fundamentalism in SAARC nations. The book attempts to theorise the military, economic and political responses at both national and international levels. The prescription for measures in the future for SAARC countries, especially to ensure security from terrorism, is the value this book seeks to add. Current and past policy makers and counter-terrorism specialists at the micro and macro levels were met and various issues pertaining to terrorism in South Asia were discussed at length. Interviews and informal discussions were focused in a manner so as to elicit different views, opinions, comments and criticisms.

CHAPTER 2

TERROR AS LOW COST OPTION

The Indian subcontinent encompassing area from Afghanistan to the north-west and extending to present-day Myanmar to its east, from the Greater Himalayas to the north and including Sri Lanka to the south has been home to some of the great civilisations and empires of history. Nearly 2,200 years before the commencement of the British Empire, the Nanda Empire[79] occupied most of the western and northern dominions whilst a scant two centuries later the Maurya kingdom stretched across most of the subcontinent.[80] The subcontinent has seen the growth of all the principal religions of the world and their adaption and amalgamation through birth, sword, or trade. The British, after two centuries of rule, left in 1947 leaving in their wake a group of nations—most of whom are members of the SAARC—bound together by physical, cultural and familial ties that have existed since time immemorial. Partition brought mass displacement of entire villages and attendant miseries—almost 10–12 million people were displaced and possibly a million were killed,[81] during relocation in the areas demarcated as Pakistan, India, and East Pakistan. Linguistic majority was the main factor for division of the subcontinent—a Muslim-majority Pakistan in the west, a Hindu-majority India at the hub, and in surrounding in three directions, a Muslim-majority East Bengal renamed East Pakistan. The Two-Nation Theory was based on the assumption that a Muslim minority could not co-exist with a Hindu majority in a representative and democratic set up. This insecurity of Pakistan remains until date and its continued efforts to secure the whole of Kashmir by force of arms in 1947-48, 1965 and thereafter through a proxy war is seen as an attempted payback to India for its loss of East Pakistan in 1971.

Since the early 1970s, Pakistan has sought to resist, or possibly outrightly retard, India's inevitable if uneven ascendance both in the region and beyond.[82] Pakistan also has territorial disputes with Afghanistan and has sought to manipulate its domestic affairs and create a regime there, since the 1960s, through Islamist proxies, that are favourably disposed towards it and limit India's influence there.[83] Pakistan's use of proxies continued during the Soviet invasion and occupation of Afghanistan; once the Soviets left, it was the turn of some of the Pakistan-trained jihadists, battle hardened in Afghanistan, to be diverted to India in the Valley of Kashmir, to start a long and bloody insurrection and seize, by force, what the Pakistan armed forces could not do earlier. Seven Pakistan-sponsored groups engaged in terror activities in India have since been identified as Foreign Terrorist Organizations (FTOs) and designated as such by the USA[84] in accordance with its Immigration and Nationality Act (INA). These groups also include Pakistani proxies like the Afghan Taliban, Haqqani Network and the Tehreek-e-Taliban-e-Pakistan who have been operating in Afghanistan. Pakistan's quest for 'strategic depth' in Afghanistan and thereby its continued endeavour to support and exercise control over terror groups and activities there (including the Taliban) has manifested into terror groups having their own strategic depth (and space) in Pakistan, which clashed with the Pakistani state's strategic vision.[85] These proxies began to turn against the state following Gen. Musharraf's decision to support the US-led war in Afghanistan, targeting Pakistani citizens, its military and institutions in retaliation.

While many foreign terrorists with links to the Al-Qaeda were handed over to the USA, local jihadists as well as the Afghan Taliban were left alone. Covert support for the Afghan Taliban was Pakistan's insurance policy to deal with the aftermath of a US military withdrawal from Afghanistan. Jihadist militancy and terrorism have traditionally been ways of enabling Pakistan to stand up to a bigger and increasingly powerful India through asymmetrical warfare. The policy of allowing militant groups to operate on Pakistani soil has proved disastrous. Jihadist militants do not accept the neat divisions between global, regional and local conflicts.[86] The consequential spiralling economic costs of supporting the jihadists, even when sponsored by the CIA, against, firstly the Russians and later the Taliban, for Pakistan are incalculable. It has been estimated that the total direct violence containment costs for 2013–2014 for the SAARC nations stood at $ 124 billion.[87]

What percentage should have been gainfully utilised was used for defending nations against terror, mayhem and instability, not only in the Indo-Pak-Afghan context, but also among its friendly neighbours, Iran and China as well as in other SAARC nations. Pakistan has the dubious distinction of having been dubbed the epicentre of Islamic terrorism.[88] Pakistan, because of its culture, customs, traditions, values, the temperament of its people and even state policies, provides an ideal ground for Islamic radicalism, extremism, sectarianism and terrorism.[89] Terrorism today has imperilled the very existence of its regional creator, Pakistan, and threatened to spiral dangerously out of control.

In Pakistan's efforts to inflict crippling damage on India's economy and retard its growing regional and economic clout, the Mumbai attacks of 2008 was planned and launched. The first seaborne terrorist assault on any country was mounted by one such proxy of Pakistan—the LeT. The effect of three days of mayhem, which brought Mumbai to a standstill, is incalculable, with just the property losses estimated at $ 113 million.[90] It cost India another $ 108 million for the trial and allied costs of the captured terrorist, Kasab.[91] It had a cascading effect on security expenditure, diverting scarce resources to deal with terror. The amount budgeted (2010) for internal security for the Central Forces alone post-the Mumbai strike was $ 6.9 billion.[92] In comparison, the annual budget (2009) of the terror strike perpetrators, LeT, was $ 5 million.[93] Even if we consider the budget for the Mumbai attack by the LeT being pegged at $ 1 million, the impact on direct costs to property was 100 times more, and was responsible for a 33 per cent hike in the internal security budget. Worldwide, the economic cost of violence containment has been assessed at $ 9.46 trillion, with the average computed percentage on Internal Security (13.7%) and Terrorism (0.1%) of the costs, i.e., approximately $ 1.3 trillion.[94] The economic cost of the conflict in Nepal till 2006[95] was computed at $ 3 billion, whereas the total cost of the peace process was estimated at $ 207 million, i.e., less than 10 per cent of the conflict.[96] Given the reach of state-sponsored terrorism, as well as the non-state actors and the extent of damage they can inflict with a profound and lasting effect on recipient nations and societies, it is no small reason that countries that perceive themselves weak, today focus on hybrid warfare,[97] at the sub-conventional level, without going through a formal declaration of war.

Impact of Terrorism in Pakistan

Ranked third in the Global Terror Index,[98] with a terror quotient at 9.37 out of 10 in 2013, Pakistan, once perceived by the West as a bulwark of anti Soviet expansionist designs during the Cold War days and a frontline state against the Taliban, is caught in a web of its own making. The Mujahideen camps that were established by Islamabad in the late 70s to take on the Soviet Army in Afghanistan with generous financial and military hardware support from the USA, expanded to form the base for exporting terror in the form of the mujahideen and jihadists into India to wage the so-called 'Proxy War' and therefore secure for Pakistan its perceived strategic depth and interests. Despite warnings from all that the hydra-headed monster created would ultimately turn on its own creator, these camps and Pakistan's involvement in exporting terror only expanded. Increasingly, Pakistan has itself become the target of several formerly state-sponsored terrorist formations that have 'gone rogue', even as international pressure has forced Islamabad to undertake visibly reluctant operations against some of these groups. The process escalated after the creation of the Tehreek-e-Taliban Pakistan (TTP) in the aftermath of the Lal Masjid (Red Mosque) operations in 2007, causing a spiral of violence that now threatens the very existence of the country.[99] Pakistan's undiminished tolerance for religious extremists has not just destroyed lives and alienated entire communities; it is destroying Pakistani society and the very idea and edifice of the nation. Afghan and Indian-focused militants continue to operate from Pakistan territory to the detriment of Afghan and regional stability. Pakistan uses these proxy forces to hedge against the loss of influence in Afghanistan and counter India's superior military.[100] The ISI sponsorship of the Indian smuggler-turned-designated-international terrorist Dawood Ibrahim, who fled to Pakistan, is well established. Dawood, who is responsible for the financing and plotting of the 1992 Mumbai bombings as well as other terror activities and money laundering (hawala transactions[101]) to support terror has been on the radar of Indian security agencies for long and it has been confirmed that his activities and movements are orchestrated and supported by the ISI, which Pakistan denies, despite overwhelming evidence to the contrary.[102]

As a consequence of its own making, Pakistan is faced with dual internal threats of sectarian and ethnic strife. This has led to increasing incidents of violence and terrorism consequent to the war in Afghanistan and its spillover. The proliferation of 44 jihadist organisations,[103] owing allegiance to Sunnis and Shias and in sync with drug mafias operating in Afghanistan and Pakistan (AfPak) regions, Al Qaeda presence and ISIS emergence, poses a grave and existential threat to Pakistan right now. Pakistan was forced to launch Operation Zarb-e-Azb, an offensive by its security forces against various militant groups, including the Tehrik-i-Taliban Pakistan (TTP), Lashkar-e-Jhangvi, Jundallah, Al-Qaeda, the East Turkestan Islamic Movement (ETIM), the Islamic Movement of Uzbekistan (IMU) and the Haqqani Network.[104] Launched in June 2014 in North Waziristan (part of the Federally Administered Tribal Areas along the Afghan border) as a renewed effort against militancy in the wake of the 8 June attack on Jinnah International Airport in Karachi, for which the TTP and the IMU claimed responsibility. Part of the ongoing war in northwest Pakistan, up to 30,000 Pakistani soldiers were involved in Zarb-e-Azb, described as a "comprehensive operation" to flush out all foreign and local militants hiding in North Waziristan. The operation received widespread support from the Pakistani political, defence and civilian sectors.[105] On 6 September 2014, an attempt by Al-Qaeda terrorists in connivance with some Pakistan Navy personnel, to hijack the Pakistani navy vessel, PNS *Zulfiqar,* in Karachi ended after a fire fight in which three attackers were killed and seven arrested.[106] The 2 November 2014 suicide attack at the Wagah border, on the Pakistani side, claimed more than 60 lives and was stated to be a revenge attack for Operation Zarb-e-Azb.[107]

Statistics of casualties over the past decade tell the story of how common people have borne the brunt of the war on terror, being the principal 'recipients' of terrorist activities, thanks in large measure to the patronage/funding by their own government.

Fatalities in Terrorist Violence 2003–2015

	Civilians	*Security Force Personnel*	*Terrorists/Insurgents*	*Total*
2003	140	24	25	189
2004	435	184	244	863
2005	430	81	137	648
2006	608	325	538	1471
2007	1522	597	1479	3598
2008	2155	654	3906	6715
2009	2324	991	8389	11704
2010	1796	469	5170	7435
2011	2738	765	2800	6303
2012	3007	732	2472	6211
2013	3001	676	1702	5379
2014	1781	533	3182	5496
2015	940	339	2403	3682
Total*	20877	6370	32477	59724

*Data until 31 December 2015.

Source: South Asia terror portal accessed via http://www.satp.org/satporgtp/countries/pakistan/database/casualties.htm

As evident from the above data, Pakistan has paid a heavy price for nurturing terrorism. Its calibrated use as an extant of state policy to further its perceived national interest has been damaging to it and has begun to unravel. Having boxed itself in, its political masters seek to find refuge in obfuscation with terms like 'Non State Actors in a Deep State', and in blaming India for promoting terror on its soil, conveniently ignoring the fact that its state sponsoring of forces has gone against them.[108] In addition, the 'battles' have also been carried forward in its heartland.

The economic hub, Karachi, resembles a fortified but embattled city and despite very heavy security presence in Islamabad, terrorists still carried out audacious strikes in 2014, killing a total of 41 and injuring more than 600 people in different acts of violence, including a strike in a court that killed a judge and 10 others in March 2014.[109] This raised doubts on the policy of negotiating with the principal terror groups, as the splinter faction that carried out the strike claimed it was not obliged to follow the ceasefire, in vogue. A terrorist assault on Karachi Airport on 8/9 June 2014, which left 28 dead and the airport in shambles was a reminder of the massive security challenge that comes from affiliates of the Al-Qaeda, holed up in the mountainous Pakistan-Afghanistan border terrain.[110] The brutal TTP attack on the Army Public School, Peshawar, in December 2014, that killed scores of innocent children and injured many others, put to rest the issue of 'Good Taliban versus Bad Taliban'.[111]

The economic costs of terrorism in Pakistan are massive, rendering it a basket case, dependent on doles and diversions to keep the country going. In a significant case study on Pakistan and Net Foreign Direct Investment (NFDI) by Omer Majeed of Australian Open University, he ascertained that terrorism in the financial hubs of Pakistan had imposed a significant cost on reduction of NFDI by around 10.7 per cent or around $ 3.0 billion (2009 prices). During the last 13 years, the direct and indirect costs incurred by Pakistan due to incidents of terrorism amounted to $ 102.51 billion, equivalent to Rs. 8,264 billion. Pakistan needs enormous resources to enhance the productive capacity of the economy by repairing damaged infrastructure and creating a favourable investment climate. The security situation will be the key determinant of any future flow of investment. Pakistan's economy needs an early end to the conflict in Afghanistan as well as its negative impact over regions bordering Afghanistan in the form of violent extremism and terrorism for the revival of the economy and to keep stability in the system.[112] This is altogether a tall order, considering that the pull-out of the bulk of the NATO/US troops will see an upsurge in violence in the Afghanistan–Pakistan (Af-Pak) region, since the withdrawal of security elements would give freer access to escalation of violence levels and diversion of terrorists and terror groups available to prosecute their violence in Pakistan and spill over to India. Pakistan, which has faced chronic current account deficits and has consequently required occasional IMF bailouts, was subject to 12 IMF programs during the 1990-2007 period (IMF 2011), and will now enter a fresh support program in summer 2016. Terrorism has cumulatively cost Pakistan 33.02 per cent of its real national income during the period 1973-2010, implying around one per cent of lost real GDP per capita growth every year.[113,114] An uncertain political environment in a fragile security environment underscores the need to urgently address issues that have undermined foreign and domestic investor confidence consequently impacting all spheres of economic and developmental activity. Adding to its troubles is the real threat of Pakistan's nuclear weapons, some or even one of them falling into the hands of one of its rogue elements or in case of the collapse of Pakistan, making its way into the hands of the Al-Qaeda or the ISIS.[115] The USA has plans for securing these weapons, should the need arise, as brought out during Senate hearings in 2005, when the then National Security Adviser, Condoleezza Rice, was asked by Senator Kerry what would happen to Pakistan's nukes in the event of an Islamic coup in Islamabad. "We have noted this problem, and we are prepared to try to deal with it," Rice had said.[116]

Pakistan's greater concerns also emerge from happenings in Balochistan, a key support base during the Afghan War, that have gone on a tailspin after the killing of Nawab Bugti, a tribal leader, ex-Chief Minister and Governor and, above all, a respected Baloch leader. Balochistan is a repository of natural gas and minerals and provides access to the Gulf through the Port of Gwadar that is being expanded through generous Chinese grants, as part of one of its economic trade routes. Baloch nationalists initially demanded greater political rights, autonomy and a share and control over their natural resources through four previous insurgencies and in 2004 began secessionist demands and activities.[117] Considering its strategic location and given its growing importance, Pakistan's counter-terror campaign in Baluchistan has exposed the vulnerabilities it faces if a political settlement is not reached soon, as a break-up of Pakistan on sectarian lines is quite possible.

Prognosis

The rapidity of the turn of events in Pakistan makes it difficult to predict the future course of that country. Whatever way one crystal gazes, it is extremely unlikely that the future will be rosy—possibilities emerge from "Bleak, Bleaker or Catastrophic"—with the best being the status quo. The events of the past coupled with the happenings in the country, given the fragility and increasing vulnerability of law and order and its political situation held hostage by maverick politicians of differing hues and prejudices, compounded by turbulent Afghanistan and the bulk withdrawal of US and NATO troops from that country, beside other pointers available, indicate that Pakistan would face increasing isolation diplomatically; a rapid downslide economically; growing intolerance and compounded violence towards minorities; strident Islamisation of the military (the real power) and the looming threat of any of the multitude of terrorist groups attempting to capture/bargain/barter its nuclear assets all justifies its tag by the Global Peace Index as one of the most dangerous places in the world.[118]

Given that 2016 is an election year in the USA, coupled with looming instability—physical as well as economic in Pakistan—domestic politics in both countries will play a major role in how they handle their bilateral relations. There are broadly two possibilities insofar as US policy towards Pakistan is concerned; first, the administration will start taking a much tougher line with Pakistan to buttress its national security credentials. This means that the USA will begin turning the screws—diplomatic, economic and even military—to force Pakistan into compliance. Alternatively, the administration may try to avoid precipitating matters and continue harbouring fond hopes of changing Pakistan's malevolence on the one hand by sweet-talking the Pakistanis, and on the other keep the aid drip-trickling in. But given that this approach has not delivered over the last ten years, chances of it working in the future are dim.

Consequent to the Gurdaspur and Pathankot attacks of 2015 and as early as in 2016, no big breakthrough can be expected in Indo-Pak relations. Both countries will, however, go through the paces of a dialogue. While there could be some forward movement on trade and the economic front, there is a strong possibility of progress being stymied by domestic political compulsions and the opposition of the Islamists. Pakistan will try to ensure that no big incident of terrorism a la 26/11 takes place because, with the Western border heating up, it would like to avoid raising tensions on the eastern front with India. However, to keep India unsettled, the pot of terrorism will be kept boiling. The only difference is that post Pathankot, instead of using Pakistani terrorists to create trouble, Pakistan will use Indians to carry out terrorist attacks inside India so that even if something goes horribly wrong, plausible deniability can be maintained. It did not require remarkable perspicacity on the part of Hillary Clinton to tell Pakistani officials in October 2011, that "you can't keep snakes in your backyard and expect them only to bite your neighbours; eventually those snakes are going to turn on whoever has them in the backyard". Comments ascribed to Indian National Security Adviser (NSA) Ajit Doval that if another serious terror attack in India would be traced to Pakistan, would lead to its losing Balochistan have also put Pakistan on notice.[119] It is in regional interests that Pakistan resolves its Baloch problem soon, as an escalation of the current conflict could effectively lead to Pakistan's balkanisation and increased instability in the Indian subcontinent. Pakistan's reining in of terror groups and its non-state actors as well as drying up their funding, easier said than done, would also require a massive de-radicalisation programme, starting from revamping education in the hate propagating madrassas. In sync with regional economic development, it can turn out to be a success story, given the participation of the state, its people and its neighbours.

Impact of Terrorism in Afghanistan

With the dubious distinction of being ranked third last in the Global Terrorism Index Peace Quotient out of 162 nations,[120] the mountainous landlocked country of Afghanistan has been on the crossroads of history since long. It emerged as a country of sorts in the mid-eighteenth century when Ahmed Khan Abdali carved out a buffer zone between Persia and the decaying Mughal Empire in the Indian subcontinent, which in later years would emerge as a buffer zone between British-ruled India and the Russia of the Czar, setting the stage for its strategic importance, not just coveted by the Russians, but also by the Iranians, Pakistanis, Americans and even Indians, each eager to expand their sphere of influence and contain that of the other.[121] The year 1979 was a turning point in international terrorism. The Iranian Islamic Revolution sparked fears of a wave of revolutionary Shia Islam through much of the monarch and dictator-ruled countries in the Arab world. The Soviet invasion of Afghanistan and the subsequent anti-Soviet mujahideen war, lasting from 1979 to 1989, stimulated the rise and proliferation of terrorist groups. Indeed, the growth of a post-jihad pool of well-trained, battle-hardened militants emerged as a trend in contemporary international terrorism and insurgency-related violence. Volunteers from various parts of the Islamic world fought in Afghanistan, supported by conservative countries such as Saudi Arabia. The CIA, according to some estimates, pumped in an estimated $ 3 billion to fight the Soviets in Afghanistan,[122] matched by equal contributions by the Saudis and other oil-rich Arab countries, who supported other Islamist groups, like as in Yemen, the Saudi-funded Islamic Front was established to provide financial, logistical, and training support to Yemeni volunteers. Battle-hardened volunteers of the Afghan War support and participate in terror activities across North and East Africa, Kashmir, Chechnya, Bosnia, and The Philippines. Afghanistan, post the 1989 Soviet withdrawal, emerged as a terrorist training ground. Pakistan, struggling to balance its needs for political-economic reform with a domestic religious agenda, provides assistance to terrorist groups both in Afghanistan and Kashmir while acting as a further transit area between the Middle East and South Asia. Since its emergence in 1994, the Pakistani-supported Taliban militia in Afghanistan was provided logistical support, travel documentation, and training facilities—all associated with State sponsoring of terrorism.

Although radical groups such as the Egyptian Islamic Jihad, Osama bin Laden's Al-Qaeda, and Kashmiri militants were in Afghanistan prior to the Taliban, the spread of Taliban control has seen Afghan-based terrorism evolve into a relatively coordinated, widespread activity focused on sustaining and developing terrorist capabilities. Since the mid-1990s, Pakistani-backed terrorist groups fighting in Kashmir have increasingly used training camps inside Taliban-controlled areas.[123] At the same time, members of these groups, as well as thousands of youths from Pakistan's Northwest Frontier Province (NWFP), have fought with the Taliban against opposition forces. This activity has seen the rise of extremism in parts of Pakistan neighbouring Afghanistan, further complicating the ability of Islamabad to exert control over the militants. Moreover, the intermixing of Pakistani movements with the Taliban and their Arab-Afghan allies has seen the ties between these groups strengthen.[124] Since 1989, the increasing willingness of religious zealots and extremists to strike targets on an intercontinental scale has brought into sharp focus the global nature and complexities of contemporary terrorism. The February 1993 bombings of the World Trade Centre, US Embassy bombings in East Africa in August 1998, the September 2001 attacks on the World Trade Centre and the Pentagon, and the Madrid train blasts of 2004 are representative of this trend.

As a precursor to American and ISAF troop withdrawals, the USA and Afghanistan signed the 'Enduring Strategic Partnership Agreement between the Islamic Republic of Afghanistan and the United States of America', on 2 May 2012, a 10-year Strategic Partnership Agreement (SPA) that underscored the US's enduring commitment to strengthen Afghanistan's sovereignty, stability, and prosperity and continue cooperation to defeat the Al-Qaeda and its affiliates. While the USA and other international partners committed themselves to continue providing extraordinary development assistance to Afghanistan through the 2014 transition and the ensuing transformational decade during the July 2012 Tokyo Conference, the US government continues to support a broad-based government in Afghanistan, whilst Afghan forces have transitioned to take the lead in combat operations, with International Security Assistance Forces (ISAF) supporting them through advisories and enabling roles by the end of 2014.

The linkages between fighting a drug war and fighting terror are starkly visible in Afghanistan. The country is the leading 'producer' of poppy with a staggering 157,000[125] hectares under cultivation of this cash crop which funds the terrorists and criminal syndicates world-wide as well as its principals, the Taliban. In Afghanistan and elsewhere, transnational organised crime groups were the main beneficiaries of the worldwide $ 320-billion drug trade in 2003.[126] In 2009, the Afghan Taliban was estimated to have earned around $ 150 million from the opium trade, Afghan drug traffickers $ 2.2 billion, and Afghan farmers $ 440 million. While UNODC findings suggest that most insurgent elements content themselves with taxing the trade rather than attempting to become active participants, it now appears that some insurgents involve themselves directly in the heroin supply chain, including in the procurement of acetic anhydride. Anti-government elements based in Afghanistan and Pakistan may gain access to only a fraction of the value of Afghan opiate exports, but this is nonetheless enough to support logistics, operations and recruitment.[127] Ultimately, the only way to beat the terrorists there is to win the war against drug cultivation.

Prognosis

India has a long-term strategic interest in Afghanistan's stability and prosperity—as with it will come development and resources. The Turkmenistan–Afghanistan–Pakistan–India (TAPI) gas pipeline project inked on 15 December 2015 will provide much-needed energy to the nations through which it will pass.[128] Mining at the Hajigak concessions, as well as extensive highway and railway construction and the Hydel Salma Dam project are some of the other initiatives, besides the construction of the landmark new parliament building in Kabul.[129] India has displayed considerable soft power initiatives through skill development, education, medical facilities and numerous other infrastructure and facilities to help Afghanistan in nation building.

With the planned departure of the USA and its allies at the end of 2016, Afghanistan needs to focus on reintegration and reconciliation of its warring clans and groups, all-round economic development, and improving relations with its neighbours, especially Pakistan, which can throw the proverbial spanner in the works, through unabated support and sponsorship of terror groups. Afghanistan's regional partners—the SAARC nations—can be useful mechanisms to its economic, cultural and social rejuvenation besides increasing the security capabilities of Afghan forces. Peace is however a far cry—four decades of non-stop war have brutalized the nation and its people and the sociological and economic costs are difficult to calculate. Two generations have grown up under the shadow of the gun as well as subject to depredations by a host of invaders, dissidents, neighbours and foreigners. The cost to the USA for the Afghan adventure from 2001 to 2015 is estimated at $ 686 billion,[130] excluding the long-term medical care and disability compensation for service members, veterans and families, military replenishment and social and economic costs and follow-up commitments. The cost of getting Afghanistan back on track will be many times more and will take longer—a stable and reasonably moderate Afghanistan will truly become a hub of not just southern Central Asia but also of Eurasia in general. The convergence of interests of Russia, China, India and Iran in favour of transport corridors through and from Central Asia[131] and to and through the sea route will spur economic development and bring about peace and stability not only to Afghanistan and Pakistan but will also result in attendant spin-offs to other SAARC nations.

Impact of Terrorism in Bangladesh

Bangladesh has no geographical defence to marshal as a state with its characteristic of a flat, aquatic landscape of paddy fields and scrub on both sides of the border with India (other than in the low hills of the southeast in the area known as Chittagong Hills Tract). This artificially-shaped blotch of territory, in succession Bengal, East Bengal, East Pakistan, and Bangladesh, could metamorphose yet again amid the gale forces of regional politics, Muslim religious extremism and climate change. Like Pakistan, the history of Bangladesh is one of military and civilian regimes, a few of which functioned well enough. Millions of Bangladeshi refugees have already crossed the border to India as illegals. Yet, the Bangladeshi government struggles on. It could yet succeed as a hub of overland trade and pipeline routes connecting India, China, and a future free and democratic Myanmar.[132]

Created out of the Partition of 1947 out of the Muslim-majority area in East Bengal, which became East Pakistan, in a format defying description, it led to calls for greater autonomy culminating in a stand-off between the two wings of Pakistan and calls for a Bengali independence movement. This movement, spearheaded by Mujib-ur-Rahman's Awami League (AL) won independence for Bangladesh, after a gruesome freedom struggle (in which a reported half a million people died [133] and approximately five million fled to India) in a brief war in 1971. Post independence, the AL government, having to re-establish the rule of law as well as returning to normalcy, could not fully meet the aspirations of the newly-independent people and was overthrown by the military in a bloody coup in 1975. This initiated a series of military coups, creation of a military-sponsored government and the birth of the Bangladesh Nationalist Party (BNP) in 1978. That government also ended in a coup in 1981, followed by military-backed rule until democratic elections in 1991. The BNP (under Khaleda Zia, wife of Ziaur Rahman and President 1977-1981) and AL alternated in power between 1991 and 2013. A military-backed, emergency caretaker regime suspended the parliamentary elections of January 2007 in an effort to reform the political system and root out corruption. The caretaker government returned the country to fully democratic rule in December 2008 following the election of the AL and Prime Minister Sheikh Hasina (daughter of Sheikh Mujib). In the January 2014 elections, the incumbent AL retained its win after the BNP had boycotted it, and Hasina was re-elected prime minister. Bangladesh has made great strides from being what Kissinger dismissed as a 'Basket Case' to substantial progress in food security since independence, and the economy has grown at an annual average of about 6 per cent over the last two decades.[134, 135]

Bangladesh is considered a developing economy. Yet, almost one-third of Bangladesh's 160 million people live in extreme poverty. In the last decade, the country recorded GDP growth rates above 5 per cent due to the development of the microcredit and garment industries. Although three-fifths of Bangladeshis are employed in the agriculture sector, three-quarters of export revenue come from producing ready-made garments. The biggest obstacles to sustainable development in Bangladesh are overpopulation, poor infrastructure, corruption, political instability and slow implementation of economic reforms.[136]

Extreme poverty levels, lack of sustainable livelihood, unchecked radicalisation programmes in madarsas, and unemployment have resulted in Bangladesh being a 'perfect place for Al-Qaeda affiliates'.[137] Between 1993 and 2015, there has been a discernible shift towards traditional forms of Islam in education, dress and deportment.[138] An inducible factor in Bangladesh politics, various local Islamic groups have alliances with parties that has given leeway for the rise of terror affiliates. In a country where the bulk of the people subsist on less than $ 2 a day, the terror group, Jama'at ul Mujahideen Bangladesh (JMB), budgets $ 1,250 per member per month.[139] Despite external pressures and internal pulls, Bangladesh has been able to improve the basic standard of living of its people. The introduction and success of micro credit (Grameen Bank) and substantial remittances from expatriates (averaging $ 1.2 billion monthly from 2012 to 2015)[140] along with the activities of NGOs has, over the past two decades, seen a large number of people climbing above the national poverty line and rise steadily; the country is on track to achieve most of the Millennium Development Goals.[141]

The exponential growth of NGOs in Bangladesh, post the 1980s (by 1998 there were 997 local and 135 foreign registered NGOs), largely to fill the space created by the failure of the Government's efforts to provide basic services to the marginalised sections of society and in rural areas, was resisted by the rural mullahs who, spurred by the Jammat-e-Islami (JEI), supported the Army rulers,[142] who began to exert influence to curb NGO activities as they felt threatened by their transformation of the countryside. Under Zia, Pakistan's ISI established links with the Director-General of Forces Intelligence (DGFI) of Bangladesh who was instrumental in supporting Indian North East terror groups. The JEI was an active collaborator with the Pakistan Army during the War of Liberation, and their reoccupation of the centre-stage, brought about increased polarisation in an already vitiated political atmosphere. The return of the AL under Sheikh Hasina to power brought about the much-needed corrections, and the JEI leadership was tried and prosecuted for their part in the genocide of 1971 by a special Tribunal. The student wing of the JEI, the Islamic Chattra Shibir (ICS), along with its parent organisation has been under the scanner for anti-national activities since the Tribunal's action and a new front of the JEI, supported by the BNP, the Hifazat-e-Islam (Saviours of Islam) was created.

Bangladesh has had to deal with increasingly fractious political groups, refugees, multiple terror organisations and strident Islamists, flush with funds from Wahhabi sponsorship, as well as India's North-East terror groups—a combination of which is affecting its security and hampering economic development.[143] The Rohingya, refugees from Myanmar concentrated in large numbers in Cox's Bazar, are reportedly being recruited by the Harkat-ul-Jihad-al Islami Bangladesh (HuJI-B), a terrorist group set up with assistance from Osama bin Laden's International Islamic Front (IIF). HuJI-B recruits are indoctrinated in the mould of radical Islam. The coastal belt from Chittagong—Cox's Bazaar right to the Myanmar border— has become a haven for all illegal, criminal and anti national activities and is the 'domain' of the HuJI-B, whose cadres also operate in North-East India. HuJI-B terrorists have been reported in J&K, Chechnya and Afghanistan.[144] The HuJI-B is also known to have enjoyed the patronage of mainstream political parties such as the Bangladesh Nationalist Party (BNP) and the Jamaat-e-Islami.

Another outfit, the Jama'at-ul Mujahideen Bangladesh aims at the Islamisation of Bangladesh through armed struggle and calls for the conduct of government under Sharia law. In March 2007, after being pronounced guilty by two judges of orchestrating terror activities, six top terrorists of the JMB, including its leader, Maulana Abdur Rahman, and number two, Siddiqui Islam, were executed. The JMB has reportedly received funds from donors in Kuwait, Pakistan and Saudi Arabia. It was also involved in the 2 October 2014, Burdwan (West Bengal) blast case. Under Sheikh Hasina, the JMB was virtually decimated and is now regrouping through modules set up inside India. The National Investigation Agency (NIA) has unearthed, following the Burdwan blast, a JMB plan to assassinate Prime Minister Hasina. The JMB was reportedly planning to establish an 'Islamic state' in Bangladesh through an armed struggle to incorporate the

West Bengal districts of Murshidabad, Nadia and Malda.[145] The NIA investigation revealed that the JMB had established its network, particularly in Murshidabad, Nadia, Malda, Birbhum and Burdwan in Bengal; Barpeta in Assam; and Sahibganj and Pakur in Jharkhand.[146] What was initially being passed off as an accidental blast has emerged as one with grave security implications for both Bangladesh and India. Coming as it is when both countries are having to contend with rising Islamist radicalisation and the spread of global jihad, the West Bengal government's clumsy attempts to cover up and play the blame game does not detract from the fact that the state government had been playing 'minority card politics' over national security. Considering the alacrity and zeal shown by the Bangladesh government of Sheikh Hasina to act against terror groups, including Indian terrorist outfits, petty Indian politicians have chosen to turn a blind eye, or worse, are complicit in allowing foreign jihadist elements to operate with impunity from our territory.

Prognosis

Bangladesh, as a struggling developing nation beset with a host of problems, has seen the consequences of allowing a proliferation of madarsas preaching a brand of radical Islam and backed by political parties of fundamentalist organisations, bent on imposing their own brand of totalitarian regressive governance. Fortunately, for the present government, it has the backing of the powerful military in quelling the rise of terror groups, as witnessed by the swift action against the JMB as also the uprising in 2014 by the erstwhile Bangladesh Rifles, since renamed as Bangladesh Border Guards. The flow of foreign funds into NGOs especially espousing Wahhabism needs to be controlled and checked and diverted to development purposes and not for proselytization or donor-driven agendas.[147] The introduction of draft laws controlling the flow of all funding to NGOs in 2014, although criticised by many, is a step in the right direction.[148] The management of Rohingya refugees in concert with the Myanmar government as well as UNHCR, and the rehabilitation of the Chakmas in India, are issues of concern. The unchecked influx of refugees into India, mainly as cheap labour, has to be addressed by both nations by a mechanism to introduce work permits as well as deportation of aliens—a carrot-and-stick policy, which requires local Indian politicians to comprehend the threat of the demographic imbalance already in place, especially in the narrow Indian corridor that lies between Nepal–Bhutan to its north and Bangladesh to the south. In addition, the growing drug trade in the CHT as well as clamping down on smuggling via Indo-Bangladesh as well as the Bangladesh–Myanmar border in close cooperation of respective governments and border guards is a priority. The present Bangladesh regime has been proactive in its approach to cracking down on Indian terror groups seeking refuge, and denying sanctuary to forces inimical to Bangladesh interests by India would be a welcome gesture. Sheikh Hasina's suggestion of a South Asia Counter Terrorism Mechanism needs to be carried forward. Similarly, bilateral initiatives to strengthen secular forces[149] in Bangladesh as well as actively wean away growing influence of China and Pakistan would work towards the mutual benefit of both India and Bangladesh.

Impact of Terrorism in Nepal

Nepal has deep cultural, social, economic and military ties with India, dating back to more than two centuries, after the British defeated the Gurkhas in the Anglo Nepalese war of 1814–1816. Nepal had traditionally been a kingdom and the root cause of terrorism there can be traced to the 1960s when the Nepalese Communists demanded that King Mahendra end the panchayat system and also draw up a new Constitution. Various events followed, but the real slide into terrorism began in 1996 which saw the emergence of the hard-line Communist Party of Nepal—Maoists led by Pushpakamal Dhamal alias Prachananda who boycotted the mid-term polls and instead opted for an armed struggle. At its peak in 2002, the insurgency saw 4,896 persons, including 3,992 Maoists, 666 security force personnel and 238 civilians, killed in a single year.[150] It finally came to an end in November 2006, with the signing of the Comprehensive Peace Accord (CPA)—violence continued thereafter until 2012; by then, more than 13,000 people had lost their lives, including 1,300 civilians and close to 2,300 security force personnel.[151] The promulgation of an interim constitution in 2007, objected to by the Madhesis[152] was followed by a nationwide Constituent Assembly (CA) election in 2008; the newly-formed CA declared Nepal a Federal Democratic Republic, abolished the monarchy, and elected the country's first president. After the CA failed to draft a constitution by a May 2012 deadline set by the Supreme Court, the then Prime Minister, Baburam Bhattarai, dissolved the CA. Instability followed and negotiations ensued until March 2013 when the major political parties agreed to create an interim government headed by the then Chief Justice, with a mandate to hold elections for a new CA. Elections were held in November 2013, in which the Nepali Congress won the largest share of seats in the CA and in February 2014 formed a coalition government with the second place Communist Party of Nepal-Unified Marxist-Leninist and with Nepali Congress President Sushil Koirala as prime minister. Nepal's new constitution came into effect in September 2015.[153]

Nepal is among the most impoverished countries in the world, with about one-quarter of its population living below the poverty line. Nepal is heavily dependent on remittances, which amount to as much as 22 per cent of the GDP.[154] Nearly 25,000 soldiers of India's Gurkha Rifles Regiment, another 20,000 from para military and police forces, approximately a lakh veterans and nearly 11,000 widows come from Nepal and get remittances amounting to Rs. 1,200 crore annually as salaries and pensions.[155] Post CPA, Nepal is ranked high in the Global Peace Index of 2015;[156] however, its violence containment costs have been high—approximately $ 1.8 billion (PPP) or almost 3 per cent of the GDP (PPP). Agriculture is the mainstay of the economy, providing a livelihood for approximately 75 per cent of the population and accounting for a little over one-third of the GDP. Industrial activity mainly involves the processing of agricultural products, accounting for just 7 per cent of the GDP. Nepal has considerable scope for exploiting its potential in hydropower, with an estimated 42,000 MW of commercially feasible capacity,[157] but continued political uncertainty, lack of skilled manpower and a difficult business climate have hampered foreign investment. Additional challenges to Nepal's growth include its landlocked geographic location, high unemployment (40%), poor communications and transportation infrastructure, labour problems and its vulnerability to natural disasters.[158]

It is not just the Madhesis who have the potential to create trouble, the eastern hill region of Nepal, the land of the Limbus too has a history different from the rest of Nepal and resist the domination by Kathmandu. As with the Tarai and its heavy concentration of Madhesis, the proportion of Limbus in the eastern hills is also considerable. The major players in eastern Nepal are also the Maoist ethnic liberation front, non-violent movements for regional autonomy and assorted armed groups.[159] Resistance to the introduction of the new Constitution saw a blockade being imposed by the UDMF of all major highways and customs check posts bordering India, its major supplier of goods and services, including essential supplies, from 23 September 2015, unless two key demands of the majority regarding proportional representation and constituency delimitation were not met. On 23 January 2016, Nepal's Parliament voted to address the two key demands of the Madhesis—proportionate representation and seat allocation in Parliament on the basis of population.

Bowing to pressure, public hardship and violence, the blockade was lifted on 5 February 2016, but the agitators claimed they would continue to press for their demand for not redrawing the provincial borders in a way that would divide them.[160] The course of the blockade saw renewed interest focused by China towards Nepal and shared its concerns at what it termed as "outside interference" (referring to India),[161] while signing an agreement to provide fuel to Nepal, beleaguered by its own people's blockade of movement of goods from India. Chinese strategic interests in Nepal have always been abiding, with its focus mainly on the 10 districts of Upper Himalayan Nepal, bordering China.[162] Nepal has also cracked down on Tibetan activists in exchange for economic aid from China, besides sponsoring the idea for a trilateral partnership between India, China and Nepal, a policy driven by national interests and not ideology.[163] Considering Nepal's location—proximity to India, Tibet, China and Bangladesh and given its fragile politico-economic condition as well as vulnerabilities being sandwiched between two powerhouses—Nepal has been more than willing to play one against the other and also against them. It has often turned a blind eye to the activities of the Pakistani embassy in Kathmandu, which directed pan-India operations, including the hijack of IC 814, and launching of terror modules for strikes in India, helped in great parts by the permeable Indo-Nepal borders. The ISI has used the Raxaul sub-division in Bihar as a recruiting ground for terrorists, with Birganj, in Nepal, being the nerve centre of such activities. Over the years, Birganj has emerged as a major hub for the distribution of counterfeit currency, narcotics, explosives, and arms in different parts of India through Bihar.[164]

Prognosis

Post promulgation of the Constitution, there has been considerable unrest with regard to the representation of the people in various elected bodies due to the new federated structure of the country. The Madhesis and Tharus, who are most affected, being dispersed along the Terai and longitudinally, are now split because the new provinces are near latitudinal, which according to them violates the spirit of what had already been agreed to by the Constituent Assembly, in 2010 and 2012. Notwithstanding this, and with the leaders having made written commitments to fulfil the rest of the demands through constitutional amendments, the strike went on and imposed tremendous hardship on the general public.[165] Concerns exist of the methodology to resolve the imbroglio, addressing the aspirations of the majority without impinging on the rights and demands of the minor parties, without it descending back into the chaos brought about by the Maoist insurrection. Of emerging concern is the mushrooming of madarsas—there are around 1,900 madarsas (seminaries) on both sides of the India–Nepal border, including 800 on the Nepal side. Muslims constitute just 4.2 per cent of Nepal's total population, of which 96.7 per cent is confined to the Tarai region bordering India, constituting 7.32 per cent of the total population of the Tarai.[166] This area is also known as a hub for anti-Indian activities, sponsored by the ISI, including smuggling of fake Indian currency notes (FICN). In addition, the rise of the Muslim population in 15 of 17 Indian border districts with Nepal gives credence to the apprehensions of Intelligence agencies that these madarsas are propagating anti-India hatred and Muslim separatism.[167] Given the security concerns that India has in Nepal relating to FICN, Maoist movements, Islamist terrorism and airport security, amongst others, the open Indo–Nepal borders and its exploitation by anti-Indian elements is a constant source of concern for the Indian security establishment. China's worry stems from the increase in the 'Free Tibet Movement', in Nepal in addition to the possible impact of federal Nepal on this movement, besides fears of instability in Nepal that it would be a threat to its security interests. Reverse migration of the Nepalese Diaspora amounting to approximately 7 million[168] (including 5 million in South Asia, the majority being in India), due to instability in the host nations is another cause of concern, as even a quarter returning would have a tremendous economic and social upheaval and consequences. The reported move of the Bhattarai government to ban the recruitment of Nepalese Gurkhas in foreign armies[169] is a short-sighted move as it is only Nepal that will be most affected—the issue of employment and foreign remittances would be most affected. It is in the strategic interests of both Nepal and India to secure their borders and to crack down on terror groups and activities within their respective nations as also assist each other to strengthen their counter-terror grids through a proactive approach.

Impact of Terrorism in Bhutan

The Kingdom of Bhutan is one of the most peaceful places on Earth, where the first time an insurrection of sorts in modern times happened when the 'Bhupalese'—Nepalese migrants settled in Bhutan, especially South Bhutan—were evicted from the late 1980s reaching a peak in 1992, for being stateless migrants who had proved their disloyalty to their host country. The origin of the trouble was a fallout of the figures of the 1981 Census, where it emerged that Bhutanese of Nepali origin constituted 53 per cent, the ethnic Bhutanese, i.e., the Sharchops (mainly from East Bhutan) comprised 30 per cent and the Ngalops (from western and Central Bhutan and who formed the dominant class) accounted for only 17 per cent. The Royal Government of Bhutan (RGB) apprehended a situation emerging wherein, if this imbalance was not checked, the native Bhutanese would be soon be reduced to a miniscule minority. There were also apprehensions of a likely demand for a greater Nepal/Gorkhaland including Sikkim, where the ethnic Sikkimese were already in a minority, and the northern parts of West Bengal. After tough citizenship laws were introduced in 1985 and enforced, approximately, 85,000 Bhupalese were evicted/fled, the majority of them settling down in refugee camps in North Bengal while some fled to Nepal.

An Indo–Bhutan friendship Treaty, first signed in 1949, was updated in February 2007 with no change in the responsibilities of each country towards the other. Bhutan continues to be guided in defence without prejudice to national security and the erstwhile clause of guidance in external affairs has been dropped. With sweeping winds of change all over and sensing environmental disquiet, Bhutan changed over from an absolute monarchy to a multi-party democracy, with the fourth king, Jigme Singye Wangchuck, stepping down in December 2006, and directing the political and legal reforms that have shaped the constitutional monarchy and democracy in Bhutan with the first elections in 2007, National Assembly election in 2008, with all levels of government democratically elected by 2011. There were rumblings amongst the Bhupalese who had fled Bhutan and settled in the foothills of the Dooars, and a tie-up with Indian terror groups, especially the ULFA and the National Democratic Front of Bodoland (NDFB) and the camps in South Bhutan in 1992-1994, especially in the Samdrup Jongkhar–Geylephug area. Joint operations with the Indian Special Forces and the Royal Bhutan Army (RBA) personnel saw a dissipation of these groups, some moving deeper into the jungles. The RBA, although trained by the Indian Army, neither has the strength nor the capacity to take on these terror groups without substantial 'collateral risks and threats' to its own people and their tenuous lines of communications.

Following the continued depredations by the terror groups of both nations, including attacks on RBA personnel by armed Nepalese dissidents, attacks on Bhutanese villagers and raiding of isolated check posts as well as ULFA activities in Assam, the Government of India exerted diplomatic pressure on the RGB to act against terror groups and camps in south Bhutan offering to conduct joint operations.[170]

The RGB preferred a peaceful solution and initiated many rounds of dialogue with the militant groups commencing in 1998. Despite repeated deadlines passing and no vacation of camps by the terror groups, the RBA finally launched military operations against the terror groups in December 2003. By the end of the year, the RGB claimed the destruction of 30 camps belonging to different terror groups and seizure of large quantities of warlike stores.[171]

Political disquiet and rumblings within Bhutan, especially by the East Bhutanese, have surfaced and with the exposure to television in 1998 and also to cross cultures, demands for more representation in governance increased. However, in a recent multi-dimensional survey that took into account the aspects of the life of the people, governance, health, living conditions, harmony with environment and, above all, governance, it was found that 91.2 per cent of the people in Bhutan are very happy.[172] Although there is a smattering of terror groups operating like the United Revolutionary Front of Bhutan (URFB), which claimed responsibility for small blasts in West Bhutan in 2007, the main threat lies from the Bhutan Tiger Force (BTF), the armed wing of the Bhutan Communist Party (BCP), formed in the United Nations refugee camps in eastern Nepal and largely comprising Bhupalese refugees.[173]

Prognosis

The situation is generally peaceful, with the last serious terror-related acts recorded in 2008.[174] It is assessed that as Bhutan progressively opens its doors to foreign influence and increasing democratisation processes and given the linkages emerging between dissident Bhupalese and Indian terror groups and political fugitives, a resurgent bout of instability is presaged. A close watch on the situation by Indian Special Forces is mandated to prevent terror groups, inimical to India's and Bhutan's interest manifesting in each others' territories. Whilst dialogue will be a way forward for resolution, cross-border joint operations should also be carried out to maintain the pressure against the terror groups. The security of the border between the two countries requires further toning up.

Impact of Terrorism in Sri Lanka

Located strategically, a pivot between the Arabian Sea and the Straits of Malacca, and occupying a dominant position in the Indian Ocean, Sri Lanka is suitably poised to be the *entrepôt* for Africa-West Asia-East Asia, and given the emergence of Hambantota, as a major focal point with Chinese aid that allows Sri Lanka to emerge from the debilitating shadows of the Long Terror War against the separatist Liberation Tigers of Tamil Eelam (LTTE) and benefit economically and strategically as a powerhouse. The development by India of the oil farms of Trincomalee, whose port faces the Andaman and Nicobar Islands and South East Asia, highlights the port's strategic access to one of the region's busiest waterways[175]—especially for trade—and ushers in developmental work in the terror conflict ravaged north.

Post-Independence in 1948, the dominant Sinhalese, backtracking on the government's granting Tamils[176] minority rights, saw a wave of violence gaining ground between the two ethnic groups. Accentuated by discrimination and the promotion of Sinhala as the official language, the Tamils had to deal with the failure of the largely Sinhalese government institutions to protect their community rights. This was followed by Buddhism being recognised as a state religion and the Hindu Tamils being largely disenfranchised.[177] Poverty, unemployment and inflation led to increasing numbers of Sinhala youth embracing an ideology, which combined Marxism with Buddhism and led to increasing communal clashes, followed by a revolt in 1971, initiated by the communist Janatha Vimukthi Peramuna (JVP). This was crushed in a brutal state crackdown within two months, and many youth were killed—by some estimates at least 15,000—some of whom had been summarily disposed off. A second revolt by the JVP in 1987-89, saw more than 50,000 killed in waves of violence, concurrent to the insurrection already launched in 1983 by the LTTE under V. Prabhakaran.

This bloody civil war lasted more than a quarter of a century and it practically devastated the economy of the eastern parts of the island, shattered the myth of 'Serendipity' and brought into sharper focus the role of India in the initial stages of militancy. The Indian Peace Keeping Force (IPKF) entered the fray in 1987, following the Indo–Sri

Lanka Accord and found itself battling the very forces that India's Research and Analysis Wing (RAW) had supposedly trained. Unable to achieve its objective of maintaining the peace, the IPKF withdrew in 1990, leaving the insurrection to be dealt with by the Sri Lankan Armed Forces (SLAF), which by now was free of the JVP-led revolt. The LTTE spread its violence far over the mainland and was very brutal in its methods but was, soon matched by the SLAF. The conflict came to an end in May 2009 under the leadership of President Mahinda Rajapakse, who had given a free hand to his SLAF to deal with the conflict, leading to horrific human rights abuses at the closing stages of the conflict.[178] By then, as per United Nations estimates, between 80,000 and 100,000 people had been killed since 1983.[179] Consequent to the end of the bloody conflict, President Rajapakse, struck a conciliatory note and stated, "This is our country. This is our mother land. No differences of race, caste and religion should prevail here.... Our aim was to liberate our Tamil people from the clutches of the LTTE. Protecting the Tamil-speaking people of this country is my responsibility. All should live with equal rights...I seek the support of all political parties for that solution...."[180] The presidential elections in January 2015 saw Rajapakse defeated and Sirisena elected, surprisingly with the backing of the Tamil North, which voted overwhelmingly for Sirisena.

Prognosis

Post election of Sirisena, and consequent to the defeat of the LTTE in 2009, efforts to reach out to the Tamil North, was one of the prime foci of the Sri Lankan Government (SLG). Despite the war, Sri Lanka's growth rate has been a steady 5 per cent and above growth dipping only in 2009, but growing to an amazing 15 per cent in 2012. During the conflict years, the tea and garment industries showed particular resilience and sustained the country substantially. The GDP is poised to grow at a steady 5.5 per cent per annum over the next four years. Unemployment being a cause of worry is pegged at 4.3 per cent by 2020.[181] The culmination of the war also led to a boom in construction. There has been a concerted effort by the Sirisena government to focus on improving the infrastructure of the island, particularly the East coast—long neglected due to the dominant LTTE presence. The development of the road network and international ports, both air and sea, represent the first semblance of a peace dividend. With assistance from India, Sri Lanka is now restoring and upgrading its railway network. India has also committed to invest substantially in Sri Lanka in non-traditional fields like information technology.[182] Remittances from the Sri Lankan Diaspora, totalling approximately 1.8 million people, amounted to $ 1.178 billion in 2014[183] and is growing at a steady pace of approximately 9 per cent per annum, and is a healthy contributor to the reconstruction efforts.

Sri Lanka's challenges in the coming years would likely manifest in a resurgent bout of Tamil nationalism. Sri Lankan Tamils (SLT) settled abroad, other than in India, account for roughly one million people, who, during the height of the war, contributed an estimated $ 200 million a year to the LTTE.[184] Sri Lanka's total population of 22 million is broadly broken down into Sinhalese 74.9 per cent, Sri Lankan Tamils 11.2 per cent, Sri Lankan Muslims 9.2 per cent, Indian Tamils 4.2 per cent, and others 0.5 per cent (2012 est.).[185] With the looming shadow of 72 million Tamils, just across the Palk Straits, as well as approximately one lakh SLT refugees still in India, and 3.7 million in Malaysia,[186] the SLG can ill afford to ignore the aspirations of the SLT without causing ripples amongst the dominant Sinhala population. SLT leaders are aware that open support for their cause by politicians in Tamil Nadu play into Sinhala hands who portray SLTs as separatists.[187] The Muslim population, mostly based in the northern and eastern parts of Sri Lanka, while not identifying themselves as Tamils, was, at one time, part of the SLT's struggle for their linguistic and political rights and had aligned with the moderate Tamil United Liberation Front (TULF). They formed their own political party, the Sri Lanka Muslim Congress, in 1986 and steered clear of separatist ideology. Driven out from northern Sri Lanka by the LTTE, the Muslims fled as refugees into the south and east.[188] However, there has been simmering discontent between the majority nationalist group Bodu Bala Sena (BBS) and the Muslims, leading to clashes in June 2014 in some Muslim pockets in the Sinhala-dominated south western coast.[189] The SLG quickly clamped down to prevent the conflagration spreading. The Muslims have not resorted to taking up arms to assert their political presence, although some of them have worked with government forces and few were members of the early Tamil militant groups, especially the TULF Apprehensions exist that younger Muslims may give vent to their anger, against both Sinhala and SLT, in the eastern province, for past grievances. SLG has to manage the environment with great political sagacity and reach out to both minorities to ensure no resurgence of the LTTE is allowed, nor emergence of any Muslim fundamentalism. Reconciliation through rehabilitation, reconstruction and a reconnect through devolution is the only way forward.

Impact of Terrorism in the Maldives

Lying in the Indian Ocean, The Maldives is an archipelagic nation consisting of 26 natural atolls, comprising 1,190 islands (200 inhabited islands, plus 80 islands with tourist resorts), about 675 km southwest of Sri Lanka, with its coral islets dispersed over an area of 90,000 sq km but with the total land area being 300 sq km. A vacationer's paradise, with more than a third of the nation's revenues coming mainly from the million-or-so tourists[190] who flock to its beaches and private islands. Global warming, shrinking of polar ice caps and rising sea levels, place the existence of The Maldives under serious threat, as none of its islands rise more than six feet above sea level. Its importance stems from its strategic geographic location, astride and along major sea lanes in the Indian Ocean. The Maldives were first settled by Buddhist seafarers from India and Sri Lanka around the 5th century BC. Islam was introduced in 1153 and the official religion is Sunni Muslim. Its population of around 4 lakh (2014) comprises ethnic stock of South Indians, Sinhalese, and Arabs. Originally, the islands were under the suzerainty of Ceylon (now Sri Lanka). They came under British protection in 1887 and were a dependency of the then colony of Ceylon until 1948. An independence agreement with Britain was signed on July 26, 1965. For centuries a sultanate, the islands adopted a republican form of government in 1952, but the sultanate was restored in 1954. In 1968, however, as the result of a referendum, a republic was again established in the recently-independent country. Ibrahim Nasir, the authoritarian president since 1968, was removed from office and replaced by the more progressive Maumoon Abdul Gayoom in 1978. Gayoom was elected to a sixth five-year term in 2003. [191, 192, 193]

In August 2008, post a new constitution under the new multi-party system saw the emergence of Mohamed Nasheed as the new president, inheriting a baggage of problems, not the least being poverty. Intra and inter-party feuds saw palace coups and counter-coups and in February 2012, Nasheed was forced to step down. The Maldives remained in a state of flux and in the elections of November 2012, Abdullah Yameen emerged as the winner, claiming his electoral victory to be God-granted, a victory for Allah and Islam.[194] Wahhabi Islam has been making steady inroads into The Maldives, even during Nasheed's time.[195] The Maldives is now in the throes of a rapid authoritarian reversal in the process of establishing Wahhabi and Salafist hegemony and has rejected democracy as an antithesis to Islam.[196] The LeT established a foothold in The Maldives, post the tsunami, through its charitable front organisation, Idara Khidmat-e-Khalq. Lack of employment (expected to top 12 per cent in 2016)[197] and higher education is pushing the youth towards jihadists and events in the Middle East, Afghanistan and Pakistan are reportedly influencing them towards Pakistan-based madrassas and jihadist groups.[198] Sufism, which is so much a part of South Asian Islam, and underpins many cultural and socio-religious practices in traditional Maldivian Islam—is discouraged in The Maldives, if not outlawed.[199]

Given the strategic location of The Maldives, astride vital sea lanes of communications of the Indian Ocean, through which pass an average of 100,000 ships a year, carrying 50 per cent of the world's container traffic as well as 33 per cent of the world's cargo traffic [200] and oil arteries to Japan, China, Australia and Western America, the necessity of its political stability cannot be overemphasised. Given its importance, post assistance requested by The Maldives in 1988 to quell a coup, India has set up a process to bring the island country into its security grid. This was prompted after its fears that one of its island resorts could be taken over by terrorists, given its lack of military assets and surveillance capabilities. Consequently, India signed an agreement permanently basing two helicopters to enhance its surveillance capabilities and ability to respond swiftly to threats; setting up radars on all the 26 atolls for seamless coverage of approaching vessels and aircraft, and networked with the Indian coastal radar system as well as the Indian Coast Guard carrying out regular Dornier surveillance sorties over the island nation.[201]

An alleged attempt on the life of the President on 28 September 2015 and the political purges that followed have only reinforced President Yameen's hold over the country's security and political apparatus, and curbed dissent and even saw Vice President Adeeb arrested for the 'plot to assassinate the President, that as per FBI sources, was nothing more than a blast in the President's speedboat not caused by any explosive substance.[202]

Prognosis

While terrorism, per se, has not struck The Maldives, the violence that led to Nasheed's ouster portends to the steady inroads made by the Salafists into the political and military fibre of The Maldives. An estimated 200 youth have reportedly joined the ISIS, radicalised by the very same preachers who followed and began preaching their brand of Islam, in the wake of the tsunami of 2004, at the smaller atolls. In Male (the capital), street gangs have contributed over 100 fighters to jihadist groups in Iraq and Syria. The main source for recruitment is prisons, where radicalisation takes place among the youth jailed for drugs and gang wars.[203] According to ex-President Nasheed, "Radical Islam is getting very, very strong in The Maldives, their strength in the military and in the police is very significant. They have people in strategic positions within both. Of the 200 people who have gone to jihad, the vast majority are ex-military".[204] Of larger concern is the return of some of the battle-hardened jihadists from different campaigns of the ISIS, LeT and Afghanistan and their joining up with already radicalised, unemployed youth in The Maldives and egged by unscrupulous politicians to impart their brand of Salafism on the Maldivians to establish a caliphate in The Maldives—funded on tourism (revenue generation of $ 1.9 billion in 2014),[205] terrorism on the seas through piracy and hostage ransom payments. The expansion of the Al-Qaeda and its affiliates or even ISIS elements seizing smaller atolls as a base to expand its operational sphere into the Indian Ocean region is a distinct possibility. They may be aided by terrorist groups operating in Southeast Asia like the Jamaah Islamiyah, the Abu Sayyaf group and the Mindanao Liberation Front who may want to enhance their area of influence in the future in an effort to find safe havens.[206] The need therefore is to ensure thorough de-radicalisation programmes for all returnees from war zones, and concurrently control the movement of youth for 'education' to madarsas abroad, especially those travelling to Pakistan and Saudi Arabia. Addressing the drug problem and generating more meaningful employment amongst youth, as well as identifying and weeding out rogue elements in the military and police are matters of priority. The Maldivian Security Forces, by themselves, will not be able to tackle a terrorist takeover or strike and will need assistance to address complex terror cases—in this case the first responders will perforce have to be the Indian Armed Forces, who should be geared up for such emergencies.

Conclusion

Financing of non-state actors by nations to carry out terror attacks against their perceived enemies has been cost effective, so to say, as it not only reduces the recurring costs of maintaining proportionately larger conventional forces, but also seeks to avoid ownership, at least in the initial stages. As investigative techniques and tools become more sophisticated, newer modes are operated to carry out terror strikes against opponents. The commission to enquire into terror financing concluded that the costs for the Al-Qaeda to mount an operation of the magnitude and complexity of 11 September 2001 that commenced the global war on terror, amounted to just under $ 500,000[207] and that the then controls to prevent abuse of the financial system did not fail. The financial impact consequent to the global war on terror, post September 2001, has been assessed to have cost the USA an estimated $ 3.7 trillion,[208] so far. The anonymity of the international and domestic financial system to move and store money for terror plotters worldwide conducted through a series of unremarkable transactions also emerged, as did the use of hawala transactions by the Al-Qaeda to transfer funds from the Gulf area to Pakistan and Afghanistan, adding to the complexities of monitoring terror funding.

To bring about stability and peace in the SAARC region, a comprehensive plan, incorporating the engagement of stakeholders and governments at national levels to address issues covering rehabilitation, reconstruction and development of social indices including health, education and poverty alleviation, followed by detailed engagements at regional levels is a prerequisite for success. People-to-people contact programmes including students, common people, intellectuals and policy makers (including military) visits and exchanges greatly enhance the scope of understanding the dynamics prevalent in regions and that of other's nations and is a useful tool in future conflict prevention.

CHAPTER 3

Rising Threats in the SAARC Region

Terrorism rarely follows a dialogue or a script. Invariably what is planned, catered for and dealt with appropriately, could possibly lead to a different calculus than war-gamed. Environmental factors such as political compulsions, regional dynamics, public and terrorist aspirations and resolve, ground realities and economics, amongst others, are some of the pulls and pressures that influence the flow of the regional or national narratives, so to say. Writing in the *Armed Forces Journal* in June 2006,[209] Ralph Peters in 'Blood Borders' alludes to the arbitrary and distorted borders in Africa and the Middle East, drawn by self-interested Europeans, that continue to provoke millions of deaths. This narrative can be easily templated to when the British drew the frontiers for the new nations that emerged from the partition of the Indian subcontinent, the consequences of which reverberate even today.[210] Just as the 'Sykes–Picot' agreement[211] between France and Great Britain come unravelling today in the Middle East, the possibility of an equivalent setting emerging in the Indian subcontinent, presently remote, could also act as a catalyst to spur unification like the European Union or a Greater India or a Union of Indian Secular States, before the middle of this century.

Concerns

A purported ISIS map outlining their plans for dominance of major portions of Mackinder's World Island, specifically the Middle East,

North Africa, most of the Indian subcontinent and parts of Europe, within the next five years, to complete its caliphate, has been doing the rounds since BBC reporter Andrew Hosken published his book '*Empire of Fear: Inside the Islamic State*'.[212] The Libyan dictator, Gaddafi, had reportedly told the TV network France 24 that if he were to be deposed, "There are millions of blacks who could come to the Mediterranean to cross to France and Italy, and Libya plays a role in security in the Mediterranean".[213] The Arab Spring unrest, which began in January 2011, led to changed regimes, instability in North Africa and a flood of refugees throughout most of Europe, in continuation with the earlier exodus of refugees post the Iraq civil war. An outflow of refugees from Syria into Turkey, Lebanon and Jordan[214] has enlarged the fragility of the area. Recent anti-refugee demonstrations in Germany, France, Norway, and Sweden have put paid, as of now, to further resettlement plans in the Schengen Nations and imposition of tighter entry controls. Connect the events in Europe to what is happening in the SAARC nations in general and the Indian subcontinent in particular over the last three decades, and a sense of the enormity of the challenges posed by just one facet of terrorism—refugees—becomes apparent.

The steady proselytisation of Saudi Wahhabism is a cause for concern in the subcontinent. Singapore's former Prime Minister, Lee Kuan Yew, pointed to Saudi Arabia as the *Queen Bee* spawning terrorism in Asia and, in the 1970s, awash with petro dollars; Saudi Wahhabi began to export this 'venomous religion' via thousands of mosques and madarsas that have radicalised Muslims in South and Southeast Asia. As a result, Afghanistan, Pakistan, Indonesia, Malaysia, Singapore and The Philippines have been victims of Wahhabi-driven extremist groups such as the Jemaah Islamiah, Abu Sayyaf, MILF, ISIS, Taliban, and others. Prime Minister Lee warned, "In killing terrorists, you will only kill the worker bees. The queen bees are the preachers, who teach a deviant form of Islam in schools and Islamic centres, which capture and twist the minds of the young".[215] With public and private Saudi funding, Wahhabism has steadily gained influence among Muslim communities and consequently, the nature of South Asian Islam has become increasingly violent in Pakistan, the Kashmir Valley, and Bangladesh—highlighting the connect of fundamentalism to Saudi money and the radicalisation of Islam with Wahhabism's spread in South Asia. Islam in South Asia is characterised traditionally with Sufism—mystical Islam—as well as elements of syncretism with Hinduism and other native religions as distinct from Middle Eastern Islam. As a result, many South Asians are now Wahhabis or members of related sects like the Deobandi movement, which, although indigenous to South Asia are influenced by Wahhabism. On the other hand, the Barelvi movement, which was formed in reaction to Deobandi, seeks to preserve the Islamic practices of South Asia, especially pilgrimages to graves and shrines. Saudi influence (government and charities) in the form of funds for Deobandi and Wahhabi madarsas and mosques initially entered Pakistan during the Soviet invasion of Afghanistan in order to educate the impoverished, create and train mujahedeen to fight Soviet Communism. The Inter-Services Intelligence (ISI) saw the spread of Wahhabism as useful to create jihadist proxies to influence Afghanistan and Indian Kashmir; consequently, even after the end of the Soviet-Afghan War in 1989, the influence of Wahhabism continued to grow in Pakistan. Today, Saudi money continues to convert Muslim groups to Wahhabism in other parts of South Asia, including India and Bangladesh.[216] It is thus evident that the uncontested erosion of the state's responsibility to provide quality and relevant education to deprived sections of society is seized by Wahhabis eager to impose their brand of radical Islam. It is essential that affected nations halt the spread of Wahhabism through Saudi funding for mosques and madarsas and institute state control and mechanism for funding education to fight radical Islam, bringing about the emancipation of the poor through modernisation.

Unemployment, the prime provider of foot soldiers for terror groups, is an increasing phenomenon worldwide. SAARC nations have high unemployment rates and equally high population growth rates—a volatile combination for the industry of Terror Inc. Taking into account low industrial and agricultural growth rates, prevailing, as well as limited scope for immediate alleviation, the figures are ominous. See Table 1.

Table 1

Country	*Population (Approx million)*	*Unemployed/ Underemployed (UE)*	*Percentage below poverty level (BPL)*
Afghanistan	25	35%	36%
Bangladesh	153	41% UE	31%
Bhutan	.75	2%	12%
India	1,224	7%	22%
Maldives	.33	28%	16%
Nepal	25	46%	25%
Pakistan	184	6.6*	22%
Sri Lanka	20	4.2%	8.9%

*Substantial underemployed (Figures not available)

Sources: 1. CIA Country Factbook for Unemployed/Underemployed and BPL figures.
2. SAARC population (http://www.saarcstat.org/content/saarc-figures-2013).

The economic drawdown in Saudi Arabia due to the crash in oil prices coincided with the exploitation of alternative sources of energy and proliferation of Asian economic highways and alliances. This includes the New Silk Route Economic Belt and Maritime Silk route Initiative, India–Bangladesh–Myanmar–China economic corridor and Asian Highway Number 1, linking India to Thailand via Myanmar that are indicators of a SAARC economic boom waiting to happen. SAARC is just one of the economic and regional alliances in the region and, as part of the ASEAN-India Plan of Action for the period 2016-20, adopted in August 2015, identifies concrete initiatives and areas of cooperation along the three pillars of political-security, economic and socio-cultural. India continues with stepped-up efforts to forge closer partnerships with concerned regional and multilateral organisations such as the Association of South East Asian Nations (ASEAN), ASEAN Regional Forum (ARF), East Asia Summit (EAS), Bay of Bengal Initiative for Multi-Sectoral Technical and Economic Cooperation (BIMSTEC), Asia Cooperation Dialogue (ACD), Mekong Ganga Cooperation (MGC) and the Indian Ocean Rim Association (IORA).[217]

Fears exist of Pakistan crumbling under the weight of weak governance, crippling debt, jihadist violence, increasing public polarisation, aggressive military and a growing unstable western frontier. With the likely re-establishment of the Taliban in Afghanistan after the US drawdown and the possibility of fragmenting into various alliances, akin to the period post the Soviet withdrawal and before the establishment of the Taliban, further uncertainty and insecurity is presaged in Afghanistan. Bangladesh has only now started getting into grips with its fundamentalists, but bogged down by a burgeoning population, shrinking land space and a truculent opposition, smarting from recent political reverses and banning of its affiliates. Nepal, sliding intermittently into chaos, anarchy and factionalism between stability. Bhutan, content with Gross National Happiness for now, but needing to reach out to the world with a Switzerland-like potential, in terms of tourism and neutrality, whilst guarding against a looming Chinese expansionist threat from Tibet in the north and an influx of Bangladeshi migrants in the south. Sri Lanka, coming to stability, post the LTTE phase and walking a tightrope between Chinese generosities, with strings attached and muted Indian support against Tamil sentiments. The Maldives, swimming against the tide of rising fundamentalism, political dictatorship, and a real threat of being swamped by rising seas. Against all this background, looms India as the centre of SAARC gravity, the region's most powerful prime mover, the world's largest and tempestuous democracy, an aspirational superpower seeking its space in the sun, but hamstrung by internal dissensions and external proxies and irrational powers, forging ahead with or without its neighbours. The dictum of Lord Acton—Great powers have no permanent friends or foes, they have permanent interests—holds good for any aspiring regional or super power. The best way therefore for India to bring about progress in the region lies in the collective unity of SAARC with a sense of cooperation and commitment to help each other grow and excise the spoilers.

Challenges in Asia

Against the SAARC scenario and the backdrop of the present and ongoing security challenges in Asia, one gets a fair idea of what might emerge in the not-too-distant future. These include the tensions across the 38th Parallel on the Korean Peninsula, and periodic threats of war by North Korea. Existent territorial disputes between China and Japan and China and India; continued Chinese claims over Taiwan; maritime security issues such as in the South China Sea, Mischief

Reef and Chinese expansionist designs on the Indian Ocean Rim (IOR), may likely escalate as the Chinese seek to increasingly challenge the USA in supremacy over Asia and the IOR.

Mostly energy rich, but internally stressed, the landlocked Central Asian Republics (CARs) or 'Sthans'—Kazakhstan, Kyrgyzstan, Turkmenistan, Uzbekistan and Tajikistan—have seen a more or less stable security situation, post the US-led Anti-Taliban Operations of 2001 in Afghanistan. However, a potential realignment of their priorities is now beginning to appear, with the CARs contemplating a future without the inbuilt security of US forces stationed in Afghanistan expected in 2016, that could have serious political implications for the stability of all five of these nations and this energy rich region. In terms of security, the major challenge in the region is terrorism. Situated next to Afghanistan and the restive Chinese province of Xinjiang, the CARs face the fallout of the volatile security situation in Afghanistan and Pakistan's Federally Administered Tribal Areas. Notwithstanding clearly defined ethnic and demographic differences, all the five countries are concerned about the spread of Islamic extremism concurrent with narcotics and weapons trafficking and the increase of terrorism and organised crime. The emergence of a potential security vacuum is, thus, real and their slide to anarchy is possible and not just hypothetical given the weak governance parameters and fragility of the region post the dissolution of the USSR. Russia is similarly concerned as its former states expose its vulnerable underbelly to a resurgent and violent Islam due to a probable worsening of the security situation in Afghanistan in the new future. While maintaining a sizable security presence in Central Asia through military bases in Kyrgyzstan and Tajikistan, Russia remains the main military and security assistance provider for most of the CARs, a criticality for their regimes to remain in power, while maintaining its influence in the region through the Collective Security Treaty Organisation, headquartered in Moscow.[218] Additionally, Kyrgyzstan and Tajikistan are deeply dependent on remittances from their nationals working in Russia. More than a million Tajiks alone work in Russia. The Chinese are also increasingly worried over the Xinjiang Region being exposed to radical Islamic forces; post the US withdrawal the region could see a spike in terror-related activities. India has been making concerted efforts to establish its presence ever since Prime Minister Narendra Modi visited in July 2015, in terms of infrastructure development, mining and energy transmission network besides the Turkmenistan–Iran–Pakistan–India gas pipeline after tepid responses by the Indian government, during an earlier initiative in 2012.

Geographically, the West Asian region stretches from Yemen and Oman in the south to Syria in the north. In the west, it includes Israel and Palestine and in the east, Iran. In the centre lie the oil-rich countries of the Persian Gulf. The largest country is Saudi Arabia. The region is volatile because of the Israel-Palestine conflict, continued instability in Syria and Iraq and the nuclear power aspirations of Iran. Shia-dominant Iran, in collusion with China, North Korea (DPRK) and Pakistan for covert supply of nuclear and missile technology, has resulted in the possibility of a sixth nuclear power in Asia. The UN Security Council has passed a number of resolutions calling for Iran to suspend its uranium enrichment and reprocessing activities and comply with its IAEA obligations and responsibilities. In July 2015, Iran and the five Permanent Members, plus Germany (P5+1) signed the Joint Comprehensive Plan of Action (JCPOA) under which Iran agreed to restrictions on its nuclear program in exchange for relief in sanctions. While the present attempts to prevent Iran from going nuclear have postponed the crisis temporarily, the process has been only delayed. The security challenge lies in a probable future confrontation between Israel and Iran with the USA factor looming over West Asia. Iran, known to be backing the Shiite Houthis against Saudi-backed Yemeni forces, is backing Syrian government forces. India has the potential to exercise a stabilising influence through diplomacy over Iran to negate a spillover of this potential conflict and to countervail Pakistani inroads into Afghanistan with Iranian support. Despite the economic downturn following sanctions, Iran has remained secure, internally stable, and would likely remain so in the near future.

However, the volatility in the Middle East is likely to persist. The Persian Gulf, a 600-mile long extension of the Indian Ocean separates the Arabian Peninsula from Iran. Sixty-six per cent of the world's known oil reserves are located in the Gulf countries, which produce over a third of the world's daily output (by comparison, North America holds 8.5 per cent of world's reserves). Saudi Arabia ranks second in reserves, with 266 billion barrels, followed by Iran (157 billion), Iraq (143 billion) and Kuwait (101 billion).[219] The Gulf is also rich in natural gas, with Iran and Qatar holding the world's second and third largest reserves, respectively.[220] This area also provides access to the landlocked Central Asian Republics, which is gaining strategic importance because of their reserves of natural gas. The colonial legacy of arbitrary geographical boundaries of the states has led to ongoing territorial disputes of which two important ones remain intractable—the Shatt-al-Arab waterway between Iran and Iraq and sovereignty over Abu Musa islands at the mouth of the Gulf between Iran and the UAE. Iran, Iraq, and Saudi Arabia are the major players in the region with competing and conflicting ideologies, instabilities and differing systems of governance and with a looming threat of the ISIS and Al-Qaeda and the happenings after Arab Spring. The Middle East faces a wide gamut of possibilities from fragile growth to chronic instability and regional conflicts. New energy technologies and lowering costs mandates oil-based economies to diversify in order to survive. Critical variables include the stability of the House of Saud; the emergence of a radical Islamist government in Egypt; and fragmentation in Iraq and Syria, which could lead to the unravelling of current borders.[221]

SAARC Concerns

Against this backdrop in the volatile region, radical occurrences have a cascading impact on its neighbouring regions and, given their proximity to the SAARC nations, it is imperative that the security environment be monitored to lessen the political, economic as well as security impact on SAARC nations. Migrant workers in the Middle East from SAARC nations totalled 7 million in 2002[222] and by 2012, the number of Indian workers there increased by 1.6 million to total approximately 5.2 million. It is safe to assume that, should there be an upheaval or political instability in the Gulf region, a sizeable work force would return to their countries of origin, bringing in their wake additional unemployment, influx or infiltration of possibly radicalised elements besides a dip in remittances (estimated currently at almost $ 25 billion for just India from the Gulf states alone). This would cause internal turmoil and instability in the smaller and less resilient SAARC economies, in the short and possibly mid-term. SAARC nations face internal and external challenges over the next two decades. Low growth, rising food prices, and energy shortages will pose stiff challenges to governance in Pakistan and Afghanistan, where youth bulges combined with a slow-growing economy, predict instability. India is in an advantageous position, benefiting from higher growth, but increasingly challenged to find jobs and food security for its large population. India's turbulent neighbourhood of smaller nations always had a profound impact on its internal political, economic and security developments, consequent to which regional mistrust prevents the development of a strong security framework for SAARC.

In the larger mosaic of emerging threats, potential game changers[223] that the SAARC nations would face would broadly fall under the following categories: Population, Employment, Food-Water-Energy Security, Urbanisation, Effects of Global Warming, Good Governance and Heightened Awareness (due to increased literacy levels and Internet connectivity).

Population

SAARC nations would grow exponentially. Table 2 shows the projected population with country rankings in 2050.

Table 2: Population Projection for 2015 and 2050

Nation	*2025*	*2050*	*World population rank 2050*
India	1.418 billion	1.620 billion	1
Pakistan	218 million (m)	271 m	4
Bangladesh	177 m	202 m	7
Afghanistan	39.5 m	56.5 m	23
Nepal	31.4 m	36.4 m	35
Sri Lanka	22 m	22.5 m	67
Bhutan	.8 m	.9 m	114
Maldives	.4 m	.5 m	158

Source: Population Estimates and Projections, World Bank, (http://datatopics.worldbank.org/hnp/popestimates.)

What is alarming is that by 2050, just eight South Asian nations will have a population of approximately 2.2 billion out of the world's projected figure of 9.6 billion, i.e., a stupendous 23 per cent of the world's population crammed in an area 3.4 per cent of the world's land area. The strain on resources, jobs, agriculture and food supply, water, infrastructure including basic hygiene, goods and service needs, would increase exponentially. With younger age profiles India, Pakistan and Bangladesh, are likely to enjoy the economic benefits of young and productive workforces over the period (Table 3). However, without the necessary social and educational policies in place to use such young populations and if inequality and corruption lead to large, young populations with limited economic opportunities but greater material aspirations, this 'demographic dividend' could become a 'demographic time bomb'. Thus, matching growth for work opportunities and immediate and drastic checks must be enforced to reduce the population as it is a calamity 'in being', ready to burst. The migration of a burgeoning middle class to other 'work stations' could well take place.

Employment

The employment of the sizable increase in the work force and the migratory shift from the rural to the urban belt, (Table 3) necessitates the creation of jobs in the skilled and unskilled sectors, domestically and abroad. Studies infer that in current advanced economies like in Western Europe and Japan, with an aging population, these countries will face difficulties in maintaining their living standards; consequently, a spurt in demand for both skilled and unskilled labour will spur global migration. Owing to rapid urbanisation, the volume of urban construction and transport services over the next 40 years is estimated to equal the entire volume of such construction to date in world history.[224] This would require nimbleness in thought and action on the part of governments and agencies to reach out, through government-to-government networking or through the reach of multi-national corporations. New jobs need to be created taking into account the increasing numbers that are added every year in the potential workforce.

Food-Water-Energy Security

All SAARC nations are highly stressed in these three vital sectors and need to concentrate on alternatives. Key technologies to be exploited will include indigenous technology in genetically modified crops, precision agriculture, improved irrigation techniques for providing food security, solar energy, advanced bio-based fuels, enhanced oil, and natural gas extraction via fracturing. Such technologies and expertise would need examination and implemented through the medium of UN agencies for greater acceptance. India particularly needs to invest more in terms of science and technology to optimise its quest for viable alternatives, especially in the Energy and Agriculture sectors, while improving on its water harvesting and management. SAARC will achieve food security through building greater resilience, trade networks, sustainable intensification, and working to improve output from the same land with fewer adverse impacts. Investing in long-term lease of land in Africa and even Australia, as well as using modern technology, hybrid, drought and pest resistance varieties would significantly boost and diversify global production thereby addressing chronic food shortages the world over. The quest for alternative sources of energy, especially wind, solar and tidal energy and efficient storage and transmission measures is essential, in view of the impact of greenhouse gases due to burning of fossil fuels. Interlinking of rivers to prevent flooding, water runoffs to the seas, as well as recharge of aquifers are some of the immediate measures to address water shortages and droughts.

Urbanisation

The urban population figures of SAARC countries are set to see a growth of almost 250 million people by 2030, having already witnessed an increase of 130 million between 2000 and 2011. Urbanisation fosters productivity through agglomeration of both people and enterprises in its towns and cities, as firms and workers experience by clustering together, enhance productivity and spur job creation, specifically in manufacturing and services. This process is clearly visible in the transformation of the region's economy, with manufacturing and services accounting for more than 80 per cent of the GDP in the SAARC nations. Major shortcomings, however, are inadequate provision of infrastructure, basic urban services, insufficient housing leading to sprawling slums and degraded environment.[225] 'Smart Cities' and 'Housing for All' are initiatives by the Indian Government, the objective being to promote cities that provide core infrastructure and give a decent quality of life to its citizens, a clean and sustainable environment and application of 'Smart' solutions. The focus is on sustainable and inclusive development and the idea is to look at compact areas[226] to address the problems of urbanisation. Table 3 (for the period between now and 2050) conveys the enormity of the employment generation and urbanisation issues that are necessary to be fast tracked.

Table 3: Actual and projected employability of rural population in South Asia

Country	*2015 population percentage*	*2025 expected population*	*Percentage employable*	*Rural of population*	*2050 expected population*	*Percentage employable*	*Rural Percentage of population*
Afghanistan	52.6 -73.3	39.5	61	68.6	70.5	56.5	54.7
Bangladesh	160 -65.7	177	69.2	58.4	202	66.5	44.3
Bhutan	0.7 -61.4	0.8	67.2	54.7	0.9	66.6	45
India	1282 -67.3	1418	67.6	63	1620	67.8	49.7
Maldives	0.3 -54.5	0.4	67.9	46	0.5	65.4	37.5
Nepal	28.4 -81.4	31.4	67.1	77.3	36.4	68.3	64.4
Pakistan	188 -61.2	218	65.6	56.2	271	69.2	42.5
Sri Lanka	20.7 -81.6	22	64.9	80.4	22.5	61.2	69.8

*Population figures in millions.
Employable population considered between 15-64years of age.
Source: http://datatopics.worldbank.org/hnp/popestimates.

From the above figures, it is clearly discernible that the shift from the rural to the urban over the next 35 years will vary from 8.5 per cent in the case of The Maldives, to 13.7 per cent for Pakistan and a high of 17.9 per cent for India. These shifts will take place because of better opportunities for employment, but will require matching infrastructure, social and transportation needs as well as advance town and urban planning to prevent overstraining of already tenuous resources. It is also apparent that the bulk of the workforce is in the 'employable age' bracket; thus suitable career opportunities at home and abroad have to be available. It has been estimated that Indian cities could generate 70 per cent of net new jobs created by 2030, produce around 70 per cent of the Indian GDP, and drive a near fourfold increase in per capita incomes across the nation.[227] Handled well, SAARC nations can reap significant benefits from urbanisation and learn from the Indian experience if shared with the expertise gained. Given that India has yet to implement its ambitious Smart Cities programmes, and considering these are going to be 'package' add-ons to existing cities, it is uniquely placed to ensure follow up on new smart cities coming up globally. Masdar, outside Abu Dhabi, is an example of self-sufficiency in terms of water, zero waste and powered by renewable energy.[228] The model needs follow-up by other SAARC Smart Cities, planned by their respective nations. SAARC nations have the potential to unlock many new growth markets in their cities, including infrastructure, transportation, healthcare, education, and recreation but to reap such benefits, unprecedented policy challenges have to be met and political consensus of parties achieved. Failure implies serious jeopardy of growth and consequent unemployment peaks, and instability in the region.

Global Warming

Effects of global warming directly influence land availability, food production, employment, rising salinity levels and shortage of potable water and threat of rising seas swamping large tracts of low-lying areas. These changes are already affecting the economic performance of SAARC countries from increased climate variability including intense floods, droughts, and storms. In addition, the melting of glaciers in the Himalayas is projected to increase flooding and affect water resources within the next two to three decades. Climate change would lead to rapid urbanisation, industrialisation, and decreased crop yields up to 30 per cent by the mid-21st century. The rise in sea levels will exacerbate inundation, storm surge, erosion and other coastal hazards.[229] Mitigation of risks associated with climate change and measures to adapt to global warming would affect every aspect of the economy and way of life. It encompasses green energy usage, efficient modes of transportation, green buildings and smart cities, forestation and green cover as well as preservation of mangrove belts along coastal belts and transition to an eco-friendly and sustainable economic growth model for current and future generations. Dramatic and unforeseen changes are already occurring at a faster rate than expected. The Maldives and Bangladesh face the brunt of rising seas and Nepal and India of rapid deforestation, in the name of development, without steps to rejuvenate. Rapid changes in precipitation patterns, such as monsoons in India and the rest of South Asia, could sharply disrupt the region's ability to feed its population. Cereal production is already facing significant challenges from environmental stresses relating to water scarcity, soil depletion, climate change, and pressures on land availability from urbanisation. The SAARC Action Plan on Climate Change identifies seven thematic areas of cooperation covering adaptation; mitigation; technology transfer; finance and investment; education and awareness; management of impacts and risks; and capacity building for international negotiations.[230] However, much more needs to be done than plain rhetoric, as implementable action plans in sync with UN protocols have to be accelerated. The ratification of the Paris Agreement of Conference of Parties (COP) 21, for climate change, over the next year and its implementation may decelerate global warming.[231]

Good Governance

As the world 'shrinks' due to the 'explosion' of new technologies enabling individuals to become vastly more connected and productive, SAARC nations have to focus on good governance and be accountable to meet the rising aspirations of their peoples. Empowerment through Education, Skills, 'right tax policies, the right investment and trade laws, the right support for research, the right intellectual property laws, and most of all the right inspirational leadership[232] through the right governance, would soon be the requirement for central and provincial/state governments to deliver. If the global middle class expands, as many experts project, the demand for rule of law and government accountability is likely to increase, as will be the demand to tackle the forces of inequality and corruption. Eradicating corruption is critical for SAARC nations if they aspire to maintain social and political stability and maintain credibility. Visionary leadership, a sound and accountable administrative establishment geared towards inclusive growth and development will be able to square up to the national, regional and global challenges that emerge. Challenges associated with managing increasing urban conglomerations will tax governing structures, but such challenges will also prompt the development of effective governing structures and smarter technologies. A growing number of diverse and dissimilar state, sub-national, and non-state actors will play important governance roles in an increasingly multipolar world.[233] The Indian Government's initiative to empower, educate and streamline governance through the 'Digital India' initiative is one such method.[234]

Heightened Awareness

K. Subrahmanyam opined that in this 21st century, in a world order of pluralism, secularism and democracy, knowledge would be the currency of power, not nuclear warheads and missiles.[235] Exponential changes brought about by the proliferation of IT use, has a flip side too—multiple and simultaneous action, instantaneous responses, and mass mobilisation of people and resources across national and linguistic boundaries. Technological dependence enhances the potential for more frequent conflict, as social networks enable citizens to challenge governments, as witnessed in North Africa and the Middle East. Concurrently, IT provides governments with enhanced capability to monitor their citizens. Increasingly, terrorism will shift its focus from the physical aspect of causing mass casualties and focus more on creating economic and financial disruptions as terrorists comprehend the scope of the disruptions that can be caused by cyber warfare, thereby ensuring the 'hardening' of potential targets from military systems to electricity grids, communications networks, and financial systems.

Likely Threats SAARC Nations May Face in the Future

Envisioning future threats likely to be confronted by SAARC nations is hazardous, because repeatedly, major events, shaped by Man or Nature, have impacted adversely on the environment and nations, and the next course of action has been dictated by national or regional response. The catalyst for Pakistan to crack down on its terror groups has not been the assassination of Benazir Bhutto, but the events of 9/11, in far-away USA—followed by the US diktat: *either you are with us or against us*. In effect, if against the USA, the threat would be being bombed back into the Stone Age.[236] Accentuated by the ghastly killings of the Army School children in Peshawar, Pakistan has shifted its focus, but still retains its Afghan-based 'clients' as a strategic asset. The impact of global warming makes its presence felt with rising seas threatening to submerge millions of acres of delta land in the Sundarbans and Bangladesh, putting pressure on already shrinking land bases, consequently leading to migrations, refugees, food shortages and their adverse impact on neighbouring provinces and nations. On the other hand, resolution of the LTTE 'problem' through highly questionable and debatable methods has ushered in a time of peace, introspection and concentrating on development of human indices in Sri Lanka. Worldwide, rapid advances in technology, interconnectivity as well as transparency has had a cascading effect on events and responses that make good and dynamic governance that much of a challenge. Weighed against the existing and emerging situation and the parameters spelt out earlier, the future for SAARC nations in dealing with terrorism and instability would be to focus on a smart strategy combining the lethality of hard power and the salutary effects of soft power. The engagement of nations outside the present association, especially regional giant China and the sole global power, the USA, has to be factored into the overall security calculus as well as take into consideration the dynamic regional alliances of

ASEAN, SCO, African Union and the Middle East, weighed in by the SAARC as an entity and the bilateral relationship of individual nations. Depending on the effectiveness of respective national responses to emerging challenges, SAARC could therefore tread any of the courses outlined below over the next three decades.

Partial Instability

The status quo of the present prevailing situation is partial stability in Pakistan with terror groups reined in, but with the threat of ISIS mutants still lingering, with the rest of SAARC states progressing to medium levels of peace and prosperity.

Ugly Instability: There could be a prolonged bout of instability in the region, given the spreading influence of the ISIS in the SAARC states, broadly taking up the following contours:

(a) ethno nationalism threatens breakup/leads to the breakup of Afghanistan and Pakistan;
(b) re-emergence of the LTTE in Sri Lanka and internecine conflicts between Buddhists and Muslims brings in prolonged instability in the island nation;
(c) Bangladesh and The Maldives confronting the twin threats of fundamentalism and global warming and the dangers of going under;
(d) Bhutan dealing with terror group sanctuaries from Assam and Bangladesh; and
(e) India and Nepal dealing with resurgent and enlarged Maoist activities propped up by China.

South Asian Market: This could take the peace and stability route, gradually ushered in after the last decade. It is possible to lead to a loose confederation, based on market-driven economies, liberal trade alliances and reduced travel restrictions. This would happen only if the state and people power prevail over fundamentalism and bigotry.

South Asian Unification: A consequence and *follow through* of the previous scenario, based on 'One South Asia' with a strong central government, and a federal system of democratic governance. While seemingly far-fetched as of now, if erstwhile animosities were to be set aside and allow people and economic power to triumph, then only would SAARC achieve a breakthrough in unification processes. Comprehensive development plans should be followed through, Sustainable Development Goals[237] achieved, leading to the region staving off the challenges of xenophobia. This would set in motion a landscape of regional alliances based on economic security, combined military alliances, political harmonisation, irrelevance of religion in the state polity and thereby lead to an era of peace all over—seemingly Utopian, but not unattainable.

When discord continues, regions and its peoples suffer. When concord is achieved, regional peace and stability have a stabilising influence on the neighbourhood besides ensuring growth and development. SAARC, as a regional platform, is an ideal endeavour to live up to its enshrined charter of consolidating democracy with the objectives of peace, freedom, social justice and economic prosperity in an increasingly interdependent world.[238]

While examining possible future courses against the backdrop of existing threats and correlating with incidents of the past, we frequently come across seemingly implausible scenarios, which, in hindsight, did not even seem as being on the horizon, but nonetheless were created due to conditions prevailing at that time. The end of monarchy in Nepal triggered by a 'Royal' slaughter followed by Maoist violence and their governance; the voluntarily ceding of space by the monarchy in Bhutan to usher in democracy; sidelining of Islamists in Bangladesh, nascent democracy in Afghanistan and the decline of martial law in Pakistan (though still controlling the key strings); with instability in The Maldives and the emergence of a right-wing democratic party in India are events that at some point seemed improbable over the past three decades. Yet they have emerged. The ending of the dictatorship of Saddam Hussein in Iraq by force of arms heralded chaos and instability in the Middle East, with no end in immediate sight just as the seemingly minor and irrational event of Mohamed Bouazizi's self-immolation in Tunisia, brought on the Arab Spring and its disproportionate fallout over dictators and countries in most of North Africa. The impact of such incidents can change the stability of whole regions with a cascading and even ripple effect on near and distant shores. Some of these *Irrational but not Improbable Events* that have serious consequences on the stability of SAARC nations are highlighted below. These events are likely to cause upheavals in the regional and possibly global landscape, leading to dangerous consequences or very different outcomes. It is quite possible that none of them is likely to take place but in a world full of uncertainties these could add up to new dynamics for the region.

(a) ***Weapons of mass destruction (WMD) in the hands of non-state actors:*** The possibility exists of a non-state actor or a group sponsored by a 'deep state' holding the region hostage to their demands, possibly disrupting trade in the IOR by seizure of an atoll in The Maldives and threatening mass destruction of transiting trade, by use of a WMD or a combination of WMDs is a grim possibility, considering the amount of literature available to fabricate DIY type 'dirty bombs'. The consequences of a retaliatory strike on sponsors would have equally horrific results.

(b) ***Collapse of Pakistan and WMD worry:*** Given the instability of the political situation and enhanced fundamentalism may force the military to take violent action against its earlier sponsored or supported groups. The resultant backlash and fragmentation of the country, inability of the military to ensure the safety of its WMDs and missiles, would bring about incalculable damage, besides likely intervention by super-powers to seize WMDs and prevent their falling into the hands of terror groups or smuggled away to other nations willing to buy them.

(c) ***War between India and Pakistan—expanded***: A Mumbai-type carnage could trigger a retaliatory air, naval strike on Pakistani economic and nuclear assets followed by an expanded canvas of war, drawing in the USA, Russia, and Israel to the conflict triggered by Pakistani-sponsored global terror groups.

(d) ***Greater Bangladesh***: Consequent to the existing refugee migration, which has brought about a change in the demographic balance with the Indian states of West Bengal,

Assam, Meghalaya and Tripura and accentuated by the submergence of already scarce land in Bangladesh or similar ecological calamities, any greater exodus of refugees will see the physical present boundaries of Bangladeshis push their settlements even deeper into the above states. This will not only cause political and administrative dissonance, but also bring about tremendous human suffering.

(e) ***Breakaway of Baluchistan and Sindh:*** Both provinces break away from Pakistan in a show of rebellion against Punjabi domination, continued state-sponsored violence, sectarian killings and inability of the national government to rein in their surrogates leading to break aways by Sindh[239] and Baluchistan.[240]

(f) ***Indian Summer:*** Inequity, burgeoning unemployment,[241] religion/caste-based reservation policies, rapid urbanization,[242] with a weak supporting infrastructure could lead to large-scale riots. Combined with a backlash against political and administrative hierarchy and aggravated by media, breakdown in law and order capacity and capability is fraught with grave consequences for the security of the region.

(g) ***Water scarcity and wars***: Several of Asia's major rivers—the Indus, Ganges, Brahmaputra, Mekong, Yangtze, and Yellow—originate in the Himalayas and due to global warming the snow/ice sheet cover in the Himalayas could thaw and it will dramatically reduce the water supply of much of Asia.[243] This will lead to famines, loss of agricultural land due to rise in sea levels and increased salinity, food shortages, famine and inter and intra-state conflicts.

(h) ***Collapse of SAARC:*** Pakistan, Afghanistan (by then a Pakistan-sponsored regime ruling it) Bangladesh and The Maldives quit SAARC on the pretext of 'Hindu' India and Nepal with 'Buddhist' Bhutan and Sri Lanka acting against Islamists. This would be a considerable jolt to India's regional standing. The flip side of this would be unfettered lack of forward movement in this regional forum, leaving most issues to be resolved bilaterally.

(i) ***Confederation of India:*** By 2050, there is the possibility of growing resistance to central government schemes and funding for increasingly laggard and fractious J&K, and Eastern[244] including North-eastern states.[245] especially since no tangible improvements are seen over a century of underwriting their expenditures. The wealthier southern, western[246] and mineral-rich central states could economically secede from the Indian Union, egged by a great power, and form a confederation of their own.

The above mentioned challenges, threats and scenarios are not exhaustive but are merely symptomatic of the malaise brought about by terrorism in its many forms. The SAARC nations have historically a common thread of prospering together in relative harmony, until invaded by foreign powers in the course of its long regional history, assimilating some cultures, defeating others, buckling down temporarily, but eventually evolving as a conglomeration of historically similar, but linguistically, religiously and demographically different nations. Individually, each nation has to tackle its broad array of social and economic issues with politically difficult and astute decisions over a long and sustained period, without spinoffs visibly accruing in the immediate period. SAARC's stability is thus by no means pre-ordained. The cohesion of efforts and congruence in methods of enhancing economic, social and political benchmarks will pave the way for peace and prosperity in the region. Cooperation, not confrontation, is the way forward for regional security.

CHAPTER 4

COUNTER TERROR: ASPECTS OF CHALLENGES AND COOPERATION

Issues ranging from societal to poor governance dog SAARC nations. It is ironic that even after 40 to 60 years of independence of the member-states, that are still mired in the same morass of poverty—economic, security, health, education, besides over-population and unemployment. Smaller countries in the neighbourhood and beyond have not only enhanced the quality of life of their citizens, but also enabled the skilled and uplifted their standing in the comity of nations, all in a shorter period than the SAARC states. Internecine discord, small wars and insurrections graduated into full-blown terrorism, state-sponsored or aggravated, that has been the bane of SAARC nations. Selective interpretation of religion has been a key driver of terrorism in the subcontinent thereby drawing recruits, willing to fight and die for a cause they believe is just. This, irrespective of the fact that the well-educated core cadre of motivators and leadership is generally secure in their own lives, distanced from the foot soldiers, who are increasingly drawn from the ranks of the unemployed and uneducated.

Considering that SAARC has an established protocol on terrorism, the SAARC Regional Convention on Suppression of Terrorism, signed on 4 November 1987, came into force on 22 August 1988 following ratification by all the member-states.[247] However, till date, there has been no tangible progress on the ground because of the intransigence displayed, especially on Pakistan's insistence, to pursue its political goals and national agenda within the regional framework. A host of protocols has however been signed. The SAARC Terrorist Offences Monitoring Desk (STOMD) was established in Colombo in 1995; its objectives are to collate, analyse and disseminate information on terrorist offences, tactics, strategies and methods.[248] The SAARC Drug Offences Monitoring Desk (SDOMD) was also established in Colombo in 1992 with the objective of setting up a desk to collate, analyse and disseminate information on drug related offences in the region.[249] An Additional Protocol to the SAARC Regional Convention On Suppression Of Terrorism was signed on 6 January 2004., Its purpose is to strengthen the SAARC Regional Convention on Suppression of Terrorism, particularly by criminalising the provision, collection or acquisition of funds for the purpose of committing terrorist acts and taking further measures to prevent and suppress financing of such acts.[250] Given the lack of consensus on defining terrorism, the Additional Protocol remains ineffective, as some of the clauses are ambiguous in definition and meaning. Article 17 of the protocol refers to non-discrimination in extradition. It states "member-countries are not under obligation to extradite or provide legal assistance if the requested state party has substantial ground to believe that extradition has been requested for the purpose to punish a person for his race, religion, nationality, ethnic origin or political opinion and the request would cause prejudice to that person's position for any of these reasons". Within SAARC nations, several groups exist, engaged in separatist movements globally or against member-nations. Thus the definition would leave them out of the purview of terrorism, since those states that are known to sponsor and shelter terrorists would be reluctant to facilitate extradition.[251] Indeed, one of the prime obstacles in SAARC protocols on terrorism has been Pakistani fears that India can destabilise its tough western frontiers—driving Pakistan to employ Islamist proxies there since the 1960s, some of whom have turned against their patrons. Its insistence on being treated as India's equal, despite being weakened with enervated governmental institutions,[252] made it adopt a hard-line stance on even the trade agreement with India. It is due to the pressure from Western countries that Pakistan finally agreed to the adoption of the additional protocol at the Kathmandu SAARC summit. However, the duality in its policy remains, as their Foreign Secretary stated, "We are mindful of our obligations of combating terrorism in all its forms and manifestations; we will not compromise on our vital national interests" (meaning its state-sponsored terrorists). This indicates the limitation of SAARC protocols, which, though impressive, remain largely symbiotic on matters of cooperation on counter-terrorism among member-countries. Mutual suspicion, trust deficit and problems of implementation among the security agencies of the member-states have become impediments. Despite SAARC having initiated cooperation in dealing with terror, before most regions and alliances, members of the Association for Southeast Asian Nations (ASEAN) share information on maritime terrorism and piracy and the Shanghai Cooperation Organisation (SCO) has implemented it through its Regional Anti-Terrorist Structure.[253]

SAARC has nine observer status nations—Australia, China, the European Union, Iran, Japan, Republic of Korea, Mauritius, Myanmar and the USA. For current member-states to derive maximum gain from such an association, it is essential that they "should build on convergences and minimise divergences and most of all seek to augment complementarities for the greater good of the people of the region",[254] said Prime Minister Sharif. This is easier said than done, considering that the globalisation of the economy, energy and terrorism bring about emerging dynamics. In addition, SAARCs inability to deal with bilateral issues between member-nations has resulted in its stagnation as such issues raked up consistently stall progress. The proposal by the Prime Minister of Bangladesh, Sheikh Hasina, for the formation of a South Asian task force to combat terrorism, is on course with India[255] and is likely to be discussed during the next SAARC meeting. SAARC countries have nevertheless found it easier to engage in extra-regional bilateral and multilateral counter-terrorism initiatives.

Bhutan was the first to start the battle against Indian insurgent groups in its southern belt in December 2003, though a loose mechanism of 'hot pursuit' existed earlier.[256] The King of Bhutan personally directed the operation, clearing out insurgent groups from

South Bhutan, which included Bodo and ULFA members. Bhutan still faces threats from the Maoists and Bhupalese who seek to rebel against the present government even after its voluntary transition from a monarchy to a democracy. India and Pakistan are members of the multilateral Global Counterterrorism Forum set up by the USA in 2011, where national counter-terrorism officials periodically participate in capacity-building programmes. However, Pakistan has consistently denied the existence of anti-India terror groups on its soil, despite overwhelming evidence to the contrary and the USA periodically considering declaring Pakistan to be a state sponsor of terrorism.[257]

Bilaterally, India-Bangladesh and India-Nepal have evolved effective counter-terrorism partnerships to neutralise terrorist groups. Soon after assuming power, Sheikh Hasina cracked down on terror groups, both domestic and sanctuary seekers. It acted against Bangladesh Islamist groups like the JMB and the HUJI as well as international terror groups like the LeT and the JeM, and, more effectively, the Bangladesh government cracked down on Indian North-east terror groups. The arrest of two high-profile terrorists, Abdul Karim Tunda and Yasin Bhatkal of the LeT and IM, in August 2013, in Nepal by joint Indo-Nepal teams, have brought into focus that more proactive and deeper cooperation between Nepal and India, since it is an acknowledged fact that terrorists enter and exit India from and to Nepal. However, bilateral cooperation is not enough, because terrorist activities take place across multiple jurisdictions. Regional cooperation through SAARC is, therefore, imperative.[258] The early adoption of the Comprehensive Convention on International Terrorism, which Prime Minister Narendra Modi spoke of at the UN General Assembly on 27 September 2014, will give added impetus to a concerted international effort to combat terrorism.

Despite challenges, SAARC nations have had some positive outcomes in counter-terror platforms. Respective financial intelligence units share information on suspicious financial transactions with inter-governmental organisations.[259] The SAARC Convention on Mutual Legal Assistance in Criminal Matters in 2008 aims at strengthening regional cooperation in the fight against cross-border crimes, especially the fight against terrorism. Unfortunately, action on the ground is lacking and SAARC as a common forum to tackle terror has been far from being a success. Whilst most SAARC states have signed the 15 UN protocols on terrorism, key protocols like the International Convention for the Suppression of Acts of Nuclear Terrorism and others, are yet to be ratified by Pakistan while the International Convention for the Suppression of Terrorist Bombings has yet to be signed.[260] The 16th international convention, a proposed Comprehensive Convention on International Terrorism, is currently under negotiation. Member-states adopted the United Nations Global Counter-Terrorism Strategy on 8 September 2006. The strategy, in the form of a resolution and a plan of action, is a unique global instrument that will enhance national, regional and international efforts to counter terrorism.[261]

Challenges of Counter Terrorism (CT) in SAARC Nations

The challenges posed by terrorist groups are increasing in complexity, scope and reach with the passage of time. The major challenges of CT in the SAARC environment and India are:

Timely Response

Issues that seem to be innocuous in the incipient stages have a tendency to go into a tailspin well before the political hierarchy acts to initiate and implement corrective measures. It was well known that the Mizo insurrection in India, because of a famine, was bound to happen; this is one such example. The renewed Baloch agitation in Pakistan is a result of perceived inequality.

Nature of Conflict

Terrorism does not follow the conventional pattern of conflict and is vastly different from Mao Tse Tung's 'Three Phase Theory of Revolutionary War—Organise, Expand and Destroy'. Today, terrorism and terrorists are unconventional, an insidious enemy that remains connected seamlessly and sometimes disconnected physically (purposively), and wreaks greater havoc than before. The emergence of the ISIS in the Srinagar Valley and the Al-Qaeda in India are prime examples.

Collapse of Governance

The physical actions of terror outfits lead to the collapse of governance, its instruments and institutions and terror groups step in to the void to provide a parallel and more efficient system of governance to manage short and long-term problems, until evicted by the re-establishment of state authority. Some cases in point are:

- The LTTE, until the public recognised it as the problem and not the solution
- The Taliban during the initial stages of their Afghan campaign

India ignored, since the mid-1970s (and sometimes encouraged) the enduring Maoist movement out of political expediency in parts of Bihar, Andhra Pradesh and Madhya Pradesh.[262] This allowed the Maoists to steadily consolidate their gains in the rural countryside, especially in Telengana, until it flared up in the early 1990s, when it became difficult for the Andhra Pradesh government to establish its writ. Naxalism suddenly loomed large in 180 districts and 10 states[263] by 2007, especially, in central India, running a parallel government until steady regrouping and concerted central and state governmental action to tackle the menace saw the numbers reduced to 34 districts that were considered the worst affected and 88 required attention.[264] Had the issue been addressed in the first phase itself, the nation would have progressed, industrially and infrastructure-wise. The challenges included protection and preservation of the environment and inclusive development of all sections of society, especially the rights of tribals. This was important since about 70 per cent of India's coal, 80 per cent of its hematite iron ore (high grade ore), 60 per cent of bauxite, 40 per cent of manganese and almost all its chromite are found in Naxalite-affected areas of Odisha, Chhattisgarh and Jharkhand.[265]

Growing Irrelevance of UN and its Peace Keeping Operations (PKO): In today's complex multi-polar and continually fractious world, the UN is incapable of dealing with local/regional issues, which quickly snowball, into international crises. The Arab Spring went into a tailspin, commencing with the suicide of a fruit seller, leading to the collapse of governments and nations. It started the refugee crises into Europe and exposed the helplessness of the United Nations in dealing with the unfolding humanitarian crisis, as is evident from its lack of nimbleness of thought and action. This has raised questions on its relevance, given the speed at which troubles erupt, globally leading to law and order problems and inability of the PKO to impose its writ to ensure an early return to normalcy. UN Observer Groups are mostly long, ongoing, irrelevant and cost ineffective. For example, the United Nations Military Observers Group in India and Pakistan (UNMOGIP) since 1949, Cyprus (1964), Lebanon (1978), and Syria (1974) involve an overall peacekeeping annual budget of $ 8.27 billion for 2015-2016. The cost for funding the UNMOGIP in 2014-2015 for its operations and staff of 115 personnel, including 47 local civilians, was a staggering $ 19,647,100, working out to a colossal $ 170,844 per head.[266] Considering that India does not recognise the UNMOGIP's mandate, it is a waste of money and resources. Similar costing measures would establish the necessity of pruning/closing down some missions and diverting the resources for better social projects in war zones. Regional peacekeeping operations operating for a fixed time and charter mandated, would be a preferred option. A review of the PKO is called for as peace enforcement, involving robust military responses, met with limited success. Calls for making the PKO more coherent, transparent, efficient, and accountable and give more influence to the countries that contribute greatly to UN peace operations is imperative,[267] if it has to contribute meaningfully to bring terror-struck and war-ravaged nations back on track.

Resistance to Law and Order

The breakdown in governance leads to law and order issues and 'No Go Zones' in such areas of internal conflict. For long, the LTTE-dominated areas in Sri Lanka and Maoist 'Red Corridor' in Central India were out of the purview of the state law and order machinery. Recent revelations of 'No Go Zones' reportedly existing in the UK[268] as well as Belgium[269] post the Paris bombings of 2014, are a reminder of the need for states to enforce their writ or risk the establishment of enclaves by terror groups and possibly the forerunner of a domestic caliphate. Malda and Burdwan districts in West Bengal have substantial 'No Go' Zones for the police,[270] due to the influx of Islamists and Bangladesh refugees and political intervention.

Warlords and Drug Lords

Afghanistan and Pakistan are prime examples of warlords and drug lords dictating the course of events in terror-affected regions by corrupting the system. Drugs finance wars and warlords direct the drug trade. Insurgents, especially the Taliban, in turn protect the 'traders' of drugs, gemstones, antiquities (dating back to the time of Genghis Khan and Alexander) and people. Secret documents released by US State Department reveal the extent of the involvement of Afghan resistance groups and the ISI in the 'lucrative' drug trade.[271] ISI support to the warlord, Jallaluddin Haqqani and his son Sirajuddin (who now heads the pro-Taliban Haqqani Faction which is fighting the US and ISAF) and controls most of the areas to the south and east of Kabul as well as being based in North Waziristan, is well documented.[272] Dawood Ibrahim ran a well-orchestrated underworld campaign in India, dealing in drugs, smuggling, and real estate before fleeing to Pakistan after masterminding the Mumbai blasts of 1993. In connivance with the ISI, corrupt law enforcement officials and politicians, Ibrahim smuggled roughly 7 tonnes of high explosives, and 300 firearms into India. Since 1993, Ibrahim and his gang have been the main link between the ISI and pan–Islamist jihadist groups in India.[273]

Prevalence of NSAs

Lone Wolf (LW) attacks are defined as the deliberate creation and exploitation of fear through violence or threat of violence committed by a single actor who pursues political change linked to a formulated ideology, whether his own or that of a larger organisation, and who does not receive orders, direction, or material support from outside sources.[274] LW capabilities have been substantially enhanced with a revolution in technology including Information Technology (IT) while bringing about qualitative improvements in lives and given unprecedented destructive power into the hands of terrorists. Physical connect has given way to connect through digital networks allowing operations in small cells or nodes, widely dispersed, invisible and away from scenes of intended terror crimes. Never before have small groups of such non-state actors had access to so much destructive power, considering the Internet gives information on every construct of crime, from instructions on bomb making to hacking the IT systems of financial services. Inimical countries' intelligence agencies and security forces serve as their proxies in their campaign to subjugate or weaken other foreign powers. They also exploit LWs and non-state actors. Their emergence may also be in response to the inadequacies or shortcomings in governance in many nations and they seek to address these shortcomings.

Maoists, the Al-Qaeda, ISIS, LTTE and their ilk, however, differ in motivation levels, and in their aims and organisational reach and structure. The LTTE had its 'offices' in European, Asian and North American countries to propagate its cause and seek funds. Others increasingly form alliances with one another including between organised crime and terrorist networks, as already given out with reference to Dawood Ibrahim and the ISI. These are likely on a temporary convenience rather than real affinity, since the state-sponsored criminal and terror syndicates are prone to discard, whenever convenient. Just as a crime syndicate can morph into a terror outfit, a terror outfit transforming to a political organisation has happened after achievement of their political goals, the cases in point being the Maoists of Nepal and the Tamil National Alliance.

Financing Terror

The lifeline of terror activities, financing operations through a wide spectrum of activities ranging from drugs, smuggling of gems, minerals, piracy, hostage taking, hawala transactions, etc., while adequate controls exist, it is in the aspects of enforcement that SAARC nations have been found wanting. Most countries are members of the Financial Action Task Force (FATF) and two FATF-style regional bodies, the Eurasian Group on Combating Money Laundering and

Financing of Terrorism and the Asia/Pacific Group on Money Laundering. Their Financial Intelligence Units are members of the Egmont Group of Financial Intelligence Units. Pakistan has approved and enacted an amendment to the Anti-Terror Act to rectify deficiencies identified by the FATF to enable the government freeze and confiscate terrorist assets, but has not yet implemented the legislation.

In fact, its UN-designated terrorist organisations continued to skirt sanctions by reconstituting themselves under different names. The FATF has determined that Pakistan needs to increase the administrative monetary penalty available or legislate for additional criminal sanctions.[275] In November 2012, India brought its domestic anti-money laundering/counterterrorist financing (AML/CFT) laws into line t with international standards by passing amendments to the Prevention of Money Laundering Act, but has to implement the legislation effectively, especially with regard to criminal convictions. Law enforcement agencies typically open criminal investigations reactively and seldom initiate proactive analysis and long-term investigations. While the Indian government has taken action against certain hawala financing activities, prosecutions have generally focused on non-financial businesses that conduct hawala transactions as a secondary activity. The degree of training and expertise in financial investigations involving transnational crime or terrorist-affiliated groups varies widely among the federal, state, and local levels and depends on the financial resources and individual policies of differing jurisdictions.[276] India's Terror Financing and Fake Currency Cell (TFFC) functions under the National Investigation Agency (NIA) and in FICN cases investigated by the NIA, the Special Court established under the NIA Act, 2008, observed that Pakistan is circulating FICN in India with the sole purpose and intention to damage and threaten the economic security and fund terror activities.[277]

Media Management

Margaret Thatcher had famously stated in a speech to the American Bar Association in July 1985, "We must try to find ways to starve the terrorist and the hijacker of the oxygen of publicity on which they depend".[278] Terrorists have exploited various media for enhancing their operational efficiency, including for information gathering, recruitment, fund raising, and propaganda schemes. In turn, media highlighting terror attacks, plots and activities receive the continued attention of the public, vital for its existence and the TRPs (or equivalent) and accrual benefits from larger audiences. It is thus fair to infer that there exists a mutually beneficial relationship between terrorism and today's media. The case of the terror attacks at Mumbai 2008 and Peshawar 2014, for example, being broadcast, live, functioned as a tool to shrink the power asymmetry between the terrorists and the state they fought against creating an atmosphere of fear in larger audiences. The ISIS' Jihadist John, with his characteristic black-hooded dress and knife, looming large over innocent victims, just before slaughtering them was meant to carry a message of submission, just as depiction of young Yazidi women as sex slaves, an act of recruitment, through enticement.

It required the Supreme Court of India to pull up the media for its negative role in the Mumbai 2008 attack and hinted that there should be some regulatory mechanism even from within the media themselves.[279] The Kandahar hijacking of 1999 heightened the emotive content; it also provoked protests against the government's inability to find a quick solution to the crisis through reportage on the crisis round-the-clock. Dominated by the *Weeping Mother Syndrome*, coverage of the trauma of terrorist victims and their families saturated by the media, built public opinion to a climax and forced the government to yield to the terrorists' demands.[280]

In Pakistan, freedom of the media has been a subject of responsibility and accountability and media ethics in the form of self-imposed restrictions and self-regulation. This has been keeping in view religious values, norms and traditions of a society. Just like in India, Pakistani electronic media enjoys unprecedented freedom, without any sense of responsibility and following any code of ethics. Questions were raised, post trials of the accused in the massacre of Peshawar schoolchildren of the revealing of information on sensitive issues.[281] While regulations exist, mostly self-controls, a clearer definition of duties and responsibilities of media towards the state and public, needs implementation.

Refugee and Migration Crises

SAARC nations have had to deal with the problems of internally displaced peoples because of zonal conflicts as well as those displaced from neighbouring nations. With the exception of Bhutan, an excess in population, which puts a strain on existing resources and employment with an influx of refugees hamstrings the already precarious situation and burdens all states. India has been home to millions of refugees who seek permanent resident status, upsetting the local demographic balance as well as introducing alien cultures and practices, resisted sometimes violently, by the ethnic inhabitants. The Maldives and Bangladesh will witness, within this century, rising seas and steady erosion of habitable and agriculture land besides displacement of substantial numbers of population. Their occupation of lesser-populated zones in the region, including island territories is a clear security threat, combined with an influx of terrorists.

Protocols need to be worked out with the UNHCR for their relocation elsewhere, for which the affected SAARC nations, notably India, have to take the lead. The UNHCR is already engaged in expanding its outreach to the Indian public and engage more prominently with new civil society actors, in order to increase refugee access to urban support mechanisms. In Nepal, the UNHCR will seek the issuance of documentation for the long-staying Tibetan population. In Sri Lanka, it will also facilitate the voluntary return of Sri Lankan refugees and those internally displaced, in safety and dignity, and will assist them to reintegrate through community mobilization projects.[282]

Rise of Internationalised but Internal Conflict

Regional and religion-based conflicts are increasingly drawing foreign fighters to their cause, however tenuous it may be. Thus we have volunteer recruits from a host of Western and Arab nations fighting in Afghanistan, Sudan, Iraq, Syria and even Libya. What is of concern is the numbers coming from other SAARC nations. India has reported

23 youth having joined the ISIS but a female Indian recruiter reached out to around 25,000 Muslim youth through Facebook and Twitter, and provoked them with stories of how Islam was under threat all over the world and how an Islamic caliphate based on the Sharia was the need of the hour.[283] Reportedly, around 500 youth have been in contact with her. Approximately, 10-12,000, Afghans are reportedly fighting with Syrian forces and 30,000 Indian Shias signed up for fighting with the ISIS and protecting the holy shrines of Karbala and Najaf.[284] What is of concern is the number of volunteers who are ready to participate in distant wars—and even if some do go and return, the impact of the presence of battle-trained and hardened veterans will have serious security ramifications of surveillance, monitoring and possibly screening for de-radicalisation programmes. The presence of JeI Bangladesh terrorists in Malda and their connect with Indian and Pakistani-based terror organisations involved in gun running, poppy cultivation and drug smuggling, bomb/IED making, transportation of FICN, smuggling of refugees and trans-national terror acts, despite initial denials by the state government, is another disturbing factor.[285]

Cyber and Nuclear Terrorism

The persisting challenges of the last century are likely to emerge as the principal threats in this. Both types of threats have a dangerously high potential for causing large-scale economic, political and demographic disasters, worldwide. The use of the Internet to further terrorist designs transcends national borders and international airspaces, amplifying the potentially devastating effect it can have on various governmental and private institutions, agencies and individuals. McAfee avers that cybercrime damages trade, competitiveness, innovation, and global economic growth. Two banks in the Persian Gulf lost $ 45 million in a few hours in 2013. A British company reported that it lost $ 1.3 billion in a single attack in 2012. Brazilian banks say their customers lose millions annually to cyber fraud. Simply adding up the losses worldwide conservatively equals $ 400 billion.[286]

India's CERT reported that 308,371 websites were hacked between

2011 and June 2013, and the Indian experience is not unique. India's estimated losses to cybercrime, though low, was pegged at 0.21 per cent of the GDP in 2013. India reportedly faces a deficiency of four lakh cyber warriors[287] (trained cyber security professionals) as practically all organisations in India have been witnessing a huge growth in cyber-attacks and intrusions. The Government, in August 2013, with the objective of creating a framework for comprehensive collaboration, released the Indian National Cyber Security Policy-2013 (NCSP-2013) to ensure collective responses to deal with the issue of cyber security at all levels within the country.[288] India faces tremendous military challenges in the realms of cyber space, as cyber technology has numerous military applications, which will be exploited in conflict situations, because of which weaker nations and even terror groups seek to offset the asymmetry of conventional forces by enhancing their offensive cyber capabilities. India is on course to set up a tri-service Cyber Command to handle both offensive and defensive cyber security capabilities and issues of cyber warfare, cyber terrorism and cyber espionage.[289] Whilst the in-house problems of cyber warfare are not so acute in most SAARC nations, as of now, maverick and terror groups regularly hack government and organisational sites with malicious intent and this threat will enhance as Internet connectivity increases its reach. With increasing numbers of mobile phone users in the subcontinent, there would be an increase in threats of cyber terror and cyber-crime.

South Asia is probably the most vulnerable to all facets of nuclear terrorism—whether by nations or terror groups. Pakistan's repeated reminders, aimed at India with a caution to the rest of the world, especially the USA and Israel "We are a nuclear armed country, we know how to defend ourselves",[290] invariably follows after a ISI-sponsored terror strike in India, but this response was triggered when India decided to call off NSA talks. Periodically, the world community has expressed concern at the safety factor of Pakistan's nuclear weapons, given the regularity with which the Tehreek-e-Taliban Pakistan's (TTP) terrorists have repeatedly attacked seemingly secure airports and naval bases exposing the vulnerabilities in its security set up. It cannot be dismissed that the TTP would not try to target

Pakistan's nuclear weapons installations. Efforts by the Al-Qaeda and the ISIS to obtain nuclear weapons or even fissile material have been documented. The range of threats include nuclear terrorism, illicit nuclear trade, *insider threats*, poor material accounting and lack of adequate commitments from several states possessing nuclear capability.[291] The presence of maverick scientists like A.Q. Khan and even rogue states like North Korea indicate vulnerability. Persistent destabilised political situations, prolonged internal conflicts and civil strife in countries possessing nuclear/radiological materials can substantially heighten risks to nuclear security. Countries with poor nuclear security provide a potential pathway for the terrorists' acquisition of nuclear/radiological materials. These challenges add new facets to the risk of nuclear security worldwide, including for India.

India's geographical location bordering Pakistan—a state with a congruence of inborn hatred towards it, terrorism running amok, political instability and an acknowledged burgeoning nuclear arsenal, would need more in an Armageddon-like exchange with India, and this gives rise to the actual motive of expanding its nuclear weapons arsenal by Pakistan. Would it arm one of its preferred non-state actors for executing the threat to destroy India and Israel in a mutually assured destructive stand-off ? Or even threaten inability to keep them secure thereby using them to continue to extract concessions to justify its existence? Alternatively, there could even be 'Sunni bombs' to extract generous largesse from Saudi Arabia!

Strengthen Investigative Systems

SAARC nations have to strengthen their investigative mechanisms and systems and make them more hi-tech, in tune with the prevailing environment of terror and crimes. The establishment of specialised laboratories at the national and state levels,[292] as well as technical agencies and equipment to monitor, process and disseminate data, besides qualified staff to deal with terror crimes, is necessary. Even now, for high-profile crimes, we depend upon the FBI Labs to provide forensic inputs to progress investigations. The outcome of investigations into the 2008 Mumbai attacks was corroborated to an extent by FBI teams provided by the USA—possibly, in hindsight, as it emerged that David Headley, one of the planners of the LeT operation, was also a double agent working for the US DEA! Prevailing IT laws should be regularly updated to deal with emergent technologies and techniques. Special attention should be given in dealing with cybercrimes, especially since the volume and value of electronic information have increased as also the business models and efforts of criminals and other adversaries who have embraced cyber space as a more convenient and profitable way of carrying out their activities anonymously. Hence, tech qualified cyber security experts to handle hi-tech cybercrimes has become an essential component of the internal security apparatus given the scope and bandwidth for the ambitious 'Digital India' programme initiatives launched by the government.

Countering Radicalisation

Considering that impressionable minds are exposed to radical beliefs and actions in certain madarsas, which preach the cult of violence, along with some returnees from ISIS-dominated areas as well as Gulf states reportedly indoctrinated to Wahhabi radicalism, it becomes incumbent on SAARC states to initiate screening and de-radicalisation programmes. De-radicalisation however does not just include ideological reorientation. Skill development, as also vocational training leading to a job, is a vital factor in preventing going back to terrorism. Periodic feedback will form an essential element to assess the success of such programmes and the necessity for mid-course corrections, as will the active support of family members of the 'not so radicalised 'elements. The inclusion of industry and the service sector to assess job suitability as part of community service in corporate social responsibility is an option. At the grass root level, formalisation and standardisation of teaching content of seminaries and madarsas would prevent the spread of hatred.

Bureaucratic and Systems Overhaul

Considering the alacrity with which terror-related issues and incidents tend to spiral out of control, a systemic overhaul of not only national and state-level bureaucracies as well as revamp and restructure of intelligence and operational systems is not only 'mission essential', but also long overdue. The age of 'generalisation' is long gone and in its stead we require subject and area specialists in all departments of governance; nor should it be the domain of single or ubiquitous civil services personnel. A quick check reveals that internal security is equally impacted.[293] Similarly, the role of central police organisations (CPO) as well as para military forces (PMF), engaged in CT operations, merit review. The Kargil Review Committee as well as the Supreme Court Directive of 2006 on police reforms need to be implemented early to streamline national security.

The overlapping of CPO and PMF roles and their burgeoning numbers without accountability necessitate the creation of effective single unit task based federal agencies to deal with border management and internal policing duties. All should be clubbed under one force for the duties and responsibilities of border management (including air space and coastal security) and another for internal security—with internal specialisation addressed concurrently during restructuring. Similarly, we need to upgrade our technical intelligence and surveillance skills and capabilities, giving more power, legal cover and, most importantly, trained manpower with 'state of the art' capabilities to the National Technical Research Organisation (NTRO), National Intelligence Grid (NATGRID), and National Investigation Agency (NIA) and set up the long-overdue National Counter-Terrorism Centre (NCTC).[294] Also long overdue is an overhaul of our judicial and legal process as part of the CT campaign. This is one of the weakest links in India's current counter-terrorism strategies. Besides strong legislative action is needed to act as a deterrent. Terrorism is an act of violence against the state and India needs stringent national legislation to counter it. In addition, there is a need for specially designated fast-track terrorist courts to dispose of these cases swiftly, as well as deterrent punishment for convicted offenders. The USA, Britain, Germany, and France have imposed stringent laws against such actions in spite of being liberal democracies. These new legislation in those countries—defining terrorism and enabling the monitoring and prosecution of terrorists and individuals or organisations supporting terrorists—has gone a long way in containing terrorism in Europe and North America. India, too, needs stringent national legislation.[295] Even Pakistan has begun trials against terrorists through Special Military Courts.[296] The monolithic Ministry of Home Affairs[297] needs urgent reconstructuring to deal with current global terror connects. Hiving off administrative departments and some divisions (20 existing) unrelated to direct internal security would prove effective.[298, 299]

Extradition Treaties

India presently has signed extradition treaties with 37 countries and has extradition arrangements with eight more.[300] Treaties with Afghanistan, The Maldives and Pakistan are pending. Treaties need to be taken up with other nations too, especially those in the Gulf States and South American nations where periodic inputs are received of terror suspects seeking refuge. India should sign extradition treaties at the earliest with the more than 100 nations not yet addressed. Terrorists and criminals must be made conscious that they cannot escape the long arm of the law. In recent years, Bangladesh, Saudi Arabia, and the UAE have deported or extradited several terrorists or criminals like Iqbal Kaksar, Ejaj Pathan, and Anup Chetia.

CT Efforts: Cooperate, Confront, Coerce & Conflict in South Asia

It has often been said that the underlying cause for the proliferation of terrorism in the subcontinent can be traced to two issues—firstly, Pakistan's insistence on being treated as an equal of India,[301] and, secondly, any Indo-Pakistan dialogue ultimately veers to the Kashmir issue,[302] even during multilateral events as in the UN and SAARC conventions. Despite existent protocols on dealing with terror and SAARC member-nations attempting to forge regional responses to common challenges, including drugs, small arms, and counter-terrorism, its efficacy is often held hostage to the relationship between India and Pakistan. Thus, member-nations have found it effective to focus on regional economic development rather than on political issues, leaving contentious problems to be addressed bilaterally. Also, historically, being hostage to colonialism in the recent past, SAARC nations are wary of external influences in the region, which adds to the resistance towards regionalisation.

The UN Global Counter-Terrorism Strategy, adopted on 8 September 2006 to address the terrorist threat is based on a four-pillar plan of action consisting of:

1. Measures to address conditions conducive to the spread of terrorism,
2. Measures to prevent and combat terrorism,
3. Capacity building, and
4. Ensuring a human rights and rule-of-law-based approach to countering the threat.[303]

The UN recognises poverty, prolonged unresolved conflicts, and dehumanisation of victims of terrorism, lack of rule of law and violations of human rights, ethnic, national and religious discrimination, political exclusion, socio-economic marginalisation and lack of good governance as conditions conducive to the spread of terrorism.[304] Whilst these issues are a consequence of national policies, mitigation measures, to a large extent, hinge on the success of the various arms of the UN as well as regional alliances along with the active support of local governments to bring about economic and social development in such an environment. Measures to prevent and combat terrorism would involve the stepping up of efforts through strengthening law enforcement agencies in cooperation with the UN and other agencies and alliances to deny terrorists the space, the means and the support to carry out their attacks on targets. Capacity building is the core element[305] of the global counter-terrorism effort and, as such, coordination and coherence with all bilateral, multilateral, technical and other assistance providers including public-private partnerships will greatly enhance support systems in place in the national narrative to bring about economic and social improvements. The UN recognises that the promotion and protection of human rights for all and the rule of law is essential to all components of the strategy, recognising that effective counter-terrorism measures and the protection of human rights are not conflicting goals, but complementary and mutually reinforcing, and stressing the need to promote and protect the rights of victims of terrorism.[306] Even with the acceptance and adoption of the UN Global Counter-Terrorism Strategy by member-states, including SAARC members, and viewed against the backdrop of the adopted SAARC protocols on terror, there has been limited headway in regional cooperation on the war on terror, principally between India and Pakistan. In a telling commentary on the situation in Pakistan, President Obama in his State of the Union Address in January 2016, said, "Even without ISIL, even without Al-Qaeda, instability will continue for decades in many parts of the world—in the Middle East, in Afghanistan and parts of Pakistan, in parts of Central America and Africa and Asia".[307] This is an alarming assessment and a damning indictment of the state of affairs in that beleaguered (self-created) nation. It is also a warning that we must put into place, mechanisms between the rest of the SAARC nations and India to ensure co-operation in strengthening CT measures.

The Bay of Bengal Initiative for Multi-Sector Technical and Economic Cooperation (BIMSTEC), founded in 1997, includes Bangladesh, Bhutan, India, Myanmar, Nepal, Sri Lanka, and Thailand. It facilitates cooperation in areas such as Trade and Investment, Technology, Energy, Transportation, Communications and Tourism, Disaster Management, Counter-Terrorism and Transnational Crime, and is a viable alternative to push forward counter-terrorism mechanisms. It recently held its sixth meeting of the subgroup on legal and law enforcement issues under counter-terrorism and transnational crime in New Delhi in December 2015.[308] This would leave aside recalcitrant Pakistan and fragile Afghanistan, both of which could be part of a more powerful CT mechanism and initiative. As Prime Minister Modi succinctly put it after the SAARC summit in Kathmandu in November 2014 became hostage yet again to Pakistan-raised bilateral issues, "The bonds will grow through SAARC or outside it, among us all or some of us".[309]

In addition to existent SAARC protocols on strengthening cooperation, India can foster closer ties by ramping up efforts in certain core areas of national building by inclusive nation-to-nation contact through the following mechanisms.

Student and Young Professionals Exchange Programmes

Student exchange/scholarship programme are needed in select national colleges and universities for up to a year for young people from SAARC nations to study or intern on aspects of disaster management, non-conventional energy, ecological sustainability, human resource development, rural development and the like. This would have a long-term effect to portray India as it is, and not propaganda. Exchange programmes in specialised fields of urban planning, medicine, engineering, agriculture, biomedicine and information technology would also be useful fields to cultivate and nurture young talent in the cross-fertilisation of ideas and initiatives. Focus on Skills training programmes would be most useful, even if such capsules were under SAARC aegis in member-nations, or in India. A programme like the US Peace Corps that was spread worldwide, duly structured to suit SAARC conditions and requirements and initially funded and fielded by India with volunteers and interns from interested SAARC nations would work at the grassroots level in sustainable development programmes, and at the same time becoming SAARC 'citizens' and their country's ambassadors of goodwill and development. They return with a broader perspective and holistic all-round development thereby becoming useful members in their country and society.

SAARC Bank

The SAARC Development Fund should transform into a SAARC Development Bank on the lines of the Asian Development Bank with an initial modest corpus to finance vocational and skill development, information technology, education, infrastructure, rural health, alternate energy sources and water supply projects being part of its core areas. This initiative would not only enhance small and micro industries, improve infrastructure, and accelerate connectivity through digitisation but also usher in inclusive growth and act as a catalyst to integrate the region.

Dealing with Common Non-Conventional Threats

SAARC nations face new and more challenging threats, which, having emerged insidiously over the past decade, have to be dealt with expeditiously to mitigate the impact posed by climate change and natural disasters such as the tsunami of 2004 and the earthquakes of 2005 and 2015. Besides, constant floods in the Gangetic and Brahmaputra basins have seen steady erosion of arable lands, putting enormous pressures on the people who live in the low-lying areas adjacent to the Bay of Bengal. The resultant impact on resource scarcity, refugees, migrations and relocations as well as attendant humanitarian crises, creates potential for inter and intra-state conflict. Thus, the necessity of SAARC nations to have disaster management teams like in India, available at short notice to deal with such calamities. Cross training, resource and expertise sharing as well as attending simulation exercises on coping with natural and man-made disasters would shorten response time. Creation of Ecological Task Forces to deal with large-scale deforestation, rejuvenation of water bodies and rivers as well as water harvesting and management and restoring ecologically degraded areas on which India has substantial expertise will also reduce migration and refugee problems, following disasters.

Dealing with Pakistan outside the ambit of SAARC is likely to pay rich dividends. Despite Pakistan being an acknowledged democracy, the power and hold of the military on politics, economy, foreign affairs, defence and national security, override the civilian authority.[310, 311] Some opinion makers have voiced the view that the Indian government may find it more prudent to initiate back channel diplomacy with the Pakistani military hierarchy, than deal with the powerless political hierarchy in resolving the terror problem. This is a tendentious argument as the Pakistan Army considers the occupation of Kashmir as an unfinished agenda for it to resolve. Thus, no military, political or diplomatic defeat that Pakistan has suffered so far, has been adequate to persuade its army to revise its beliefs, not only on its claims to Kashmir, but also its unwillingness to accept India's rise (economic, military, social and political) in the region and much beyond. For the Pakistan Army, acquiescing to India is tantamount to accepting that the basis of two nations is illegitimate or defunct.[312] For the well-being of the Pakistani people and SAARC nations to see peace and progress, the presence of a strong democratically elected Pakistani government, with the will and determination to eradicate terror groups, and its army stepping back to cede space in domains it has institutionalised to itself, (besides rein in and roll back their strategic assets, a challenge in itself), will therefore be substantial progress towards peace in the region. With the drawdown of NATO and ISAF forces from Afghanistan, and a resurgent Taliban, current trends in Pakistan indicate increased levels of violence, which could lead to political instability and in the worst-case scenario, internal collapse of the state posing a threat to the safety of Pakistan's nuclear weapons. Even a partial loss of 50-60 kg of highly enriched uranium (HEU) is enough to make a crude gun type device, considered the most accessible nuclear terrorist weapon.[313] Such a loss will have terrifying consequences for not only the safety and security of the world, but also for the Pakistani people and the Indian subcontinent. Besides the soft options outlined, some of the Pakistan-specific options along with suggested hard options are given below:

Reviewing Extant Treaties

Pakistan's Kashmir obsession has less to do with the Muslim population and more related to its water supply sources. All its life-sustaining and agriculture-based water systems are dependent on rivers, which emerge from India. The Indus Water Treaty (IWT) signed in 1960 is one such pressure point, which although having survived three wars without disturbance, would have a salutary effect on the policies of support for its non-state actors. India should prepare for its ramifications—including the threat of a nuclear war. The exploitation of the loopholes of the IWT to reduce the flow of waters from India is an effective medium. Similarly, Afghanistan must seek to review its Helmand and Kabul Eastern Basin[314] water-sharing arrangements with Pakistan.

Status of Gilgit, Baltistan, and Baluchistan

Pakistan's repeated raising of the bogey of status of the whole of Jammu and Kashmir should be dealt with by Indian questioning, in international forums, the legitimacy of Pakistan's forcible occupation of Baluchistan, the illegality of ceding the Shaksgam tract to China, territory belonging to India. Hosting events that highlight the plight of the locals of these areas under Pakistani occupation and oppression as part of a subtle but sustained Psy–ops campaign, besides sponsoring rebel speakers from these areas to air their grievances in international events, would need calibration.

Human Rights Violations

Pakistan's record of human rights violation should be regularly brought up whenever it chooses to bring up Jammu and Kashmir during multi-lateral meetings, particularly relating to those occurring in the provinces of Balochistan, Sindh, Khyber Pakhtunkhwa (KP and formerly known as the North West Frontier Province), and the Federally Administered Tribal Areas (FATA). Pakistan's record of brutal suppression of minorities as well as the Shias, Ahmediyas, people of Gilgit Baltistan and their demographic displacement necessitates highlighting in national and international forums and media. The Indian High Commissioner in Pakistan should also invite dialogue with Balochi and other separatist leaders, and publicly in other world capitals to highlight their plight.

Some hard options for dealing with Pakistan, should it continue using non-state actors as well as sponsoring terrorists for strikes in India, is as suggested. Since they fall outside the scope of this research, they are not in detail. However their viability and practicability, as well as application of select options, should be based on getting affected nations on board, including China, who has recently been warned by the former Afghan Intelligence Chief, Amrullah Saleh about the presence in Pakistan of members of the banned Xinjiang extremist group, East Turkestan Islamic Movement.[315] Hard options could include a combination of one or more of the following, appropriately calibrated along with soft power as well as Pakistan-specific options suggested. The list is not exhaustive for obvious reasons.

(a) ***Target terror infrastructure through air and precision missile strikes.*** The trigger has to be related to a terror attack launched in India or Indian assets abroad and, for maximum effect, be directed at training camps or offices of such groups, in Pakistan or even in Afghanistan, since some surrogates would be based there. Target identification has to be a regular process.

(b) ***Employment of special forces for snatch and grab/destroy camps.*** The physical aspect of the previous option runs the risk of compromise, but the mere striking of terror assets in their own lairs, deep in Pakistan, will have a cascading effect on their standing, effectiveness, as well as morale.

(c) Covert and selective killing of terrorist leaders or their families

(c) ***Terror groups in Pakistan.*** This option can be useful where such targets are located deep inside urban areas and the risk of collateral damage due to air or missile strike is greater.

(d) ***Coordinate with Israel and the US for removing nukes.*** A hazardous, but essential element of any campaign, whenever the collapse of the Pakistani government or state or nukes are in imminent danger of being snatched by radical elements/ terrorists—this option is also important to know the exact location of weapon grade plutonium as well. Seizure of the area through air and helicopter assault, and maybe in connivance with saner elements in the Pakistani establishment, will result in greater chances of success.

(e) ***Sustained Psy-ops campaign to turn Pakistan people's perceptions and opinion.*** The centre of gravity in any counter-terror operation is the people—the passive many who are the base, neither for recruitment and shelter, nor for sustenance and finance. The Pakistani people having savoured democratic ideals and freedom should be subject to subtle TV programmes as well as Indian movies that project the negatives of terror and especially of state-sponsored terror. The use of medium like Facebook, Twitter and other forms of social interactions to attune the people of not only perceived hostile nations, but also hostile agencies. This would bring direct or indirect pressure demanding a change in the form of a more accountable government, focused on the well-being of its citizens and not of its policy makers, politicians and military rulers—none of whom are accountable for the mess Pakistan has been placed in.

SAARC's campaign on counter-terror will take time to achieve its goals of reducing and eradicating terror-related violence in the subcontinent. The spread of jihadist culture and Maoism has deeply affected the lives of all and permeated the psyche of the few who seek to perpetuate a myth of invincibility, even at the cost of self-destruction. As elucidated earlier, various dimensions and facets of statecraft and governmental and regional polity and protocols be brought to bear in the quest for harmony and stability in the region. Nations have to set their own houses in order, and governments should cooperate with its opposition, protect their minorities, especially against human rights abuses and violation of fundamental rights, and bring about socially uplifting measures to alleviate their lot. Judicial processes strengthened and rule of law prevailing in a time bound manner, without infringing on human rights, is essential. Mooting of regional and international courts of justice to try state sponsors of terror or leaders of such terror groups, besides imposing financial and UN sanctions would be preferred options, when dealing with rogue nations.

The focus of the international community is shifting towards punitive actions against non-state actors and their sponsors. The formerly sponsored non-state actors have gone rogue in some cases and, in some, just changed their modus operandi to project themselves as NGOs, espousing social causes. Whatever be the case, nations are responsible and made accountable for the acts of their citizens. Clamping down on hate schools, deterrent laws, and exemplary punishments to those preaching and spreading the cult of violence would have a salutary effect. Politics cannot trump national security at any cost, if the state has to survive. Cooperation should be the mantra for SAARC in spheres of intelligence-sharing, law enforcement, joint operations, border management, drug control, illegal financial deals (hawala) as well. SAARC nations should also work towards new extradition treaties, which would send the right signals to international terrorists hiding abroad. While most measures are in place between India and other SAARC nations, we need to coerce a shift in Pakistan's ambiguous policy towards terror. India's principal failure in the counter-terror campaign against Pakistan-based terror modules has primarily been its inability or unwillingness to exact a punitive price on Pakistan. A sustained soft power and selective and effective use of hard power, direct or indirect would work, especially where it hurts more. Pakistan should also be made aware that its nuclear sabre rattling would not work any longer and that sponsored cross-border adventures will have painful repercussions on its people and economy. Its public and politicians, being made continually aware of the disastrous consequences that have befallen them, because their state-sponsoring terror as an instrument of coercion has begun to hurt their interests more.

The international community, especially the USA, Saudi Arabia and China, need to be reminded that the consequences of their continually supporting Pakistan, economically, politically and militarily, has tragic spinoffs for their own people, as most terror incidents worldwide owe their origins in Pakistan or in the training fields of Afghanistan. The expansion of *Terror Inc.* worldwide, including Iraq, Syria, North Africa and Yemen, has a direct relationship with the jihadists churned out from Multan and other radicalised schools. Coordinated, strategic, and deliberate engagements by different bodies of the UN system, especially those dealing with education, development, health care, sanitation, and refugees, at the level of headquarters, and in the field, and those in between will need to coordinate their efforts with that of the state to ensure that the Sustainable Development Goals (SDG) are achieved. The state and UN agencies must monitor this implementation of SDG to ensure that funds are not diverted.[316]

The successful implementation of the UN Global Counter-Terrorism Strategy amongst SAARC nations and its overlapping its protocols ensures comprehensive coverage in dealing with root-and-trigger factors that contribute towards the growth and proliferation of terror. Nations and regional alliances have to calibrate their response mechanisms and executing agencies in their efforts to counter terror through a mix of soft and hard power. Periodic reviews with stake holders is a must to ensure mid- course corrections so as to optimise capabilities, effort and finances and bolster efforts to bring about peace and stability. South Asian nations will be able to enhance their spheres of influence and concentrate on development through a mix of cooperation and partnerships and by enhancing capacities and capabilities from a whole gamut of operations, ranging from poverty alleviation programmes to skill development, rural health, and judiciary. To be able to holistically address key issues in a spirit of cooperation and not confrontation amongst member-nations as well as domestically, will lead to success in the overall CT campaign.

CHAPTER 5

THE ROAD AHEAD

"History also teaches us the importance of peace, because peace is ultimately the best guarantor of security."[317]

—John Kerry, former Secretary of State, US Department of State

A prognosis of the environmental conditions that prevail in the SAARC nations reveals that mind-sets and strategies have to change and the political and security apparatus has to be geared to deal with terror groups in a spirit of regional cooperation, as the only way forward. Whilst nations focus on the debilitating effects that terrorism, as an instrument of state policy, has had on the rebound, the world at large is taking serious notice of addressing terror through a combination of hard and soft power. The UN, while holding regular interactions on defining terrorism, still struggles to find an acceptable definition.[318] This holds up categorising more 'states as sponsoring terror' which would lead to invoking and imposing diplomatic and economic sanctions on those that stoke the fires of terrorism. It is equally the responsibility of the great powers to refrain from initiating reckless adventures, which bring matters to a tailspin like in Iraq,[319] Afghanistan, Libya,[320] and Syria, and jeopardise peace and security of the region and afar. In South Asia, the SAARC nations, minus Afghanistan and Pakistan, have brought in some measure of stability within their boundaries to control the spread of terror, but more has to be done in the political, economic, social and security domains and also address non-traditional challenges to security, i.e., food, water, health, environmental security and disaster management.

Terror in the Af-Pak region and its continued fragility is not merely a SAARC and Indian problem. Should Islamabad's power continue to disintegrate, and extremist forces are strengthened, instability could quickly spread across South Asia and the Middle East. Regional developments in neighbouring Afghanistan will also have a profound impact on Pakistan, with increasing concerns over the ability of a weak Afghan government to consolidate power and preserve stability. The prospect of enhanced instability in Afghanistan, as well as concerns over increased Indian, Russian, and Iranian influence in that country as the US and NATO presence draws down, has fuelled Pakistan's reluctance to give up its own instruments of influence, which include control of subversive militant groups. Recent moves by the civilian governments in Pakistan and India towards improved relations will affect the dynamics in Pakistan as the anti-India driven foreign and military policy has been the linchpin for entrenched stakeholders within Pakistan's military-intelligence establishment and generated support for state-sponsored terror groups out to destabilise India. A rapprochement between Pakistan and India would not be in the political, ideological, or economic interests of these factions and may inadvertently contribute to increased efforts to destabilise the civilian government in Islamabad as well as antagonise India through support for increased extremist activities—or even military incursions—on Indian territory.[321] The recently conducted 'Hearts of Asia' conference in Islamabad in December 2015, addressed issues concerning Afghanistan's security and its future, post the withdrawal of US forces. The issues covered included stability operations, denial of sanctuaries; preventing proliferation of narcotics, peaceful resolution of disputes, and respect for international laws as well as the reconstruction of the Afghan economy and solving the refugee problem in Afghanistan, brought about by recent Pakistani military offensives against terror groups in FATA.

It is in the interests of peace, enduring stability, and development that SAARC nations collectively seek the cooperation of the UN agencies to not only strengthen regional security, but also actively cooperate within and across the framework of established regional protocols to defeat terrorism, whilst simultaneously addressing non-traditional threats to security. Whilst it is easier said than done, considering the antipathy of the two central nations, nonetheless, it is time that such an effective counter-terror (CT) mechanism is created, which should be explored beyond the SAARC. Individually and internally, SAARC nations must strengthen their CT mechanism, running the gamut from law,[322] [323] intelligence, de-radicalisation and the like to enhancing development and bringing peace and stability in their citizens' lives. Cooperation and assistance from SAARC, UN agencies and the neighbourhood, especially India, will be a prime driver to usher in stability and greater economic enhancement in the region. India's geo-strategic location is such that, despite being conventionally seen as a predominant power in the South Asian region, its security and economic interests straddle Central Asia, West Asia, the IORA, and the Indo-Pacific, cutting across major strategic neighbourhoods in Asia, in an expanded geopolitical theatre, making it uniquely positioned to engage with SAARC nations, positively. Thus, in the post-cold war context of emerging threats and opportunities, all these neighbourhoods are important—from the point of view of energy security, piracy, terrorism, and search for markets and investment for Indian entrepreneurs as well as employment opportunities for its growing young population.[324] Terrorism that has plagued South Asia can be best ameliorated through cooperation at various levels, and India and Pakistan have to cooperate with each together, because neither can tackle this problem unilaterally. SAARC urgently needs consensus and the collective will of the politico-military-bureaucratic leadership and captains of industry, as well as the determination to implement the endorsed counter-terrorism measures, overcoming past hostility, 'deep state' adherents and 'non state actors'. Various initiatives need to be taken at the regional level to get the 'ball rolling'. The establishment of a regional training centre for technical and CT experts as well as defence and intelligence officials, with member-countries from and outside the SAARC region but affected by terror, could be one such appropriate platform.[325] Utilising the Bay of Bengal Initiative for Multi Sectoral

Technical and Economic Cooperation (BIMSTEC) is perhaps another such mechanism, which while strengthening the territorial integrity of member-states, would also bring about regional cooperation in fighting terror, including piracy, along with poverty.

A duly authenticated and chartered road map, by all member-states to achieve this measure of cooperation would first involve a consensual definition of terrorism—preferably within the UN Charter. In the absence of such a clearly defined classification of terrorists and terrorism, SAARC should strive for defining through consensus, as without a defining term of terrorism and terrorists, the next step of an implementable and viable regional counter-terrorism strategy will make no headway.

The establishment of a SAARC counter-terrorism centre by enhancing the scope and responsibilities of the SAARC Terrorism Monitoring Desk as well as the Regional Training Centre could be the first initiative, irrespective of the progress of defining terrorism. This centre could be structured like the UN Counter-Terrorism Committee[326] and along with the respective national institutes of security studies become a recognised regional hub for training CT specialists and enhance the capacity building initiatives of law enforcement agencies. These initiatives would set the stage for the development of an effective, regional mechanism for fostering sustained counter-terrorism cooperation amongst SAARC nations and the expertise gained here should be shared with similar institutions and government agencies/alliances.

As explained earlier, 'soft power' plays a vital role in CT efforts—thus, the requirement of increasing people-to-people contacts, and not just 'cultural programmes' but more youth exchange programmes at National Cadet Corps levels, premier education institutes and higher educational institutes of trade, humanitarian assistance and disaster management, agriculture as well as science and technology, should take place. Extension of a model of the Colombo Plan,[327] as pertinent to SAARC for human resources and skill development would be an appropriate initiative. Such 'people-to-people' contacts as part of a subtle CT campaign not only enriches civil society but also benefits domestic society. A youth exchange programme akin to the US Peace Corps[328] is appropriate to carry forward SAARC development programmes in the fields of climate change, health care, hygiene and sanitation, green initiatives and ecological sustenance besides food security, gender equality, and women's empowerment.

In line with the UN Global Counter Terrorism Strategy Review 2014,[329] and the importance of joint action to combat terror, conflict and political violence in South Asia, it is imperative that SAARC leaders explicitly endorse the UN strategy and initiate and implement measures proposed to develop a regional strategy to address the terrorist threat and counter conditions conducive to terrorism, prevent and combat terrorism, build state capacity, and ensure a human rights approach to all counter-terrorism measures.[330] It has also been advocated that engagement holistically by the UN on CT issues with host nations should fall within the General Assembly's UN strategy as a framework rather than Security Council Resolutions 1373[331] and 1624[332] with their Chapter VII mandate. Such a 'kid glove' approach while addressing political sensitivities of the region should pave the way for SAARC and BIMSTEC to become effective meaningful and legitimate regional partners on counter-terrorism while drawing on the experiences and best practices from other parts of the globe, and design regional training programs or workshops aimed at addressing regional problems,[333] in the proposed counter-terrorism centre.

Despite a common heritage going back several centuries, South Asia has today emerged as the least integrated and one of the more unstable regions in the world. As the region's dominant power, India has to take the lead in initiating dialogue and action and assume charge to ensure economic growth and stability in the region, as without peace in the neighbourhood, India does not prosper—this has a cascading effect on the well-being of its regional neighbours—and will not be able to achieve its objectives of rapid, inclusive and sustained growth and improvement in the people's living standards.

Taking the lead demands a clear articulation of the National Security Policy[334]—spelling out the national aims, intent, strategic interests, and strategic thought. It is from our national aim that intent and vision will flow, which will dictate national interests, and the conduct of foreign policy. A country's national aim and interests also has a direct impact in the way we address our external and internal security concerns. Unfortunately, we have often diluted our national interests for narrow, short-sighted political compulsions. This can be directly attributed to the lack of strategic culture and thought in India[335], which has been reflected in the spasmodic reactions that successive governments respond to in security situations. Massive defence budgets and Home Ministry allocations are not passed without adequate feedback on previous utilisations, 'value for money received', nor is there any Parliamentary discourse or debate by our lawmakers on the delayed progress of implementing various committee measures to enhance security both at the central and state government levels.

To be a strong regional power, India's internal and external security elements have to be geared up and structured to tackle challenges and, as the repeated failures of the past show, we have yet to implement the recommendations post major terror strikes. We, thus, need to refocus on engagement of terror afresh. An aspiring great power cannot allow itself to be hobbled by inaction against terror nor it be shackled by regional ties and constrained by local politics. It has to reach out beyond its shores and engage constructively. India must also articulate a comprehensive and robust national counter-terrorism (CT) strategy based on a sound assessment of the threats—present and emerging—including their nature and scope. National affiliations and transnational linkages, the ideologies, capabilities, tactics, funding and support motives should be highlighted along with periodic reviews of worldwide terror activities, modus operandi and national responses. Issues like surrender policy, negotiations with terrorists, and peace initiatives with local groups should be factored into the overall strategy. Military initiatives, internally and externally as well as command and control during joint CT operations should also be articulated. Our own CT architecture has to be regularly assessed and audited for its capabilities in enabling proactive and robust response mechanisms, by subject specialists and not generalists, as it all too often happens. We are only adding on increments/new elements/ forces, without assessing and auditing capabilities and capacities of existing architecture. Periodic audits of performance capabilities will enable security agencies to respond more effectively and prevent them from continuing to function on the basis of preconceived notions. Another reason for carrying out periodic net assessments of the threat of terrorism is to ensure that a well thought out counter-terrorism strategy and counter-terrorism measures are adopted proactively instead of in knee jerk fashion in the aftermath of an attack,[336] as is invariably the case in India.

Countering terrorism and internecine warfare can no longer be confined to the physical domain alone but has to be extended beyond the borders, besides internally encompassing the full spectrum of engagements—psychological (including pride in national identity), developmental activities, the use of information technology-driven tools, good governance, revamp of intelligence gathering/sharing, police force revamping and re-skilling, expeditious and separate judicial processes, neutralisation of radicalism, and border and access controls besides financial strangulation. The active involvement of industry and trade, NGOs, societies—religious, cultural, and social—as well as the public as vital components of the overall CT campaign, will add major incremental efforts to central government and regional initiatives.

In its dealings with nations that sponsor or subsidise terror groups, India must exploit the entire gamut from soft power to hard force, more often than not, concurrently, but not necessarily, in graduated scales. The signing of extradition treaties with Pakistan, Afghanistan, and The Maldives and progressing with countries providing safe havens is an initiative, which should be taken up seriously by the Ministry of External Affairs to bring terror fugitives to justice. Internally as well as while dealing with neighbours racked by terror, cooperation and not confrontation would be the preferred medium. India is often referred to as a 'soft state' given its perceived inability to systematically and categorically deal with several threats to the country's homeland security as evidenced by a plethora of state security agencies with minimal ability to coordinate in dealing with these threats in an effective manner.[337] Domestically, India needs to get its house in order and dump existing strategy based on political expediency that have arisen out of electoral considerations. Attacks like Mumbai 2008, would not have been accomplished in such an efficient and coordinated manner without the help of sleeper cells. Grandstanding politicians need to accept this and acknowledge the ground realities and act in the national interests. Similarly, the removal of tough national laws (such as POTA) that allowed for enhanced witness protection and extended detention of suspects in terrorist cases sent out a signal to domestic terrorist groups also that India lacked the political will to fight terror. This also demoralised the security forces and law enforcement agencies who felt they would not have the backing of the state in the campaign against terror. Even basic policing assistance from the public, to report illegal and unlawful activities, take on communal overtones and harassment of the 'minority' card is flashed.

Terrorism today is an act of war against India and aggression against the state. It cannot be treated as a law and order crisis anymore. It is about national security rather than law enforcement and therefore needs to be viewed and responded to in that manner.[338] India thus needs to confront the challenges forced by terrorism in a more proactive, focused and vigorous manner, to deter and deny terrorists the means and support mechanisms to plan and execute attacks, while, at the same time, maintaining an adequately robust response mechanism should they occur. To deal with the proponents of terror, India needs a strong national legislation backed with specially designated fast-track anti-terrorist courts that dispose of cases swiftly and with exemplary punishments. The USA, Britain, and France have imposed stringent laws against terrorist actions despite being liberal democracies; even Pakistan has cracked down hard with special laws and anti-terror courts. Thus, it is imperative that India shed all pretensions of politics in sham secularism through appeasement policies of minorities, curtailing the ability of law enforcement and counter-terror agencies and enforce hard-line policies.

India has a large, unwieldy, and complex bureaucratic set up[339] to manage its counter-terrorism efforts. The responsibility for maintaining law and order is a part of the state list with the first responders to a terror strike being the local police, who can best deal with local crimes and gangsters. Post Mumbai 2008, states equipped, trained and fielded special anti-terror teams, but so far their performance has not been tested, other than in Gurdaspur in 2015. Information being a key component of the CT campaign, despite a plethora of intelligence agencies, mostly structured for law and order and to spy on political and other rivals, instead of being investigative and intelligence units.[340] Reluctance in sharing information, poor coordination and latitudinal layers and echelons[341] ensure highly cumbersome and slow response mechanisms. Besides, lack of adequate analysts,[342] intelligence agencies are understaffed, undertrained and technologically challenged. India's police-to-population ratio is well below international standards. It stood at 138 police personnel per 100,000 people in 2014. The acceptable international standard is between 225 and 500 police personnel per 100,000 people, and the UN recommends it at 220 per 100,000 people.[343] While policing depends on several variables like crime, law and order and traditional local problems and therefore benchmarking figures and ratios may not be idealistic. However what is definitely required is enhancing their core capabilities and competence and equipment profile, including digitisation of surveillance systems. The shortage of technically trained officers in the Intelligence Bureau (IB) is even more. In 2013 there was a shortage of around 8,000 officers in the IB, which had 18,795 personnel on its rolls, against a sanctioned strength of 26,867, a shortfall of over 30 per cent.[344] The IB has since gone on a recruitment drive, but it takes years to gain competence in specialised tradecraft.

Recommended Measures to Counter Terror—Internal

A slew of measures is suggested, taking into account the existent deficiencies as well as future threats that may emerge to counter the multifaceted terror challenges that India confronts at present and those likely to rise in the future. These measures are part of the numerous directives and initiatives that can be taken at central, state (regional), corporate and societal levels and are not exhaustive in themselves.

Measures—Central Government

To begin with, terrorism, insurgency, insurrections, and the like have to be treated as federal crimes and dealt with by the central government keeping in mind that the balance of the law and order component remains with the state. Secondly, the army must not be utilised as first responders for CT tasks inside the country; it should be the domain of respective state police SWAT teams, supplemented by the NSG. The army should be the second responder in all establishments, other than in their own, for which they should be responsible and accountable. This extension of clear-cut accountability and responsibility must extend over all domains and periodic reviews and exercises to sharpen skills and response must be carried out with the active participation of all stake holders; regular audits and feedback should be obtained and implemented. The army must take the lead in handling all facets of chemical, biological, radiation and nuclear (CBRN)-related activities and train central and state disaster management teams and select state police personnel in the initial handling and reporting of such threats. Periodic disaster management exercises incorporating CBRN threats also need to be carried out to assess the capabilities of responders, including that of medical response teams. It is also appropriate to establish a separate National Security Administrative Cadre of technical and subject specialists, enrolled, directly recruited or taken aboard on contractual basis to strengthen the manning and handling of complex skills required in today's hi-tech world in the various technology-driven specialised agencies existed and those to come up The generalised cadre of 'one size fits all' should be abandoned. Strengthening the economic offences wing for targeting the terrorists' 'centre of gravity', i.e., their financial inflows through different medium is a priority of the central government. Transfer of funds from abroad through the hawala and NGO route as well as targeting terrorists' 'revenue generating models' like the drug trade, trafficking in gems, extortion and the like, should be clamped down upon ruthlessly. Additional measures at the central government level are suggested below.

(a) Creation of an Internal Security Ministry

The monolithic Ministry of Home Affairs having six departments (including the Department of Internal Security and a separate Department of J&K Affairs) with a total of 20 divisions[345] including three on police, two on internal security, one each on J&K, the North-East, Left-Wing Extremism, Border Management and Disaster Management, besides other equally important divisions, is a ministry which urgently requires paring. Presently, vital security-related components like the Intelligence Bureau, Central Bureau of Investigation, National Investigation Agency, National Intelligence Grid, seven Central Armed Police Forces of which the 'sword arm' for Counter-Terror operations, the National Security Guards, is a part of, leads it to a unique ministry where reorganisation is necessary to ensure cogency and efficacy. Hiving off border management to the Ministry of Defence with reconstituted forces (Assam Rifles, Border Security Force, Sahastra Seema Bal and Indo-Tibetan Border Police as one border guards formation), as well as regrouping the Central armed police forces into one single and leaner agency under the Internal Security Ministry could lead to better functioning. Besides reorganization of internal and external intelligence and investigative agencies (Central Bureau of Investigation and National Investigation Agency), and ensuring a balance among the police forces (the Central Industrial Security Force could be shared by the Ministry of Industries and the Ministry of Civil Aviation) and retaining the National Security Guards as well as a more effective and less bloated Central Reserve Police force would surely yield better policing and results.[346]

(b) Securing Boundaries

The notion that only land boundaries need physical securing was dispelled by two landmark events: The Purulia Arms Drop case of 17 December 1995[347] and the Mumbai terror attack of 26 November 2008,[348] both of which laid bare the urgent necessity of having a coordinated inter and intra-agency counter-terror approach to secure the maritime boundaries and air space.[349] The Air Force should be responsible for all aspects of air defence and airspace management control, excluding civilian traffic. The creation of an Air National

Guard as an auxiliary to the Air Force for local air space management, considering the envisaged extensive use of drones, should also be factored. The Navy should be responsible for maritime security, including anti-piracy operations on the high seas with the Coast Guard being the lead agency responsible and accountable for coastal security, with the marine police of respective states placed under their command and control for better coverage and coordination.

(c) Creation of National Counter-Terrorism Centre (NCTC)

This federal agency should be the lead organisation to deal with all aspects of intelligence connected with terrorism-related cases occurring in any part of the country or abroad. Like its US counterpart, it should serve as the repository for a central and shared knowledge bank on terrorism information, providing all-source intelligence support to government-wide counter-terrorism activities, as well as integration, dissemination, and use of, terrorism information, besides serving as the primary organisation for strategic operational planning for counter-terrorism.[350] The NCTC should have its own dedicated satellites for electronic surveillance and communications for real-time data to be linked to all CT agencies in the country. This agency would be the focal point for developing a specialised cadre of intelligence analysts specialising in terrorism. The establishment of the NCTC would mean streamlining intelligence with unambiguous responsibility, authority, and accountability. Overlapping with the existing Multi Agency Centre (MAC) functions should be resolved to avoid turf wars and if operational streamlining requires merging, it should be done. Linkages with the National Technical Research Organisation (NTRO, functioning under the National Security Advisor) in providing technical intelligence inputs must continue.

(d) Fine-tuning of National Intelligence Grid (NatGrid)

Set up in 2014 and intended to integrate existing databases, which the government claimed would help 'fight terrorism', NatGrid has so far failed to take off. Its potential impact on terrorism is, moreover, debatable, and its efficacy has been questioned even within the intelligence community.[351] NatGrid is nonetheless set to become a secure centralised database to stream sensitive information from 21 sets of data sources such as banks, credit cards, and visa, immigration, (including train and air travel details), as well as from various intelligence agencies. The database would be accessible to authorised persons from 11 agencies on a case-to-case basis, and only for professional investigations into suspected cases of terrorism.[352] Considering that India has acknowledged expertise in designing Artificial Intelligence (AI) tools, its meshing into a specially-created national information exchange grid, (gathering data from varied sources such as telecom, banking, immigration, national identities, electronic spectrum, and existing intelligence, police, paramilitary and other government and even private security agencies) and thereafter funnelling it through powerful AI analytics would bring about the capability to predict trends, events and create 'over the horizon' visibility[353]. The overdue initiative to revive NatGrid should address the longer-pending demand to have effective oversight of intelligence agencies by Parliament or an eminent group, so that misuse of personal information and violation of an individual's privacy does not take place.

(e) Enhance Capabilities and Charter of National Investigation Agency

The National Investigation Agency (NIA), which was established in the wake of the 26/11 attacks, has failed to impact significantly on the trajectory of terrorism, despite occasional successes. The total cases registered by the NIA as on 31 December 2015, since 2011, currently stand at just 114 in a country where thousands of terrorist-related offences are committed every year. Charge sheets have, thus far, been filed in only 61 cases, with some cases dating back to 2011 still under investigation![354] The cumulative CT impact of the NIA—if at all measurable—would at best be negligible. The total strength of all crime investigation departments (CID) in the state police across the country stood at 11,729 personnel in 2011, with as many as 6,252,729 offences registered that year; yielding a ratio of 533.09 cases per officer (it is no surprise that most of these cases go un-investigated).[355] It is thus mission essential to not only sharpen the investigative skills of the NIA, but also impose time lines for investigations and leave lesser relevant cases to be dealt with at local state police levels.[356] NIA staffers face the non-cooperative attitude of respective state level apparatus, cooperation from whom would be forthcoming once terrorism is categorised as a federal crime and local police and administrative obstructionists, jailed for non-cooperation.[357] Also, many offences, including major Indian Penal Code crimes and some specific terror-financing models, which may be linked to terror activities, have yet to be brought under the NIA's jurisdiction.[358]

(e) Introduction of Strategic Culture

There is an overwhelming need to introduce the culture of a grand strategy, national strategy as well as aspects of counter-terror operations amongst our political, administrative, legal, industry fraternity and intellectuals through the medium of discussions, seminars and interactions with subject specialists from India and abroad to generate awareness as well as provoke thought on these national and regional security subjects. The same can be also introduced at more institutions of higher learning, with the active participation of universities and think tanks.

(f) Laws

It is indeed a paradox of our times that India, which has been one of the worst sufferers of terrorism for more than three decades, has an acknowledged weak judicial system hampered by activism and slow legal processes and is accepted the world over as being notorious in its dispensation of exemplary justice and early resolution. Even the Administrative Reforms Commission, in its recommendation, averred thus, "A comprehensive and effective legal framework to deal with all aspects of terrorism needs to be enacted. The law should have adequate safeguards to prevent its misuse. The legal provisions to deal with terrorism could be incorporated in a separate chapter in the National Security Act, 1980".[359] In the same report, the Law Commission was quoted as being of the opinion that a legislation to fight terrorism was a necessity in India and that it was not as if the enactment of such legislation would by itself subdue terrorism. It would however, arm the State to fight terrorism more effectively. The Supreme Court has repeatedly held that the mere possibility of abuse cannot be a ground for denying the vesting of powers or for declaring a statute unconstitutional.[360] The trial by a special court for the Mumbai attack of 2008 lasted three years ending with the hanging of the only surviving Pakistani terrorist on 21 November 2011. One of the principal accused of the Mumbai blast of 1993, Yakub Memon was finally executed on 30 July 2015, twenty-two years after the crime. Therefore, there is a requirement for enacting separate and stringent laws to deal with all aspects of terror and terror-related crimes, through special courts and investigative agencies (NIA) in a time-bound manner. Review and revitalisation of the judicial system is also necessary to weed out colonial-era laws as well as introduce the admissibility of electronic evidence. The necessity exists of creating a state and central cadre of competent investigating officers and criminal and terror law prosecutors, besides enacting a federal law to deal with increasing economic offences, as they are avenues for terror funding.

(g) Involvement of State Governments

Each state should tone up its counter-terror architecture in line with the central CT strategy and road map and ensure implementable time lines, to deal with allocated responsibilities at regional levels. The establishment of a state-level version of NatGrid and the introduction of technology and analysts to monitor communication systems utilised by anti-national elements, the setting up of advanced forensics laboratories with qualified technicians as well as dealing with fake Indian currency notes (FICN), money laundering (hawala transactions), and curbing the preaching and teaching of radicals are some of the state-level initiatives that could fall in the domain of local expertise in the overall CT campaign. National security should under no circumstances be compromised by state and regional 'politicking' as there has already been a progressive erosion of the professionalism of the state police forces because of day-to-day political interference in the functioning of constabularies. Such interference has taken a toll of the accountability, morale, and integrity of state police forces.[361] There is thus an urgent need to restore public perception and confidence in the state police forces and their functioning by streamlining their channels of response as well as clearly-defined responsibilities and accountabilities for law and order. Implementation of various pending projects to enhance state policing capabilities is long overdue. In making respective state police forces tech savvy as well as enhancing capabilities, capacities, and numbers to deal with a range from petty crime to violent terror actions will also require regular reviews and audits of existing systems.

Monitoring of social networking sites and mobile traffic, especially emanating from known terror centres as well as seminaries and select population enclaves and foreigners, will likely yield substantial results. As far as physical security is concerned, state-level CT teams, trained and equipped, should be available at each police district with adequate reserves at bigger towns and cities. The tendency to divert them to VIP protection duties should be discouraged. Human Intelligence (HumInt) should play as vital a role as Technical Intelligence (TechInt), as HumInt gleans more from local-level policing and initiatives through interactions with community, caste and religious leaders, personages and elders, besides common people. Community policing, screening, and de-radicalisation programmes, especially of returnees from identified vulnerable nations and Sunni-dominated areas, is a must. The compulsory registration of all religious and minority education and connected institutions including their sponsors, attendees, and curriculum needs scrutiny to prevent hatred being preached in the name of religion. The reach and capabilities of the Internet and mobile phones must be fully exploited in the policing aspects, including introduction of applications to generate inputs connected with hawala transactions, especially for incendiary speeches at religious and political gatherings, terror activities, passing fake currency (FICN), terror modules/activities, incendiary speeches, extortion and the like. The technology available in the open market is substantial to meet present and future requirements. This has to be harnessed for maximum benefit.

Coastal security and marine police have assumed national importance since the 26/11 Mumbai attacks. An elaborate network has been envisaged and put into place. Its efficacy is patchy, to say the least, as it is common knowledge that it is still vulnerable and suffers from serious deficiencies.[362] Until now, Identification Friend or Foe (IFF) systems are not available in boats, nor is there any codified method of passing distress signals while at sea when engaged by terrorists, pirates or witnessing suspicious activity. The use of unmanned aerial vehicles (UAVs) and drones, especially with night-vision capability, by smaller Coast Guard vessels and even marine police for shore patrols in inaccessible areas and creeks will be a force multiplier with deterrent effect.

(h) Corporate Initiatives

The 'Made in India' drive launched by the government is an ideal platform for corporate involvement in the improvement of the internal security and counter-terror architecture of the country. There are tremendous growth opportunities in the high-tech sector for providing state-of-the-art defence and security-related equipment, hardware, and software for India as well as for SAARC nations and other regional partners. Other combined initiatives include encouraging greater public-private participation, access to and adoption of latest technologies and leveraging the growing defence sector-specific competencies created within the country,[363] including their involvement in research and development activities for different platforms and systems. Considering the considerable competence that the Indian IT industry wields, it will be prudent for the Indian security establishment to involve IT in working out various computing models to deal with various facets of the war against terror. Regular interactions and exercises between agencies connected with preventive actions for disaster management and against terror strikes generate environmental awareness and streamline reporting of incidents. Companies should also devote a considerable part of their corporate social responsibilities (CSR) towards community development projects in the rural areas in sync with government initiatives especially in terror-struck areas and in those fields where rehabilitation is required, for example, by running vocational and skill development establishments in such areas. All these initiatives generate employment opportunities, which is a vital component of the 'Made in India' campaign.

(i) Additional Initiatives

The involvement of the country's youth in rural development schemes re-establishes a connect between the urban and the rural besides bringing about a sense of personal achievement. The creation, through legislation, of a national development service wherein all those selected for state and union civil services compulsorily serve for a year in rural areas as part of a national effort in rebuilding, making that a precondition for joining civil services at central and state levels, would be an innovative game changer. In addition, compulsory rural service for all medical graduates, irrespective of whether from government or private institutions, would strengthen rural health care, which is dismal.[364] Besides, PG medical students from all institutions should be mandated to do a rural internship stint. Concurrently, the development of infrastructure to enhance the facilities of National Rural Health Mission clinics would go a long way to ameliorate conditions in backward areas, which are generally the 'prime spots' of LWE dominance. A comprehensive rural development plan involving all final year students/fresh graduates from government and private technical institutes to do 'rural time' in departments of their chosen field and whose contours can be enlarged to include those joining government banking services—a stint in rural micro finance and those with IIMs, IITs, and RECs carrying out educational classes in government-run schools in rural areas, will greatly expand the concept of involvement in national development efforts. This can also be kept open for people of all ages to volunteer their time, energy, and skills for national development.

(j) Societal Responsibilities

Society nurtures individuals and those who plan to or tread the path of violence can be brought back to the mainstream by a system of peer and community elders counselling and guiding them, besides demotivating them through the efforts of family and friends. Weaning away potential terrorists is through the process of de-radicalisation, disengagement and ultimate rehabilitation into the society with a 'paternal' eye kept on their activities. Society is also responsible to assist in a revamp of a radicalised education system and bring it back into the mainstream, while community elders and family members are made responsible and accountable for missing youth or reporting suspicious activities and reporting the presence of radicalised elements as a part of community policing initiatives.

(k) Media Responsibilities

In an increasing era of global transparency a modicum of controls and self-restraint of media is called for. The media should refrain from live coverage of terrorist events as it jeopardises planning and operations and imperils the safety of those in the line of fire. In addition, an analysis of ongoing and past operations often gives away tactics and plans that help terrorists in their future plans. Nowadays, terrorist mentors/handlers are attentive to media and communicate details to the terrorists to take appropriate counter-measures. The establishment of a media desk, away from the scene of operations, to communicate delayed information should be the norm. There is a need for legislation to have checks and controls of what constitutes security breaches by the media, besides guidelines for 'red lines' in reporting as a step towards increased ethical and professional conduct by reporters and editors. Deterrent punitive fines as well as banning channels from broadcasting for specified periods depending on the severity of the infringement to completely proscribing channels is an effective measure to check runaway reporting and biased coverage.

(l) Additional Measures to Enhance Governance

Effective governance is possibly one of the most essential drivers in a CT campaign and also to enhance peace, prosperity, progress and attain stability through elimination of poverty. Elimination of corruption is one of the major enablers in successful development activities.[365] Transparency in institutional functions as well as clear-cut responsibility and accountability of government officials is a prerequisite for successful execution of government initiatives. Rewards and punishments are a must for good governance and the meritorious must be recognised and the inefficient weeded out, irrespective of caste or other considerations.

Additional Measures to Counter Terror—External

Concurrent to domestic measures, India must reach out to expand its global footprint as a service and technical provider in the CT domain, especially amongst the other SAARC nations and in the IOR as part of our calculus for long-term security projections. With the emerging shift in economic power from west to east and changing climatic conditions, the world's geographic focus will also change. The Pacific and Indian Ocean basins are already the fastest-growing commercial hubs for exchange of goods, services, and people—a trend that will intensify. With the growing competition for resources, the region is becoming an important avenue for global trade and an arena for geopolitical competition. It has significant deposits of primary raw materials that are vital to the world's economy such as bauxite, chromite, coal, copper, gold, iron ore, natural gas, nickel, oil, phosphates, titanium, tungsten, uranium, and zinc. The region's fisheries are also a key part of food security and regional livelihoods.[366] Increasing SAARC membership to include some of the IORA and BIMSTEC nations, especially Myanmar, Thailand, Malaysia, Seychelles, and Mauritius is an option to push forward development-linked CT initiatives. BIMSTEC is an important vehicle to facilitate integration between South Asia and South-East Asia, the realisation of which is essential for the achievement of Pan-Asian regional cooperation and integration. Some of the 'soft power' options available to enhance the standards of living in the region and bring about economic stability are elucidated below. The key areas where cooperation can assure shared interests include:

- Trade and transport policy through trans-border linkages and enhanced connectivity.
- Establishment of private but SAARC-backed banks at the regional level for microfinance, which could enhance the quality of lives at rural levels.
- Cooperation in disaster management and ecological sustainability initiatives.
- Enhance people-to-people contacts, especially of youth, women, technocrats and policymakers and SAARC volunteer programmes as well as scholar exchange programmes.

These will go a long way in bridging any trust deficit; besides generating goodwill and mutual understanding of a country's aspirations. The possibilities of enhanced cooperation are endless and are only limited to the extent of political will to meet aspirations of their people and regional goals for development and prosperity.

The motivation for greater integration in the South Asian region stems from four distinct factors:

1. Economic gains through efficient use of capital and labour and freer cross-border movement of goods and services.
2. Greater regional integration results in increased flow of FDI.
3. Strategic gains when the South Asian countries negotiate as a unified group in multilateral forums.
4. Developmental and environmental efficiency gains arising from adopting a regionally integrated approach.

These regional issues cannot be effectively addressed individually and are best addressed in a cooperative framework.[367] Taken together, these factors have an exponential effect on the economies of the region, bringing about greater economic freedom and enhanced standards of living, which should push back the efforts of the proponents of violence, and idealistically, contain and ultimately isolate terror groups and their sponsors. However, as long as a country's terrorist is another nation's freedom fighter, the prospects of an effective regional counter-terrorism strategy will remain dim.

The range and impact of generating terror through various mediums are endless and it requires nimble minds, proactive action and dedicated people and agencies to thwart terror, especially in the nascent stages itself. Vital components of India's existing internal security apparatus suffers due to the ignorance and incompetence of a politically compromised and sometimes corrupt executive. The present CT system is woefully short of capabilities, capacities and competence in dealing with existing challenges and those looming in the horizon. Our system needs to be able to engage, handle, and defeat current and emerging threats, especially the violence emanating from a threatened holocaust by new-generation terrorists armed with computers and CBRN technology. A holistic national counter-terrorism policy as part of a comprehensive national security policy, with clear-cut delineations and responsibilities must be urgently finalised taking states on board and embracing aspects of management, funding and accountability to deal with the increasing dangers of terrorism.

SAARC, as a regional forum, must live up to the expectations of its founding fathers, and bring about a quantitative and qualitative change in the lives of the South Asian people. Rectifying gaps in bilateral relations[368] while engaging trilaterally, as in the case of Nepal with India and China,[369] and multilaterally, as in the SAARC charter, are the ways forward in sustaining the region's cooperative resolve towards development, economic stability, peace and prosperity and, above all, living up to and exceeding the potential of this ancient and richly historical land, which at one time generated a quarter of the world's wealth, less than half a millennia before.[370]

CHAPTER 6

INFERENCES

"Great power is not a standing achieved easily or by many countries. With a modicum of economic strength, and natural attributes of size, population, and location, what separates great powers and would-be great powers from the rest are a driving vision, an outward thrusting nature backed by strong conviction and a sense of national destiny and matching purpose, an inclination to establish distance presence and define national interests within the widest possible geographical ambit, the confidence to protect and further these interests with proactive foreign and military policies, the building up of meaningful conventional armed forces backed by a proven and tested thermonuclear arsenal, and the willingness to use coercion and force in support of national interests complemented by imaginative projection and use of both soft power and hard power to expansively mark its status in the external realm."

—Bharat Karnad[371]

This book has endeavoured to evaluate the challenges faced by the SAARC nations and suggests some of the approaches to be adopted to overcome the scourge that has afflicted this once prosperous region, severely affecting the tolerance and harmony that once characterised the sub-continent. The canvas whilst encompassing the sub-continent seeks to expand on the need for India to look beyond the prism of narrow regional aspirations, and redefine spheres of influence and alliances and focus its efforts towards attaining superpower status, whilst concurrently addressing the aspirations of its peoples. Nimbleness of thought and action is generally not associated with governments, but that is the precise requirement of the day to deal with rapidly emergent situations, worldwide. The Indian Diaspora, dispersed the world over, constitutes a remarkable 'force multiplier' that should be factored in during planning and execution processes, especially in the economic and security calculus of national policy.

SAARC

Issues that are central to the growth and proliferation of terrorism in the SAARC region were the focus and their ascent was highlighted and steps to usher in peace and tranquillity recommended. Whilst harmonising the uniqueness that each nation's identity brings to a common platform, the core issues that spur radicalisation and violence, need to be addressed at the state and regional level, so that spillovers can be contained and eventually neutralised by a judicious mix of hard and soft power and through collusive efforts. India, being in a unique position, and sharing boundaries with all the SAARC nations, is thus eminently placed to assist in these endeavours through various mediums, including achievement of the 17 Sustainable Development Goals set out by the UN over the next 15 years.[372]

Despite the various protocols of SAARC, not much headway has been made consequent to the joint declaration made by the SAARC heads at 15th summit in Colombo in August 2008.[373] The political complexities and animosities of the region, other than those of Pakistan, has encouraged all member-states to actively cooperate and join hands in working towards the eradication of terrorism. Terrorism has to be contained by making nations fully accountable for their acts of omission in turning a blind eye to the activities of their citizens and commission in sponsoring such activities. International consensus has to be built up and, wherever required, a movement to declare such nations as state sponsors must be pressed for and economic sanctions imposed. Under the circumstances, India has to take a more vigorous lead to ensure that Pakistan is given this dubious distinction —nukes notwithstanding.

Domestic

Over the years, India's approach, especially towards domestic terror, has been knee-jerk reactions, motivated more often than not by populism and politics rather than national interests. Progressive developmental activities in the Maoist belt, without leaving it to business houses to ravage the countryside in their exploitation of natural resources, with effective social development programmes to ameliorate the lot of the affected tribals as well as afforestation programmes would maintain a balance of ecological sustainability. Indeed, it would be preferred, in the long run, to leave vast areas under-developed with tribal reserved forests designated in consultation with the stakeholders—the tribals, government, national NGOs, and eminent personalities acceptable to all. Nuanced in time, with effective legislation and counter-actions against all forms of terror will deliver a stern message to domestic perpetrators as well as supporters, sleeper cells and purveyors of anti-nationalism of the serious and disproportionate consequences of challenging and compromising on the security and stability of the nation.

Politically, India needs to emerge expeditiously out of its petty factionalism, bureaucratic mindset and vote bank appeasements to deal with national issues instead of myopic priorities. The Ministry of Home Affairs has to be revamped and bifurcated into two, to make it responsive to changing security concerns and staffed with specialists. India needs to also set its internal security structure in order and make it responsive to environmental requirements, rather than bloating the number of central forces. Land border management agencies should be clubbed into a professionally-managed single unit, rather than several forces looking after different sectors without accountability. Revamping of the intelligence apparatus and reorganising intelligence agencies to make them more proactive, including expanding RAW's capabilities in covert operations, the Intelligence Bureau's numbers and focus on, as well as strengthening investigative agencies and local policing numbers and competence is mission essential. Coastal security under the Coast Guard and the support of the Customs and respective marine security police should be better equipped to be effective, proactive, and competent to handle security up to the Exclusive Economic Zone. Emerging aerial threats that include drones, para motors; balloons, microlites, and the like require a different set up for coordination with existing air space management and control systems. Setting up an air national guard would be a step in that direction. The security of our island territories has to be upgraded, as some may be vulnerable to occupation by terror groups as well as refugees and 'boat people', alongwith infringements in our EEZ.

The ramping up of military capabilities to deal with current and emerging threats rather than handling so-called conventional operations (of the past) is essential. A bloated military with huge mechanised formations, strike corps (including mountain strike corps) are difficult to conceal, costly to maintain and inefficient in current war-fighting requirements have no role in future conflicts [374] and require to be dumped. Air mobility of our Army, especially for insertion in high altitude and stealth operations, needs to be effected in a big way, through extensive increment in rotary and fixed wing aircraft. Our military planners' myopic focus towards Pakistan and lip service towards the main threat—China, the IOR and Fourth Generation Warfare has to change.

Administratively, our policies towards those taking to the cult of violence have to be analysed to address the root and trigger causes. The government would find it extremely cost effective to invest more on meaningful social welfare issues like primary and secondary education and midday meal schemes for all children all the year round. Skills and vocational training, besides a modicum of NCC or NSS training to instil national character and pride, will have long-term positive outcomes. Compulsory rural service for all medical graduates, irrespective of whether from government or private institutions, would strengthen rural health care; schemes that are currently in operation are dismal. The creation of a volunteer national development service, and making it a precondition for joining the civil services at the central and state levels would be an innovative game changer. This can also be kept open for people of all ages to volunteer their time, energy and skills for national development. Similarly, all those joining government banking services and IIMs, IITs, RECs and the like must do a stint in rural environment before placements. CSR projects should focus on these core groups taking their initiatives forward to address the inequalities that exist in our rural and urban areas.

Issues of economic deprivation, unemployment, underdevelopment and urban rural divide have to be addressed holistically if we have to end internal dissent and rebellion. A statute to treat all forms of terrorism in India as federal crimes, whether, planned, sponsored, financed, supported or executed in or outside India, impacting India or any UN member-nation, should be introduced expeditiously. Terror can also be taken out of the purview of the state list and so should introduction of trial courts to exclusively deal with terrorist related crimes in a time-bound manner. It is understood that the fundamental rationale of any nation's counter-terror measures is to protect human rights and democracy. Therefore, the states must ensure that counter-terror measures do not undermine the same democratic values or violate human rights and thereby subvert the very law they seek to protect through their actions. Ending of the draconian Armed Forces Special Powers Act, 1958, especially in the North-east states where it was first imposed more than half a century ago is a must; the military must be made more accountable for misdemeanours and human rights violations. The relevance of this Act in Jammu and Kashmir only in terror-affected areas, while leaving out peaceful zones and districts, will have a salutary effect. A standard 'No Negotiations Policy with Terrorists or Terror Groups' as well as a comprehensive Surrender and Rehabilitation policy and follow-up are equally important components of any counter-terror strategy.

International

Internationally too, India has to emerge out of its hesitation to deal and operate jointly with Israel and other terror-affected nations in striking at terror groups and individuals inimical to India's security interests. This could be in the form of pacts, alliances or even covert and overt support. The substantial Indian Diaspora in the West (Canada and the USA included), and African, Southeast Asian regions and the Gulf should be tapped by the Indian government to canvass for support in respective parliaments (or their equivalents) locally seeking diplomatic and economic isolation of those countries sponsoring terror. The USA, which is eager to seek India's assistance as a net security services provider in the IOR, should be pressurised to get Pakistan to back down on terror and ease on its terror engagements in Afghanistan, after the total US pullout from the strife-torn state. Similarly, the collective known as the Indian Ocean Rim Association (IORA) should be actively engaged to exert diplomatic pressure on states sponsoring terror or piracy. Article 51of the UN

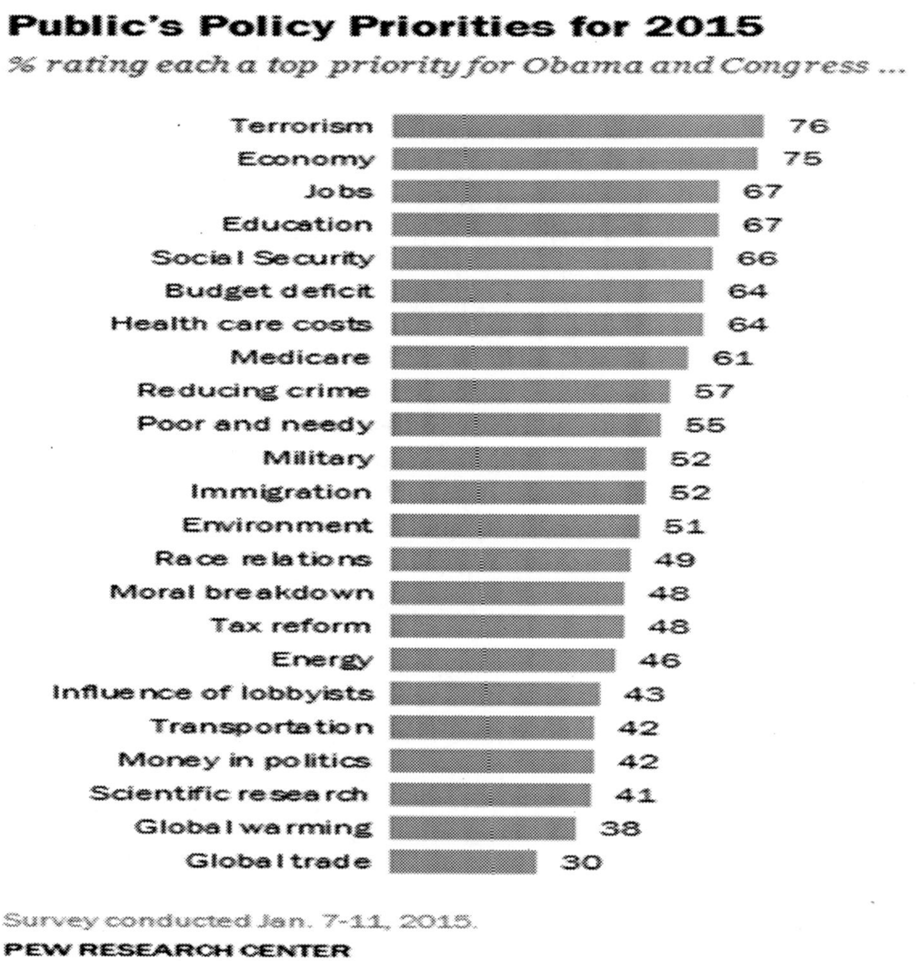

Charter[375] logically allows a nation acting in self-defence to conduct pre-emptive strikes against terrorists, their infrastructure, and funding processes as well as their cells and networks operating anywhere. Dismantling of terror groups in neighbouring nations by force, deep penetration and compromising of funding has to be aggressively followed up. Unconventional military and non-military responses and practices of dealing with terrorists and terror groups have to be ensured, dealing with their psyche and religious beliefs is another option.

Pakistan

Dealing with Pakistan requires a firmer approach. In addition to raising international awareness and Indian voices on human rights violations in Sindh and Baluchistan and against minorities, overcoming hesitancy to name Pakistan publicly in all international forums as a purveyor of jihad against the tenets of Islam, and drawing its own people's opprobrium against the boomerang effect brought about by sheltering, harbouring and financing international terror groups, would probably see some positives emerging. The engagement with the Pakistani establishment should continue, but with caveats which should foreclose the option of its usage of terror as an extension of state policy. These caveats should run the spectrum of responses from rescinding water treaties, disproportionate response by forces to terror attacks (including likely collateral damages), working towards its diplomatic isolation, imposing economic sanctions and costs (banning civilian overflights is one), strict visa regime and, if required, recasting SAARC without Pakistan's presence. The continued engagement with China, Iran and the 'Sthan' nations on the dangers posed by state-sponsored terror and propagation of jihadist violence by Pakistan-trained terrorists and the impact of expansion of the ISIS, Al-Qaeda and their domestic terror groups to their security, will bring more pressure on Pakistan to crack down on terror. "The past stereotype of a militant as a tribesman from the mountains in traditional garb with bandoliers of ammo slung over his shoulder has been replaced",[376] said analyst Bruce Hoffman, Director of the Centre for Security Studies at Georgetown University in Washington. The new generation comes from "well-educated, cosmopolitan, university-educated Pakistanis from middle-class backgrounds who can navigate our globalised space whether virtually or physically with facility and confidence".[377] They can use social media, cross borders and fit "seamlessly into global societies.... They are the new force multipliers of terrorist groups",[378] he said. The ISIS is courting university students, doctors, lawyers, journalists and businessmen and using women groups for fundraising.[379]

Afghanistan

The Afghan people and their need for assistance in the fields of education, water supply and health should be specially considered. The effective engagement of all warlords, alliances—tribal and regional—accentuated by an oversight of generous aid and skilled support including co-operation with stakeholders in the region is necessary, because, in the stability of Afghanistan lies the security of Central Asia and SAARC nations.

Nepal

The efforts of the Nepal government in addressing issues emerging out of the adoption of the new constitution would likely see some instability—but it is in the interests of both India and Nepal, not to aggravate the Madhesi problem but seek an early resolution through political means. Infrastructure development, especially of hydropower resources, even if sponsored by countries other than India, should be encouraged, in sync with the water-sharing treaties along with ease of trade and transit through Indian points of access. The increasing jihadist support, presence and ease of transit to and from Nepal for terrorists and criminals alike, especially for assignments in India and Bangladesh, has to be neutralised by stricter border controls by both India and Nepal, besides denying transit facilities by air by upgrading security in airports. Human trafficking should be curbed, as should the resettlement of Muslim communities along either side of the Terai belt.

Bhutan

Bhutan, India's only all-weather ally, has to be supported in all its endeavours to grow economically as well as industrially to realise its potential of being the ultimate tourist and Buddhist religious destination. India should engage with its terror groups from Assam to prevent them from making periodic forays from the plains to Bhutan's sparsely populated south as well as discourage Bhupalese from making inroads back to South Bhutan. Whilst strengthening Bhutan's miniscule military, it should ensure that the Chinese do not make any further inroads into their already substantial claims. Bhutan should also be encouraged to pursue an active foreign policy, guided by its own policies and security concerns, without ignoring the Chinese threat to its territories and that of India.

Bangladesh

Bangladesh, on the road to economic recovery and democratic stability, has made sterling progress in its counter-terror campaign, especially in its crackdown on Indian terror groups, which once got state-sponsored sanctuary during the rule of Khaleda Zia. It needs India's assistance to see that terror groups do not get support and sanctuary in India, especially in West Bengal and Assam. Its ability to manage its border controls and keep the refugee migration into India under check would be the single-most contributory factor towards good neighbourliness. Trade and transit, as well as water-sharing issues, are focus points for improvement as well as assistance in managing climate change leading to rising sea levels and the impact of global warming. Sanctuaries for the Rohingya, some of whom are being recruited by the JeI against the Bangladesh government, as well as piracy and human trafficking in the coastal belt, are some of the other concerns that need addressing.

Sri Lanka

Sri Lanka's emergence from near economic and domestic ruin after a long and bloody war against the LTTE sees its path to reconstruction galvanised by economic and infrastructural support from India as well as China. Internal dynamics of discord between the Muslims and Buddhists, Sinhalas and Tamils need sagacious and mature political handling to prevent a slide back into civil war. The resettlement of Tamil refugees and healing the wounds of the brutal last few months of a 'No Holds barred' war, is a priority as is the development and restoration of a greater degree of autonomy in local governance.

The Maldives

The Maldives has to come to grips to quell its internal disequilibrium, consequent to three major issues impacting its future—its bleak political outlook, growing jihadist culture and global warming. Its strength and fragility are both in its location and the government of the day has to take immediate steps to restore its credibility and stability, lest the jihadists seize the opportunity to topple the government, and expose the vulnerabilities of sea-borne trade in the IOR.

Other Neighbours

Countries contiguous to SAARC nations play a vital role in the peace and stability of the region. Myanmar, ushering change after long decades of military rule, has a host of internal problems to tackle, most of it brought about by its six decades of lack of democratic processes and the military regimes' policy of isolationism and poor economic management. Rampant poverty, crumbling infrastructure, endemic corruption, huge drug trade, underdeveloped human index and skills and poor financial conditions of the country necessitates a total overhaul of its administrative and monetary systems for which it requires extensive support from neighbours like India and China and world financial bodies.

India needs to act with alacrity on Prime Minister Modi's 'Act East Policy' if it has to make an impact as a regional and global player. Infrastructure development in the region as well as military and political engagements, and disaster management, in addition to application of soft power, will see a tremendous growth of a requirement for Indian expertise, especially by the Indian Ocean Rim countries. Anti-piracy operations, especially in the Horn of Africa and the Andaman Sea is an important facet to keep trade routes open and deny terrorists the capacity to seize vessels for launching terror operations, especially against India.

Shri K.M. Pannikar, a well-known and deeply regarded diplomat, remarked well before India's independence, "The interests of India in the Indian Ocean are different from those of other countries whose shores are washed by its waters. The other countries are not as entirely dependent as India is on this ocean. The peninsular nature of this country with its extensive coast line, and a rich and fertile littoral makes India entirely dependent on the Indian Ocean...while, to other countries, the Indian Ocean is only one of the important oceanic areas, to India it is a vital sea. Her lifelines are concentrated in that area, her freedom is dependent on the freedom of that water surface. No industrial development, no commercial growth, no stable political structure, is possible for her unless her shores are protected".[380] The Indian Navy has to emerge as the primary service to show the flag in the IOR, and its expansion to a bigger and more lethal force is essential for our economic survivability as well as force projection. It is thus necessary that besides the carrier battle groups, submarines and more lethal surface combatants planned—an impressive sealift capability in terms of dedicated amphibious forces to support naval operations, be they for coming to the aid of small maritime nations facing coups or even a show of strength or presence in distant lands, is a deterrent worth the investment. Trade and commerce existed from time immemorial among India, East Africa, and the Gulf states and up to Indonesia and beyond; this necessitates that Indian presence be felt as far away as Fiji. In addition, it raises the confidence levels of our Diaspora residing in these distant shores, especially when engaged in mercy missions and disaster relief operations. Such mercy missions can also be in the form of hospital ships paying port-of-call visits to remote islands in the IOR as well as our own islands. Efforts of late suggest that India is upgrading the Andaman and Nicobar Islands into a strategic outpost to improve its reach into the Indian Ocean. In 2012, with the commissioning of INS *Dweeprakshak* in the Western seaboard and Lakshwadweep Islands, and the recently-released Navy document, 'Indian Maritime Security Strategy' brings out the perspectives of developing India's island territories. Effectively, the islands in the western and eastern seaboards already form part of the strategic fulcrum of India's maritime ambitions.

Future Research

Future analysis in the area could be organised around a review of the efficacy and relevance of SAARC, given the existing regional dynamics that are likely to persist. The correlation between failing states and non-state actors with focus on effects of radicalisation needs to be understood. De-radicalisation programmes and national intervention in seminary-imparted education in the Indian context could be examined. The security of borders and island territories together with handling of migration and refugees; military restructuring for India; enhancing Indian maritime power, including coastal security power; meeting tribal aspirations, mining, environment issues and development and dealing with LWE (conflict and resolution); bringing all para military forces and central police organisations together for internal and border security (force restructuring versus force proliferation); police reforms in capacity-building initiatives in handling modern criminals, crime as well as terrorism can all be areas that address various aspects of the terrorism menace.

These studies together would contribute towards enhancing capabilities and capacities in the counter-terror domain as well as enhancing regional cooperation and in addressing nation-building issues whilst retaining an interest of archival value for subsequent works.

In summary, this book has studied the issues concerning terrorism as they impact SAARC nations and the courses of action available in tandem or where relevant, with specific reference to India's role as the key to unhinging this instrument of state-induced or sponsored terror. India's political hierarchy must be engaged in proactive foreign policy making, in sync with a resurgent administrative machinery (adequately equipped legally, technically as well as in terms of competence and skill) and suitable military and para military forces structured to deal with external and internal threats, with adequate early warning assets, and upgraded intelligence capabilities. These, in addition to the political will to cooperate with regional and extra-regional alliances to exercise hard and soft options to prosecute and maintain its capabilities to ensure safety of its borders, assets, citizens and Diaspora—will contribute to India taking its rightful place as a global power.

India should seek to leverage its substantial 'soft power' capabilities in infrastructure development, IT and technical education. This may encompass but not be limited to the setting up of institutes of higher learning in select SAARC states, development of small scale industries, including placement of substantial orders to these nations. As a net security provider in the IOR and SAARC region, India is unparalleled. Military-to-military cooperation must be another area of focus, which will foster regional security through joint training exercises. Navy and Coast Guard operations like joint anti-piracy operations, disaster management exercises and actuals, using the considerable reach and capabilities of the Air Force and sizable civil aviation assets should be undertaken. The UN Police and Military Training is another suitable area of cooperation. The launch of communication satellites as well as tie-ups to utilise our satellite-based communication systems, weather applications and warning and other geographical information systems applications are where Indian expertise can globally benefit.

Thus, an effective counter-terrorism strategy should include all the aspects of cooperation, political will, economic development, regional security and elements of national power. In the formulation of individual and joint strategies, effective and timely judicial processes with a SAARC court functioning similar to the International Court of Justice (ICJ) to hear terrorist-related joint issues will go a long way in addressing this pressing regional and global travail.

In Memory

The year was 1976, a new battalion of the Indian Army was being raised. On reaching the Regimental Centre to take over the command I was informed that a young officer has been attached to the Centre waiting to be assigned to the new raising—The 28th Battalion of the Madras Regiment. I sent word for this youngster to come and meet me.

When he reported, little did I know that I was setting eyes on a future General of the Indian army who would one day lead the Republic day parade on the Raj path as Gen officer commanding Delhi Area. This bright boy from Bengal with cheerful countenance and an amiable disposition displayed a confident outlook and balanced judgement which soon endeared him to the gallant Thambies.

Soon after he joined the unit, terrorism had started rearing its ugly head in western India. The Battalion had by now moved to Nagaland where, yet another type of terrorism and militancy prevailed. They were attacked by the Naga rebels. The battalion rose up with a roar and a successful beating back of the rebels took place. This was the first time when Nagas had failed to execute their intent of looting an Army camp. (Then Capt.) Mitra along with his brother officers had made an outstanding contribution to reestablish the supremacy of Indian army in Nagaland where it had been badly bruised by frequent sorties by the rebels.

This operation where he had played a sterling role has been made a case study in college of combat Mhow.

That was when he was awarded his first gallantry award- The Sena Medal.

Looking back one could see that even as a youngster he was exceptionally motivated and receptive to the guidance of seniors and peers. His many experiences in counter insurgency operations played their role in shaping the soldier in him.

It was but desirable that he shared his plethora of military know how with rest of the Indian Army. Considering his deep understanding, it was an appropriate subject for his doctoral thesis: TERRORISM IN INDIA AND ITS IMPLICATIONS ON NEIGHBOURING COUNTRIES and consequently to translate that as a readable material for the benefit of the Indian army with a view to planning future operations against prevailing terrorism. Given his vast experience and military acumen, eye for detail combined with his literary flair, the work has culminated in this book which is a matter of pride for the nation!

(Col Shanti Swaroop)
1st Commanding Officer of 28 Madras – The Daring

In Memory

I take this opportunity to convey my felicitations to Mrs. Pushpita Mitra, wife of late Lt Gen Subroto Mitra, PVSM, AVSM, SM, VSM and all members of the family on the posthumous award of PhD to the General Officer by the University of Madras. His thesis on "Terrorism: Security Challenges to India and Its Neighbouring Countries", is an exceptional piece of research work, which has been validated by the examiners of three overseas universities as well.

Lt Gen Subroto Mitra had served in almost all insurgency afflicted states of our country and as such, had rich hands-on experience in the planning and execution of counterinsurgency and counter terrorism operations. As an analytical, innovative and reflective thinker, he was endowed with the strategic frames of reference and had a deep understanding of the multipronged national strategy for asymmetric conflict management and its resolution. As a Captain, he had served in Nagaland, where he was awarded Sena Medal gallantry in 1983. Later, in the ranks of Brigadier and Major General, he went on to hold important command and staff appointments in J&K. While he commanded 87 Mountain Brigade (then deployed at Rajouri) and 28 Infantry Division in the valley, on staff, he was the Brigadier General Staff of 16 Corps, which is responsible for the counter infiltration and counterinsurgency operations south of Pir Panjal range.

Although I had met Lt Gen Subroto Mitra on many occasions, I got to know of his outstanding professional acumen and stellar leadership traits essentially during his tenure as the GOC of 28 Infantry Division under me in 15 Corps. Under his command, the formation conducted successful people friendly operations to neutralize the terrorists and ensured effective domination and sealing of the Line of Control. Given his affable nature and intellectual sophistication, he maintained healthy interagency relations in his area of responsibility, which helped achieve optimal operational and intelligence synergy. The awards received by the officers, JCOs and other ranks of his formation during his command, bear apt testimony to his remarkable leadership in an extremely challenging environment.

I am sanguine the book - 'The Lurking Hydra: South Asia's Terror Travail', based on Subroto's research paper will be a priceless guide for all those seeking deeper understanding of the subject.

Gen Bikram Singh PVSM, UYSM, AVSM, SM, VSM, ADC
Former Chief of the Army Staff

In Memory

I have known Lt Gen Subroto Mitra since his early service days as a young Captain. In 1982, when I assumed Command of the 28th Battalion of the Madras Regiment, he was my Adjutant in Mon, Nagaland. Thus began our association which spanned for more than 30 plus years.

Matured far beyond his age, Subroto was a forthright Gentleman Officer who never hesitated to express what he felt to be right. A man of all seasons, his wit and charm could disarm the toughest of people and allow him to forge everlasting relationships with all he met. Very clear perception and forthright in expression, I have seen him growing up in the Army from a young, enthusiastic and energetic Capt to the rank of Lieutenant General, leading the Republic Day parade in the capital for three consecutive years as General Officer Commanding Delhi Area.

All along he lived with high moral values and never compromised on his convictions.

His experience in various Command and Staff appointments in the Army, at High Altitude and Counter Insurgency areas, gave him a unique perspective to the role of India in the subcontinent, which is well reflected in his thesis.

I wish to compliment Mrs Pushpita Mitra, for the effort she has put in to ensure a logical conclusion of the PhD thesis paper of her late husband being published as a valuable book for academics and professionals alike.

Best Wishes.

Brig P V Sahadevan AVSM, VrC, VSM (Retd)

In Memory

This is a colleague reminiscing a special brother from amongst the Band that is the Indian Army. The bonding and recognition began at the Defence Services Staff College in Wellington in 1987/88. Bike rides, adventure treks andtours together as part of the Singlescomplement of DSSC served to highlight character and understand each other. A special bond was formed.Academic routine at the College served to highlight professional acumen that came to the fore.Subroto was the epitome of an Officer and a Gentleman.

There were brief associations along the way, especially a very personal one when Subroto was Deputy Commandant at the Madras Regimental Centre. It culminated with our tenure together in North Kashmir during the years 2009-2010 with Subroto as GOC 28 Infantry Division and me as GOC K Force. Professional interaction was intenseduring a period when the focus of activity was North Kashmir. I was witness to the cool professionalism that was on display in managing what was an immensely challenging operational assignment.

Early hands-on experience of insurgency that was followed by command at the operational level brought out the best in the Soldier Scholar that was Subroto. A voracious reader and practitioner of the art of warfare, Subroto only naturally decided to document his learnings and analyses therefrom in his thesis for his Doctorate.

The thesis that follows is a document hugely acclaimed at Madras University and advised to go to print. It will undoubtedly serve as excellent reading for just about anybody interested in the profession of Arms, especially for those directly or indirectly involved in its practice.

Maj Gen N George (Retd)

ENDNOTES

1. Robert Kaplan: "Monsoon"; New York, Random House, 2011, page xii.
2. Ibid.
3. Sergei DeSilva-Ranasinghe: Fact Sheet–The Indian Ocean region and Australia's National Interest; 29 May 2012, http://www.futuredirections.org.au/publications/indian-ocean/539-fact-sheet-the-indian-ocean-region-and-australias-national-interests.html
4. George Lenczowski: The Arc of Crisis: Its Central Sector, accessed on 25 April 2014, https://www.foreignaffairs.com/articles/russian-federation/1979-03-01/arc-crisis-its-central-sector
5. Alex P. Schmid: Root Causes of Terrorism: Some Conceptual Notes, a Set of Indicators, and a Model; Routledge, *Democracy and Security*, 1: 127–136, 2005.
6. Sood Vikram: Radical Islam in South Asia and Implications for the Region, Observer Research Foundation.
7. Michelle Nichols: U.N. Security Council plans to suppress foreign extremist fighters, accessed on 10 September 2014, http://www.reuters.com/article/us-iraq-crisis-un-idUSKBN0H408E20140909
8. The organization's name transliterates from Arabic as al-Dawlah al-Islamiyah fi al-'Iraq wa al-Sham (abbreviated as Da'ish or DAESH). In the West, it is commonly referred to as the Islamic State of Iraq and the Levant (ISIL), the Islamic State of Iraq and Syria, the Islamic State of Iraq and the Sham (both abbreviated as ISIS), or simply as the Islamic State (IS). *Choices for America in a Turbulent World*. James Dobbins and others. Executive Summary Page xiii. Published by the RAND Corporation, Santa Monica, Calif. © 2015 RAND Corporation.
9. Bill Roggio: Pakistan launches 'comprehensive operation against foreign and local terrorists' in North Waziristan, accessed on June 15, 2014, http://www.longwarjournal.org/archives/2014/06/pakistan_launches_co.php
10. Lars Berger: Al-Zawahiri hopes an Indian franchise will revive al-Qaeda,8 September 2014; http://theconversation.com/al-zawahiri-hopes-an-indian-franchise-will-revive-al-qaeda-31330
11. World Bank Report on South Asia, *South Asia Economic Focus* Spring 2015: Making the most of cheap oil; http://www.worldbank.org/content/dam/

Worldbank/document/SAR/saef-final.pdf
12. SAARC Group on Statistics, SAARC Secretariat, Kathmandu: http://saarcstat.org/db/statistics
13. World Bank: Overview; http://www.worldbank.org/en/region/sar/overview ; 29 May 2015.
14. World Bank: Annual report 2015; page 50.
15. Institute for Economics and Peace: Global Peace Index 2015, Measuring Peace, its Costs and Economic Values; table 8, page 16.
16. Ibid, pp. 8-9.
17. Ibid, table 30, page 113.
18. Ibid, page 72.
19. Ibid, box 4, page 72.
20. http://hdr.undp.org/sites/default/files/hdr_2015_statistical_annex.pd 14 December 2015.
21. U.N. Chief Silent on Longstanding Failure to Define Terrorism, Patrick Goodenough, http://cnsnews.com/news/article/un-chief-silent-longstanding-failure-define-Terrorism, 4 June, 2012.
22. Prime Minister Narendra Modi urges UN to 'define Terrorism', TNN & Agencies 15 November 2015, http://timesofindia.indiatimes.com/india/Prime-Minister-Narendra-Modi-urges-UN-to-define-Terrorism/articleshow/49786744.cms. accessed on 16 November 2015.
23. League of Nations 1937 Convention for the Prevention and Punishment of Terrorism.
24. The Unlawful Activities (Prevention) Amendment Bill, 2008.
25. Government of India, Second Administrative Reforms Commission, Eighth Report: Combating Terrorism Protecting By Righteousness, June 2008, pp. 4-6.
26. Vivek Chadha: *Low Intensity Conflicts in India: An Analysis*, United Services Institution and Sage Publications, New Delhi. 2005; pp. 55-62.
27. Pakistan Supported, Trained Terror Groups: Pervez Musharraf, World, Press Trust of India, Updated: 28 October 2015 ; http://www.ndtv.com/world-news/pakistan-supported-trained-terror-groups-pervez-musharraf-1237173
28. Sushil Kumar Sharma: Insurgency in North-East India: External Dynamics, *Journal of Defence Studies*, vol. 8, no. 4, October-December 2014, pp. 111-131.
29. Ibid.
30. Arijit Mazumdar: Left Wing Extremism and Counter Insurgency in India: "The Andhra Model", Institute for Defence Studies and Analyses, New Delhi, *Strategic Analysis* 2013, volume 37, number 4, pp. 447-448.
31. Ibid, p. 449.
32. Pramod Jaiswal, Caught in The India China Rivalry–Policy Options for Nepal; Institute of Peace and Conflict Studies, New Delhi, Issue Brief #249, March 2014, p. 3.
33. E.N. Rammohan: Spring Thunder in Bangladesh, *USI Journal* April–June 2013, New Delhi, p. 259.
34. Pakistan Blames India's RAW For Karachi And Other Terror Attacks: Indo-Asian News Service; Pakistan's Foreign Secretary Aizaz Ahmad Chaudhry alleged that Indian foreign intelligence agency Research and Analysis Wing

(RAW) was "involved in various terrorist activities" in his country; Updated 14 May 2015. http://newsworldindia.in/world/pakistan-blames-india-on-recent-terror-attack/35023/

35. James Lamont: Clinton warns Pakistan on militant 'snakes'; *Financial Times*, London, 21 October 2011.
36. Dr. S. P. Sinha: Indo Nepal Relations, *Indian Defence Review*, April–June 2007, vol. 22 (2), p. 95.
37. Jaswant Singh: *India at Risk*, Rupa Publications, New Delhi (2013), pp. 152-157.
38. Adam Roberts: Addressing Violent Extremism–Lessons from Sri Lanka; *Strategic Analysis*, 2014, vol. 38, no. 4, p. 412.
39. Government of India, Second Administrative Reforms Commission, op. cit, p. 44, Recommendation para 4.1.6.9.
40. Ibid, p. 52.
41. Ibid, p. 41.
42. U.S. Department of Justice, Federal Bureau of Investigation, Terrorism 2002-2005, https://www.fbi.gov/stats-services/publications/Terrorism-2002-2005, accessed on 17 August 2012.
43. Congressional Record, vol. 148 (2002), PUBLIC LAW 107–296—25 November 2002, http://www.dhs.gov/xlibrary/assets/hr_5005_enr.pdf
44. http://www.satp.org/satporgtp/countries/pakistan/document/actsand ordinences/anti_Terrorism.htm
45. World Pakistan Photos Video Blog: New York Diaries (8 July 2009). "Zardari says Pak created and nurtured militants–CNN IBN News". Ibnlive.in.com.
46. http://mha.gov.bd/wp-content/uploads/2013/10/Anti-Terrorism-Act-2009.pdf
47. http://mha.gov.bd/wp-content/uploads/2013/10/Anti-Terrorism-Rules-2009.pdf
48. Draconian anti-Terrorism bill passed into law, Ahmed Naish, 27 October 2015. http://maldivesindependent.com/politics/draconian-anti-Terrorism-bill-passed-into-law-118990.
49. http://www.myanmarlegalservices.com/wp-content/uploads/2015/01/Myanmar-laws-enacted-in-2014-Thaw-Dar-update-9-Jan-2015_1465344_3.pdf
50. https://www.fincen.gov/statutes_regs/patriot/
51. https://www.gov.uk/government/publications/the-Terrorism-act-2006
52. Prem Mahadevan, *The Politics of Counter Terrorism in India*, I. B. Tauris, London, 2012, p. 123.
53. Yakub Memon executed for 1993 Mumbai bombings, 30 July 2015, http://www.bbc.com/news/world-asia-33704435
54. Rasheed Kidwai: Sonia Mercy Plea For Mother Nalini; New Delhi, 18 November 1999,http://www.telegraphindia.com/991119/front_pa.htm
55. Centre for Disease Control and Prevention: BioTerrorism Overview, Atlanta, USA, 12 February 2007; http://emergency.cdc.gov/bioTerrorism/overview.asp
56. http://www.ncbi.nlm.nih.gov/pmc/articles/PMC1200679/table/T1/
57. Stefan Riedel: Biological warfare and bioterrorism: a historical review; Baylor University Medical Centre Proceedings, Dallas, USA, Proc (Bayl Univ Med

Cent). 2004 October; 17(4): 400-406.f

58. Reshmi Kazi: *Nuclear Terrorism The New Terror of the 21st Century*; Institute for Defence Studies and Analyses, New Delhi, December 2013.
59. Dorothy E. Denning: Cyber terrorism, Testimony before the Special Oversight Panel on Terrorism Committee on Armed Services, U.S. House of Representatives, 23 May 2000.
60. Chris Uhlmann: China blamed for 'massive' cyber-attack on Bureau of Meteorology computer, 2 December 2015, http://www.abc.net.au/news/2015-12-02/china-blamed-for-cyber-attack-on-bureau-of-meteorology/6993278
61. Ryan Fleming: Bits before bombs: How Stuxnet crippled Iran's nuclear dreams; 2 December 2010, http://www.digitaltrends.com/computing/bits-before-bombs-how-stuxnet-crippled-irans-nuclear-dreams/#ixzz3w1RhWcDo
62. Communications and IT Minister Ravi Shankar Prasad told Lok Sabha in a written reply, 11 March 2015, http://www.businesstoday.in/technology/internet/over-700-indian-govt-websites-have-been-hacked-since-2012/story/216802.html
63. James F. Jarboe: Testimony Before the House Resources Committee, Subcommittee on Forests and Forest Health, Washington, DC; 12 February 2002.
64. Lorraine Elliott: Eco Terrorism; http://www.britannica.com/topic/ecoTerrorism
65. Express News Service: Aggressive green stand is eco-terrorism; 25 June 2011, http://www.newindianexpress.com/states/karnataka/article445481.ece
66. Brian A. Jackson and others: Economically Targeted Terrorism; RAND Corporation Technical Report, Santa Monica, USA, 2007.
67. http://www.tracking terrorism.org/article/narcoterrorism.
68. Government of India, Second Administrative Reforms Commission, op. cit, p. 6.
69. Martha Crenshaw: Explaining Suicide Terrorism: A Review Essay; *Security Studies* 16, no. 1 (January–March 2007): p. 134; https://fsi.stanford.edu/sites/default/files/Crenshaw_Explaining_Suicide_Terrorism.pdf
70. Bureau of Counterterrorism: Foreign Terrorist Organizations; downloaded on 10 August 2015.http://www.state.gov/j/ct/rls/other/des/123085.htm
71. Government of India, Ministry of Home Affairs, Banned Organisations: List Of Banned Terrorist Organisations Under Section 35 Of Unlawful Activities (Prevention) Act, 1967 (As On 30-03-2015), http://mha.nic.in/bo
72. http://tribune.com.pk/story/456294/list-of-banned-organisations-in-pakistan/ 24 October, 2012.
73. Khurram Husain, *Dawn*: Analysis: Wrangling persists in listing terror groups; published 9 March 2015, http://www.dawn.com/news/1168347
74. http://www.saarc-sec.org/SAARC-Charter.
75. Kripa Sridharan: Regional Organisations and Conflict Management: Comparing ASEAN and SAARC, National University of Singapore, March 2008, LSE, DESTIN Papers.
76. http://www.state.gov/j/ct/rls/crt/2011/195547.htm State Sponsors of Terrorism, Office of the Coordinator for Counterterrorism, Country Reports

on Terrorism 2011, Report 31 July 2012.

77. www.saarc-sec-org
78. Talk by General Sir Richard Gannett: "A Perspective of the Nature of Future Conflict"; Chatham House, 15 May2009.
79. R.C. Majumdar: *Ancient India*, M. Banarsidas, Delhi, 2013, pp. 95-97.
80. John Keay: *India, A History*, Harper, London, 2010, p. xxi.
81. Simon Denyer: Rogue Elephant–Harnessing the Power of Democracy in the New India, Bloomsbury, London, pp. 6-7.
82. C. Christine Fair: *Fighting to the End – The Pakistan Army's Way of War*, Oxford University Press, New York, 2014, Kindle edition.
83. Ibid.
84. US Department of State: Foreign Terrorist Organizations. http://www.state.gov/j/ct/rls/other/des/123085.htm. These include the: Harkat ul-Mujahidin (HUM), Jaish-e-Mohammed (JEM), Lashkar-e Tayyaba (LeT), Lashkar i Jhangvi (LJ), Harkat ul-Jihad-i-Islami (HUJI), Harkat ul-Jihad-i-Islami/Bangladesh (HUJI-B) and Indian Mujahedeen (IM).
85. Abubakar Siddiqui: *The Pashtuns – the Unresolved Key to the Future of Pakistan and Afghanistan*; Random House, India, 2014, pp. 58-60.
86. Hussain Haqqani: Pakistan's Tolerance of Jihadis Backfires Badly, *The Huffington Post*, 17 December 2014.
87. Institute for Economics and Peace (IEP): Global Peace Index 2015, Sydney, pp. 112-113.
88. Fareed Zakaria: Pakistan is 'epicentre of Islamic terrorism'; CNN, 5 May 2010.
89. Mohammed Shehzad: The State of Islamic Radicalism in Pakistan: *Strategic Analysis*, 2013, vol. 37, no. 2, p. 186.
90. Most expensive terrorist attacks worldwide as of 2014, by insured property losses (in million U.S. dollars), http://www.statista.com/statistics/276731/most-expensive-terrorist-attacks-based-on-insured-damage-since-1970/
91. Sreeja V. N: Kasab Hanged: India Had Spent $108 Million To Give The Mumbai Attacker A Fair Trial, *International Business Times*, 21 November 2012, http://www.ibtimes.com/kasab-hanged-india-had-spent-108-million-give-mumbai-attacker-fair-trial-894414
92. V.K. Kapoor: Homeland Security: India's Internal Security Reforms; *CLAWS Journal*, winter 2009, p. 11.
93 PTI: LeT's annual operations budget is $ 5.2 million, 6 December 2010, http://articles.economictimes.indiatimes.com/2010-12-06/news/27629741_1_mumbai-attacks-planning-terror-attacks-private-fund
94. Institute for Economics and Peace: The Economic Cost of Violence Containment; Sydney, 2014, pp. 9-13.
95. Nepal was historically governed by a series of royal dynasties until the early 1990s when several political parties launched a popular pro-democracy movement, the Jana Andolan (People's Movement). Following a turbulent period of street protests, multiparty democracy was restored in May 1991. Traditionally, social life in Nepal has been highly stratified, marked by caste and other hierarchies which shaped much of the country's social, economic and political life. The dramatic political changes of 1990 raised popular

expectations of social progress and greater equality, but although some statistical indicators from the early 1990s show positive developments in the economy, the living conditions of most people remained poor. Around this time, some analysts were noting that deep-rootedsocio-economic conditions favourable to armed conflict existed in Nepal, and warned of the possibility of a radical movement rising up to channel longstanding grievances. In March 1995 the newly named Communist Party of Nepal (Maoist) ("CPN (Maoist)") began to draw up plans to launch an armed struggle, the so-called "People's War", against the State. On 4 February 1996, the CPN Maoists submitted a 40-point demand to the Government which addressed a wide range of social, economic and political agendas, and warned that a militant struggle would follow if the demands were not met. Just one week later, on 13 February 1996, the CPN (Maoist) launched an armed insurgency against the Government. Over the course of the following decade, what was initially regarded as a minor problem of law and order in a distant part of rural Nepal developed into an entrenched and often brutal armed conflict that affected the entire country. Violations and abuses by both government Security Forces and by the CPN (Maoist) were widespread throughout the conflict; conflict–related killings were recorded in all but two of Nepal's 75 districts, Manang and Mustang. Source: Nepal Conflict Report, United Nations Office of the High Commissioner for Human Rights, Geneva, October 2012, pp. 14-15. http://www.ohchr.org/Documents/Countries/NP/OHCHR_Nepal_Conflict_ Report 2012.pdf

96. Ibid: pp. 28.
97. N. Kumar: Changing Face of Conflict: Need to Reshape Military philosophy, *CLAWS Journal*, Winter 2013, pp. 122-123. Hybrid conflicts are full spectrum wars in the physical and conceptual dimensions: the former, a struggle against an armed enemy and the latter, a wider struggle for control and support of the combat zone. It is waged through the indigenous population, with the support of the intervening nations and the inimical international community. It will prove to be one of the most difficult to combat because it is a mixed war, with conventional war, insurgency and terrorism, fought from the hinterland and from the population centres. Frank Hoffman categorises Hybrid Warfare thus: "Its chief characteristic—blurring and convergence—occurs in several modes. In the blurring of combat and conflict, combatants and non-combatants, and the physical and the metaphysical. The convergence of various types of conflict will present us with a complex puzzle until the necessary adaptation occurs intellectually and institutionally. *4GW as a Model of Future Conflict*, Frank Hoffman, http://smallwarsjournal.com/blog/4gw-as-a-model-of-future-conflict.
98. Institute for Economic & Peace: Global Terrorism Index 2014, p. 8.
99. http://www.satp.org/satporgtp/countries/pakistan/index.htm assessed on 25 November 2015.
100. U. S. Department of Defence: Progress towards Security and Stability in Afghanistan, October 2014, p, 95.
101. Gretchen Peters: *Seeds of Terror – The Taliban, The ISI and the new Opium Wars*,

Hachette, pp. 169-175.

102. *The Economic Times*: ISI shifts underworld don Dawood Ibrahim to Pakistan-Afghanistan border, 27 October 2014.
103. SATP: Terrorist and Extremist Groups of Pakistan; this includes 12 domestic organizations and 32 Transnational organizations operating or based in Pakistan and Four "Trusts" classified as extremist groups. http://www.satp.org/satporgtp/countries/Pakistan/terroristoutfits/group_list.htm
104. "US commander commends Zarb-e-Azb for disrupting Haqqani network's ability to target Afghanistan". *The Express Tribune*, 6 November 2014. Retrieved 6 November 2014.
105. "Pakistan Launches Offensive against Militants near Afghan Border". Huffington Post. Associated Press. 15 June 2014. Archived from the original on 30 June 2014. Retrieved 23 June 2014.
106. http://online.wsj.com/articles/al-qaeda-militants-tried-to-seize-pakistan-navy-frigate-1410884514, updated September 16, 2014
107. http://www.dawn.com/news/1142006 of 0 November 2014.
108. Rezaul H. Laskar: Pakistanis say time for tough questions instead of blaming India, *Hindustan Times*, New Delhi, 21 January 2016. Hours after the assault on Bacha Khan University, Brigadier Asad Munir, a former ISI official-turned-columnist, surprised many by tweeting that Pakistanis would do well to look for the attackers among themselves instead of blaming India. Munir, with long experience of serving with the Inter-Services Intelligence agency in Pakistan's volatile northwest, blamed the terrorism afflicting his country squarely on Islamabad's policy of using jihadists for issues such as the war in Afghanistan and the move to "liberate" Kashmir.
109. Jon Boone, Lahore: *The Guardian*, 3 March 2014, accessed on 25 November.
110. Imtiaz Gul, Centre for Research and Security Studies: What's behind Karachi airport attack? 10 June 2014, CNN.
111. A differentiation of Taliban, coined by the Pakistani establishment, which averred that the Good Taliban were those Taliban factions fighting (and protecting Pakistani interests in Afghanistan, and the Bad Taliban comprising elements who were attacking Pakistani interests, within). In reality, both are hurting Pakistan interests. Also refer to Taha Siddiqui: 'Good Taliban' and 'Bad Taliban.' New dynamic inside Pakistan?, dated 9 November 2014, http://www.csmonitor.com/World/Asia-South-Central/2014/1109/Good-Taliban-and-Bad-Taliban.-New-dynamic-inside-Pakistan
112. Pakistan Economic Survey 2013-2014, M/o Finance, M/o Interior, M/o Foreign Affairs, Joint Ministerial Group Annexure III.
113. Foreign Financial Flows and Terrorism In Developing Countries, Anwar, A. I. and Mughal, M. Y. Shannon School of Business, Cape Breton University, Canada, 2013, p. 8.
114. An amount of $50 Billion is due in 2016, reports Bloomberg. Around $30 billion is due between July and September, of which $8.3 billion will need to be in foreign currency, depleting 40pc of the nation's $21 billion in foreign-exchange holdings.
115. Shamil Shams: Is Pakistan's nuclear stock safe? *Deutsche Welle*, 7 October 2013,

http://www.dw.com/en/is-pakistans-nuclear-stock-safe/a-17143032. Safety of Pakistan's nuclear weapons is one of the principal concerns of many industrialized nations, who fear that given its dangerous geopolitical situation and its increasing support to terrorist organizations, they could end up with nuclear weapons in the hands of terrorists, who would use it or threaten its use in a dangerous trade off. Also see Akhilesh Pillalmari's article in *The Diplomat* titled "Pakistan's Nuclear Weapons Program: 5 Things You Need to Know", dated 21 April 2015, http://nationalinterest.org/feature/pakistans-nuclear-weapons-program-5-things-you-need-know-12687

116. Jeffrey Goldberg and Marc Ambinder: The Pentagon's Secret Plans to Secure Pakistan's Nuclear Arsenal; *National Journal*, Nuclear Threat Initiative, 9 November 2011, http://www.nti.org/gsn/article/the-pentagons-secret-plans-to-secure-pakistans-nuclear-arsenal/
117. Mickey Kupecz: Pakistan's Baloch insurgency—History, conflict drivers and regional implications; International Affairs Review, vol. XX, no. 3, Spring 2012, pp. 96-104, http://www.iar-gwu.org/sites/default/files/articlepdfs/Pakistan's%20Baloch%20Insurgency.pdf
118. Global Peace Index 2015: Ongoing Domestic And International Conflict Domain, Most Peaceful To Least, table 31, p. 114,
119. Ravi Menon: Doval's comments raise serious misgivings; *Gulf News*, 22 January 2015.
120. Ibid: A Snapshot Of The Global State Of Peace, p. 9.
121. Robert Kaplan: *The Revenge of Geography*, Random House, New York, 2012, pp. 245-248.
122. Steve Galster: Afghanistan: The Making of U.S. Policy, 1973-1990, 9 October 2001, *The National Security Archive*, http://nsarchive.gwu.edu/NSAEBB/NSAEBB57/essay.html
123. Hussein Haqqani: Magnificent Delusions, *Public Affairs*, New York, 2013, pp. 287-290.
124. Ibid. pp. 293- 297.
125. Gretchen Peters. op.cit., p. 235.
126. United Nations Office on Drugs and Crime: World Drug Report 2012, Vienna, p. 60.
127. United Nations Office on Drugs and Crime (UNODC): The Global Afghan Opium Trade. A Threat Assessment, 2011, Vienna, p. 8, http://www.unodc.org/documents/data-and-analysis/Studies/Global_Afghan_Opium_Trade_2011-web.pdf. accessed 2 December 2014.
128. Gulshan Sachdeva: TAPI gas pipeline may become game changer in South Asian geopolitics; *Hindustan Times*, 20 December 2015.
129. Discussions with former Indian Defence Adviser in Afghanistan on 15 December 2014.
130. Mark Thompson: The True Cost of the Afghanistan War May Surprise You; TIME, 1 January 2015. Other estimates put the true figure at $ 1 trillion with many billions to be paid. See Geoff Dyer and Chloe Sorvino: $ 1 tn cost of longest US war hastens retreat from military intervention, 14 December 2014, http://www.ft.com/intl/cms/s/2/14be0e0c-8255-11e4-ace7-

00144feabdc0.html#slide0

131. Kaplan: op.cit., pp. 247-248.
132. Ibid. pp. 252-253.
133. http://www.bbc.com/news/world-asia-16207201
134. Bangladesh GDP Growth Rate 1994-2016; http://www.tradingeconomics.com/bangladesh/gdp-growth
135. Author's discussion with former Indian Defence Adviser to Bangladesh, 15 December 2015.
136. Op. cit. http://www.tradingeconomics.com/bangladesh/gdp-growth
137. Kaplan: op.cit, p. 143.
138. Author's discussions with Dr. Sharmila Mitra, 14 January 2016.
139. Kaplan: p.cit., pp. 146.
140. http://www.tradingeconomics.com/bangladesh/remittances
141. http://www.adb.org/publications/bangladesh-fact-sheet
142. E.N. Rammohan: Spring Thunder in Bangladesh, *USI Journal*, April–June 2013, pp. 256-261.
143 Op. cit., former Defence Adviser.
144. U S State Department : Country reports on Terrorism, ; http://www.state.gov/j/ct/rls/crt/2011/195553.htm#huji_b
145. Saikat Datta: Ending the suspense: Mystery of Burdwan blast explained, *Hindustan Times*, 2 December 2014.
146. Shiv S. Singh: Charge sheet filed in Bardhaman blast case, *The Hindu*,, 31 March 2015.
147. Anand Kumar: Terror Financing in Bangladesh, IDSA Fellows Seminar, 13 February 2009. Dr. Kumar cited the steps taken by the USA to halt the flow of funds to terrorist organizations through Executive Order 13224 and related elements of the US Patriot Act. He argued that as oversight mechanisms were absent, no financial scrutiny of the Islamic charities is undertaken, which further complicates the problem of tackling terror financing. The Saudi Government's patronage of charities such as International Islamic Relief Organization (IIRO) and the World Association of Muslim Youth (WAMY) was also brought to attention. He cited the example of Al Haramain, a Riyadh-based Muslim charity, which was opened in Cox Bazar in 1992 to help Rohingya refugees but continued to operate in Bangladesh uninterrupted despite it being banned by the USA and Saudi Arabia. The connection between Al Haramain and terrorism was revealed in 2002, when linkages were made between Al Haramain and its suspected links to terror funding and trafficking of women and children under the garb of providing Islamic education. As far as individual support is concerned, links to Bin Laden were cited. Dr. Kumar argued that funds were flowing into Bangladesh in the form of hundi through Jessore, Chittagong and Dhaka.
148. On 1 December 2014, the Bangladeshi cabinet gave the final approval to the draft "Foreign Donations (Voluntary Activities) Regulation Bill, 2014" making registration with the NGO Affairs Bureau mandatory for all NGOs receiving foreign funds. The new legislation would combine the Foreign Donations (Voluntary Activities) Regulation Ordinance, enacted in 1978, and the Foreign

Contributions (Regulation) Ordinance, enacted in 1982. Both laws were adopted through military proclamations. On June 2, the cabinet approved in principle the draft Foreign Donations (Voluntary Activities) Regulation Bill, 2014, which later drew criticism from donor agencies and NGO activists.
Source: http://www.omct.org/human-rights-defenders/urgent-interventions/bangladesh/2014/12/d22942/

149. Jaideep Saikia: Circle of Treason–Bangladesh Beyond the Threat of Illegal Migration, CLAWS Maneckshaw Papers, no. 41, 2013, p. 19.
150. Fatalities in Maoist Insurgency 2000-2016 : http://www.satp.org/satporgtp/countries/nepal/database/fatalities.htm
151. Ibid.
152. Deepak Thapa: Cycles of Violence: Conflict in 'Post-Conflict' Nepal; The Terror Challenge in South Asia and Prospect of Regional Cooperation, IDSA 2012, pp. 86-87. Soon after the draft of the interim constitution was made public in December 2006, the Madhesis from the southern Tarai plains made their discontent known. Federalism was a key issue for the Madhesis. As the draft of the interim constitution did not even mention it and neither did it look into the issue of increasing the number of electoral constituencies in the Tarai, despite the significant migration from the hills to the plains over the years, protests erupted in Nepalgunj in western Nepal. It took 19 days of protests and rioting during what has been called the Madhesi movement, which led to a complete shutdown in this vital region of Nepal, before the government reached out to Madhesi groups to seek a political resolution to the issues. But it took one more round of agitation by the Madhesis before the government responded by fulfilling their two major demands: redrawing of electoral districts and including federalism in the interim constitution. The Madhesi Movement was concentrated mainly in the 10 districts of central and eastern Tarai. These 10 districts are home to nearly 25 per cent of the population of Nepal, and almost three-quarters of them are Madhesis. It is this numerical clout that became evident during the agitation.
153. SATP: Timelines–Nepal; http://www.satp.org/satporgtp/countries/nepal/timeline/index.html
154. Dependency on remittances, Nepal; http://sitreport.unescapsdd.org/remittances/dependency-remittances
155. Rajat Pandit: Nepal may ban Gorkhas from joining foreign armies, *Times of India*, 20 March 2012.
156. Global Peace Index 2015: Measuring Peace, its Causes and Economic Value, p. 9.
157. Madeline Bergner: Developing Nepal's Hydroelectric Resources, Policy Alternatives, 2014.
158. CIA World Fact Book–Nepal, https://www.cia.gov/library/publications/the-world-factbook/geos/np.html
159. Thapa: op.cit., pp. 87-89.
160. Gopal Sharma: Nepal's Madhesis call off blockade over charter; Kathmandu, 8 February 2016, http://in.reuters.com/article/nepal-blockade-idINKCN0VH13W

161. Sunil Raman: Madhesi protest in Nepal: Why India needs to step back a little, 9 November 2015. http://www.firstpost.com/world/madhesi-protest-in-nepal-why-india-needs-to-step-back-a-little-2501544.html
162. Monalisa Adhikari: Politics and perceptions of Indian Aid to Nepal: *Strategic Analysis*, vol. 38, no. 3, May-June 2014, pp. 336.
163. Daaman Thadi: Nepal Fast Becoming the Dragon's Lair, CLAWS Focus, no. 9, 2013, pp. 5-6.
164. Ajit Kumar Singh: India-Nepal: Subversion without Borders; *South Asia Intelligence Review*, Weekly Assessments & Briefings, vol. 5, no. 19, 20 November, 2006.
165. Ameet Dhakal: Nepal's new Constitution: Fallout beyond borders, *South Asia Monitor*, 24 September 2015, http://southasiamonitor.org/detail.php?type=in&nid=13525
166. Ajit Kumar Singh: op.cit.
167. Author's interaction with Intelligence Analyst, 2 July 2014. According to the officer, Kishanganj with 70% and Araria with 41% Muslim population, 2011 Census, have seen the maximum rise with Balrampur 38%, Bahraich 34%, and Shravasti 31% equally affected because of migrant Bangladeshi population as well as increase in numbers of local Muslims. Other than Champawat and Pithoragarh, the remaining 10 districts have Muslim populations of between 17 and 30%, a cause for concern as they are slowly taking over all the jobs from the locals.
168. T. Subedit: International Migration and Development–Prospects and Challenges to Nepal, *International Migration and Development in South Asia*, Routledge, London, 2015, pp. 187-188.
169. Rajat Pandit: op.cit.
170. Bhutan: The External Threat, http://www.satp.org/satporgtp/countries/bhutan/backgrounders/index.html
171. BBC News : Bhutan 'seizes top Indian rebels', 19 December 2003, http://news.bbc.co.uk/2/hi/south_asia/3333251.stm
172. S. Chandrasekharan: Bhutan: In praise of Gyalpo IV, Update no. 114, note no. 758, 12 January 2016, http://www.southasiaanalysis.org/node/1923
173. Author's interaction with Intelligence Officer on 12 April 2015.
174. Bomb Blasts in Bhutan, 2008: http://www.satp.org/satporgtp/countries/bhutan/datasheets/bombblasts.htm
175. C.S. Kasturi: Delhi toehold in key Lanka port, at last–IOC role in strategic weathervane; *The Telegraph*, 14 March 2015.
176. S. Muthaiah: The Indo Lankans; Indian Heritage Foundation, Chennai, 2003. Muthaiah contends that invasions by the Sangam Cholas in the 2nd century BCE saw numerous soldiers and camp followers, besides recruited mercenaries from Tamilakam, who settled in the east and northwest of Lanka. They predated the labourers brought in for the tea gardens by more than two millennia.
177. Kaplan: op.cit. pp. 198-201.
178. SATP: http://www.satp.org/satporgtp/sair/Archives/sair13/13_6.htm#assessment2. On 27 March 2014, the 47-member United Nations Human Rights Council (UNHRC), by a vote of 23 states in favour, 12 against and 12

abstentions, adopted a resolution for launching an inquiry into war crimes allegedly committed by both Sri Lankan Forces and the LTTE rebels during the last phases of the civil war as, according to them, the Sri Lankan Government had failed to investigate the issue properly. Consequently, on 12 June 12 2014, the United Nations High Commissioner for Human Rights, Navi Pillay, established the Office of the United Nations High Commissioner for Human Rights (OHCHR) Investigation on Sri Lanka (OISL), an investigative team comprising 12 members, including two forensic experts, a legal analyst, a gender specialist and investigators as mandated by the UNHRC to conduct its operations for a 10-month period, beginning mid-June 2014 and ending mid-April 2015. However, according to Human Rights Watch, the Sri Lankan government has made little progress in providing accountability for wartime abuses. The government's failure to comply with a March 2013 United Nations Human Rights Council resolution led to a new resolution in 2014. The resolution calls on the UN Office of the High Commissioner for Human Rights (OHCHR) to investigate serious violations of international human rights and humanitarian law and related crimes by both sides during Sri Lanka's civil war, which ended in 2009. https://www.hrw.org/world-report/2016/country-chapters/sri-lanka

179. SATP: Sri Lanka Assessment 2010; http://www.satp.org/satporgtp/countries/shrilanka/assessment2010.htm
180. President's speech to Parliament on the defeat of the LTTE: http://www.satp.org/satporgtp/countries/shrilanka/document/papers/president_speech_parliament_defeatofLTTE.htm
181. http://www.tradingeconomics.com/sri-lanka/forecast
182. Indian investments in Sri Lanka have been substantial of late. The areas include petroleum, retail, IT, financial services, real estate, telecommunication, hospitality and tourism, banking and food processing (tea and fruit juices), metal industries, tyres, cement, glass manufacturing, and infrastructure development (railway, power, water supply). A number of new investments from Indian companies are in the pipeline or under implementation. The Government of India put in place a robust programme of assistance to help the IDPs return to normal life as quickly as possible and it also consistently advocated the need for them to be resettled in their original habitations as early as possible. India's immediate humanitarian assistance to IDPs included supply of 250,000 family relief packs, establishment of an emergency medical unit, which treated over 50,000 IDPs, supply of over one million roofing sheets, as well as 400,000 bags of cement for constructing temporary housing and provision of 95,000 starter packs of agricultural implements. India also assisted in the revival of agricultural and economic activities in areas affected by the conflict. Source :http://www.mea.gov.in/Portal/ForeignRelation/SrilankaBrief_August2015.pdf
183. World Bank : Migration and Remittances Data ; 24 September 2015, http://www.worldbank.org/en/topic/migrationremittancesdiasporaissues/brief/migration-remittances-data
184. International Crisis Group Report: The Sri Lankan Tamil Diaspora after the

LTTE, *Asia Report*, no. 186, 23 February 2010, pp. 1-3.

185. CIA: World Fact book; https://www.cia.gov/library/publications/the-world-factbook/geos/ce.html
186. Tamil Ethnologue: http://www.ethnologue.com/language/tam
187. Smruti Pattanaik: The Tamil Nadu Factor in post-war Sri Lanka: Perspectives of Tamils and Muslims; *Strategic Analysis*, 2014, vol. 38, no. 5, pp. 637-639.
188. Thirumalai Manivannan: Analysis: Tamil-Muslim divide, 27 June 2002, http://news.bbc.co.uk/2/hi/south_asia/2070817.stm
189. Buddhists vs Muslims: Sri Lanka deploys army as riots spread in country; *Times of India*, 17 June 2014.
190. http://data.worldbank.org/country/maldives#cp_fin
191. CIA: World Fact Book; Maldives, https://www.cia.gov/library/publications/the-world-factbook/geos/mv.html
192. John Kirby: Press Statement, Department of State: Maldives: State of Emergency; 4 November 2015.
193. http://www.infoplease.com/country/profiles/maldives.html
194. Alok Bansal: Maldives: End of Uncertainty; CLAWS, November 2013, vol. IX, pp. 45-47.
195. Author's discussion with Senior Intelligence official on 6 February 2012 and subsequently on 4 May 2013.
196. Azra Naseem: Maldives in South Asia: Let's talk about Saudis,; 3 December 2015, http://maldivesindependent.com/feature-comment/maldives-in-south-asia-lets-talk-about-saudis-120392
197. Maldives Unemployment Rate Forecast 2016-2020, http://www.trading economics.com/maldives/unemployment-rate/forecast
198. N. Manoharan: Presidential elections in Maldives and the Future of Islamic radicalization in the atoll state, CLAWS, September 2013, pp. 1-3.
199. Naseem: op. cit.
200. Admiral R. K. Dhowan: Indian Ocean Region: Emerging Strategic Cooperation, Competition and Conflict Scenarios; *USI Journal*, October- December 2014, pp. 545.
201. P. K. Ghosh: Maritime Security Trilateralism: India, Sri Lanka and the Maldives, *Strategic Analysis*, May-June 2014, vol. 38, no. 3, IDSA, pp. 283-284.
202. S. Chandrasekharan: Maldives: Democracy Back Sliding; South Asia Analysis Group, Paper no. 6053, 5 January 2016.
203. Praveen Swami: From Maldives, road to Islamic State goes via drugs, gangs and jail, 15 April 2015, http://indianexpress.com/article/india/india-others/video-from-maldives-road-to-islamic-state-goes-via-drugs-gangs-and-jail/
204. Oliver Wright; Islamic State: The Maldives–a recruiting paradise for jihadists, 14 September 2014, http://www.independent.co.uk/news/world/asia/islamic-state-the-maldives-a-recruiting-paradise-for-jihadists-9731574.html
205. World Travel and Tourism Council: Economic Impact 2015, Maldives, Travel and Tourism's Contribution to GDP, p. 7, source https://www.wttc.org/-/media/files/reports/economic%20impact%20research/countries%202015/maldives2015.pdf
206. Mohamed Ziad: Countering Terrorism–The Maldivian Perspective; The Terror

Challenge in South Asia and Prospect of Regional Cooperation, IDSA Publication, 2012, p. 64.

207. John Roth and others: Staff Report to the Commission, National Commission on Terrorist Attacks upon the United States–Monograph on Terrorist Financing, 2004, pp. 131-136.
208. Mark Thompson: The $ 5 Trillion War on Terror, TIME, 29 June 2011.
209. Ralph Peters: Blood Borders: How a better Middle East would look, *Armed Forces Journal*, 1 June 2006, http://www.armedforcesjournal.com/blood-borders/. Peters goes on to aver that "While the Middle East has far more problems than dysfunctional borders alone—from cultural stagnation through scandalous inequality to deadly religious extremism—the greatest taboo in striving to understand the region's comprehensive failure is not Islam but the awful, but sacrosanct, international boundaries worshipped by our own diplomats. Of course, no adjustment of borders, however draconian, could make every minority in the Middle East happy. "
210. Jaswant Singh: *India at Risk*, Rupa, New Delhi, 2013, pp. 5-6.
211. Tarek Osman: Why border lines drawn with a ruler in WW1 still rock the Middle East, BBC, 14 December 2013, http://www.bbc.com/news/world-middle-east-25299553
212. PTI: ISIS map of areas it wants to take over by 2020 includes India, 10 August 2015, http://indiatoday.intoday.in/story/india-in-2020-if-isis-plans-succeed/1/457594.html
213. Joe Wiesenthal: Qaddafi Warns France, If I Go Down, You Will Be Flooded With "Millions Of Blacks" ; 7 March 2011, http://www.businessinsider.com/qaddafi-warns-france-if-i-go-down-you-will-be-flooded-with-millions-of-blacks-2011-3?IR=T
214. Arab Renaissance for Democracy and Development: The Arab Spring's Refugee Crisis, Carnegie Endowment, 22 December 2011, http://ardd-jo.org/sites/default/files/resource-files/the_arab_springs_refugee_crisis.pdf
215. Christina Lin: ISIS and the Saudi Wahhabi Threat to Asian Security, July 2015, Institut für Strategie- Politik- Sicherheits-und Wirtschaftsberatung, Berlin, ISPSW Publications, no. 361.
216. Akhilesh Pillalamarri: The Radicalization of South Asian Islam: Saudi Money and the Spread of Wahhabism, Edmund A. Walsh School of Foreign Service's Centre for Security Studies at Georgetown University, 20 December 2014, http://georgetownsecuritystudiesreview.org/2014/12/20/the-radicalization-of-south-asian-islam-saudi-money-and-the-spread-of-wahhabism/. The author brings into focus the spread of Wahhabism in the State of Jammu and Kashmir where Saudi influence has led to 1.5 million people, from a population of 8 million, to affiliate with Wahhabi mosques. A Saudi-funded group, Jamiat Ahl-e-Hadith, claims 16 per cent of Kashmir's population as its members and has built 700 mosques and 150 schools. Police in Jammu and Kashmir believe this is the result of a $ 35 billion plan approved by Saudi Arabia's government in 2005 to build mosques and madrassas in South Asia. Additionally, Saudi Arabia distributed free religious literature and provided stipends to Wahhabi preachers.

217. Ministry of External Affairs: Act East Policy, Press Information Bureau, 23 December 2015.
218. Sameer Patil: After Modi's Visit, Is Central Asia Open for Indian Business? *The Pulse*, 28 July 2015, http://thediplomat.com/2015/07/after-modis-visit-is-central-asia-open-for-indian-business/
219. OPEC share of world crude oil reserves, 2014, http://www.opec.org/opec_web/en/data_graphs/330.htm
220. ISIS Almeida: Iran Is No Qatar, Even With World's Second-Biggest Gas Reserves, *Bloomberg Business*, 15 July 2015, http://www.bloomberg.com/news/articles/2015-07-14/iran-no-qatar-even-with-the-world-s-second-biggest-gas-reserves
221. National Intelligence Council: Global Trends 2030, *Alternative Worlds*, pp. 73-76.
222. Anisur Rahman: Migration and Human Rights in the Gulf, Middle East Institute, 2 February 2010. Although it is difficult to know the exact size of the migrant worker population in the GCC countries, available information suggests that it was about 12.5 million in 2002. Of this total, there were 3.6 million Indians, 1.7 million Pakistanis, almost one million Bangladeshis, and over 700,000 Sri Lankans. http://www.mei.edu/content/migration-and-human-rights-gulf. However, by 2012, India had over 5.2 million workers in the Gulf States. Accessed online at http://moia.gov.in/writereaddata/pdf/Population_Overseas_Indian.pdf on 7 August 2015.
223. Also see South Asia Development Matters World Bank Report--Leveraging Urbanization in South Asia, Managing Spatial Transformation for Prosperity and Liveability, 2015; *Brookings Report*: Reinvigorating SAARC India's Opportunities and Challenges, November 2014, Development, Concepts and Doctrine Centre (DCDC). South Asia out to 2040, October 2012, Asian Development Bank; Asia 2050: Realizing the Asian Century, 2011, Institute for Defence Studies and Analyses, New Delhi Grand Strategy for India 2020 and Beyond, 2012.
224. National Intelligence Council: Global Trends 2030, *Alternative Worlds*; Washington, 2012, p. iv.
225. World Bank: Leveraging Urbanization in South Asia–Managing Spatial Transformation for Prosperity and Liveability, 2014, pp. 2-14. www.worldbank.org/southasiacities
226. Government of India, Ministry of Urban Development: Smart Cities–Mission Statement & Guidelines; June 2015 p. 5.
227. McKinsey Global Institute: India's urban awakening: Building inclusive cities, sustaining economic growth, April 2010, http://www.mckinsey.com/global-themes/urbanization/urban-awakening-in-india
228. Ibid., pp. 207-208.
229. World Bank Report: Managing Climate Risk–Integrating Adaptation into World Bank Group Operations, 2006.
230. Dhaka Declaration and SAARC Action Plan on Climate Change (2008): http://saarc-sec.org/areaofcooperation/cat-detail.php?cat_id=54
231. United Nations: Conference of the Parties Twenty-first session, Paris, 30

November to 11 December 2015, Adoption of the Paris Agreement, FCCC/CP/2015/L.9/Rev.1. https://unfccc.int/resource/docs/2015/cop21/eng/l09r01.pdf

232. Thomas Friedman: *The World is Flat*; Penguin, London, 2006, pp. 342-343.
233. National Intelligence Council: Global Trends 2030, *Alternative Worlds*, pp. 49-52, 2012.
234. http://www.digitalindia.gov.in/content/about-programme
235. K. Subrahmanyam: *Grand Strategy for the First Half of the 21st Century*, Institute For Defence Studies & Analyses, Pentagon Press, New Delhi, 2012, pp. 21-22.
236. Steve Kroft interview of Pervez Musharraf for CBS News: Pakistan's President Tells Steve Kroft U.S. Threatened His Country; 21 September 2006. http://www.cbsnews.com/news/musharraf-in-the-line-of-fire/
237. Resolution adopted by the General Assembly on 25 September 2015: Transforming our world: the 2030 Agenda for Sustainable Development, United Nations, 21 October 2015, A/RES/70/1.
238. SAARC Charter; http://saarc-sec.org/SAARC-Charter/5/
239. South Asia Terrorism Portal–Sindh Assessment 2015: Karachi, Sindh's premier city, has been in a state of crisis for decades now. Criminalization of the state in Pakistan, and the unwillingness to abandon Islamist extremism and terrorism as instruments of state policy that have resulted in the unbridled and self-destructive violence in Sindh. Its increasing fragility has the potential of transforming into a civil war, engulfing the entire province, and dispersing into the country at large. Karachi's other problems are drug trade and a rapid urbanization and burgeoning population, http://www.satp.org/satporgtp/countries/pakistan/sindh/index.html
240. Abubakr Siddiqui: *The Pashtuns*; Random House, Gurgaon, 2014, pp. 203-205.
241. India Economic Forecasts 2016-2020 Outlook: India's population pegged at 1,324 million in 2020–unemployed is expected to rise to 55.96 million, overall unemployment rate estimated at 4.6%. http://www.tradingeconomics.com/india/forecast In addition, the unemployed youth is expected to be around 15.5%.
242. McKinsey: op. cit.
243. Asian Development Bank: Asia 2050: Realizing the Asian Century, Philippines, 2011, p. 47.
244. Analysis–Greater Pacific: India's Hidden Economy–The India within India; 2014. http://greaterpacificcapital.com/indias-hidden-economy-the-india-within-india/
245. Tridivesh Singh Maini: India's laggard states need attention, too; East Asia Forum, 27 December 2014, http://www.eastasiaforum.org/2014/12/27/indias-laggard-states-need-attention-too/
246. Dhiraj Nayyar: India's Two-Speed Economy, 27 November 2014, http://www.bloombergview.com/articles/2014-11-28/indias-twospeed-economy
247. SAARC Regional Convention on Suppression of Terrorism and its Additional Protocol: http://saarc-sec.org/areaofcooperation/detail.php?activity_id=21
248. SAARC Terrorist Offences Monitoring Desk:; http://saarc-sec.org/areaofcooperation/detail.php?activity_id=24

249. SAARC Drug Offences Monitoring Desk (SDOMD): http://saarc-sec.org/areaofcooperation/detail.php?activity_id=23
250. SAARC Regional Convention on Suppression of Terrorism and its Additional Protocol: http://saarc-sec.org/areaofcooperation/detail.php?activity_id=21 (Additional Protocol to the SAARC Regional Convention on Suppression of Terrorism came into force on 12 January 2006 following its ratification by all Member-States).
251. Smruti S. Pattanaik: Making Sense of Regional Cooperation, SAARC at Twenty, *Strategic Analysis*, vol. 30, no. 1, Jan-Mar 2006, pp. 148-150.
252. C. Christine Fair: *Fighting to the end: The Pakistan Army's Way of War*, Oxford University Press, Oxford, 2014, p. 2.
253. Sameer Patil: Combating terror financing through SAARC, 25 November 2014, http://www.gatewayhouse.in/combating-terror-financing-through-saarc/
254. Press Trust of India: Pakistan pushes for active role for observers in SAARC, Kathmandu, 26 November 2014,, http://indianexpress.com/article/world/neighbours/pakistan-pushes-for-active-role-for-observers-in-saarc/#sthash.N9Mbd6ea.dpuf
255. Press Trust of India: India, Bangladesh discuss terrorism, water management, New Delhi, 2 February 2016.
256. Author's discussion with Intelligence Officer, 12 April 2015.
257, Fair: op. cit., pp. 3-4.
258. Patil: op.cit.
259. Anand Kumar: The Terror Challenge in South Asia and Prospect of Regional Cooperation, Institute for Defence Studies and Analyses, New Delhi, 2012, p. 5.
260. https://treaties.un.org/Pages/ViewDetails.aspx?src= TREATY&mtdsg_ no= XVIII-9&chapter=18&lang=en
261. United Nations General Assembly Adopts Global Counter-Terrorism Strategy; http://www.un.org/en/terrorism/strategy-counter-terrorism.shtml
262. Robin Jeffrey and others: *More than Maoism*, Manohar, New Delhi, 2013, p. 6.
263. Press Information Bureau, Government of India: Naxal problem needs a holistic approach, 22 July 2009. http://www.pib.nic.in/newsite/erelease.aspx?relid=50833
264. Ministry of Home Affairs: Annual Report 2014-15, pp. 21-23.
265. Rich lands, poor people: http://cseindia.org/mining/pdf/miningpub.pdf
266. Peacekeeping Fact Sheet as on 31 August 2015, http://www.un.org/en/peacekeeping/resources/statistics/factsheet.shtml.
267. Brett Schaeffer: Time for a New United Nations Peacekeeping Organization, February 2007, http://www.heritage.org/research/reports/2007/02/time-for-a-new-united-nations-peacekeeping-organization?aliId=1454129639
268. Soeren Kern: European 'No-Go' Zones: Fact or Fiction? Part 2, Britain, 3 February 2015, http://www.gatestoneinstitute.org/5177/no-go-zones-britain
269. Kimiko De Freytas-Tamura and Milan Schreuer: Belgian Minister Says Government Lacks Control Over Neighbourhood Linked to Terror Plots, *New York Times*, 15 November 2015.
270. *The Statesman*: Mamata under fire over Malda violence, Kolkata, 29 January 2016.

271. Gretchen Peters: *Seeds of Terror*, Hachette, New Delhi, 2009. pp. 140, 237.
272. Carlotta Gall: *The Wrong Enemy*: Penguin, New Delhi, 2014, pp. 258-261.
273. Prem Mahadevan: *The Politics of Counter Terrorism in India*, I B Tauris, London, 2012, pp. 97, 120.
274. Security Studies Programme: Report: Lone Wolf Terrorism, National Security Critical Issue Task Force, Georgetown University, June 2015, pp. 7-9.
275. US Department of State: Country Reports on Terrorism–South and Central Asia Overview 2014, http://www.state.gov/j/ct/rls/crt/2014/239408.htm
276. Ibid.
277. Ministry of Home Affairs: Annual Report 2014-15, p.28.
278. Margaret Thatcher: Speech to American Bar Association, 15 July 1985, http://www.margaretthatcher.org/document/106096
279. S. Ahmed Ali: 26/11 attack: Media pulled up by Supreme Court for its role, *Times of India*, Mumbai, 31 August 2012.
280. Kanchan, L: The Media in Terror–Analysing Reportage from Theatres of Conflict, South Asia Terror Portal, http://www.satp.org/satporgtp/publication/faultlines/volume8/Article2.htm#
281. Shabbir Sarwar: Terrorism and the role of media, *The Daily Times*, Lahore, 23 December 2014.
282. UNHCR: 2015 UNHCR Sub-regional Operations Profile–South Asia, http://www.unhcr.org/cgi-bin/texis/vtx/page?page=49e4878e6&submit=GO
283. S. Rama Krishna: ISIS recruiter has data of 25,000 Indian Muslim youth, *The Sunday Guardian*, Hyderabad, 19 September 2015.
284. Jijo Jacob: 30,000 Indian Shia Muslims Ready to Fight ISIS 'Bare Handed' in Iraq, *International Business Times*, 27 June 2014, http://www.ibtimes.co.uk/30000-indian-muslims-ready-fight-isis-bare-handed-iraq-1454415
285. Sanchita Bhattacharya: West Bengal: Malda–Locus of Instability, *South Asia Intelligence Review*, Weekly Assessments & Briefings, vol. 11, no. 27, 7 January 7, 2013.
286. Centre for Strategic and International Studies: Net Losses: Estimating the Global Cost of Cybercrime, June 2014, p. 4.
287. PTI: India facing shortage of 4 lakh cyber warriors, *The Hindu*, New Delhi, 20 January 2014.
288. Annual Report 2014, Indian Computer Emergency Response Team: http://www.cert-in.org.in/.
289. P.R. Sagar: India readies cyber command service to combat espionage threats online; *DNA*, 15 January 2014.
290. Shalini Chawla: Why does Pakistan threaten India so often with nuclear attack? *Daily Mail*, UK, 18 September 2015. http://www.dailymail.co.uk/indiahome/indianews/article-3240567/Why-does-Pakistan-threaten-India-nuclear-attack.html
291. Reshmi Kazi: Global Centre for Nuclear Energy Partnership: India's Gift Basket of Nuclear Security, *Asian Strategic Review* 2015; India as a Security Provider, Institute for Defence Studies and Analyses, New Delhi, 2015. Pp. 330-332.
292. Dr. Gopal Ji Misra & Dr. C. Damodaran: Perspective Plan for Indian Forensics, Ministry of Home Affairs, July2010.

293. To give just an –Secretary Border Management, as per Executive Record Sheet Generator has not been posted in any contentious border state, (http://persmin.gov.in/ersheet/MultipleERS.asp?HiddenStr=01AM017000). Similarly, Special Secretary, Internal Security, has limited experience in states having internal security issues. This lack of exposure, irrespective of the officers' competence, impacts on the efficiency of the officer and his department, especially in the initial phase.
294. Policy Brief: Internal Security Priorities for the New Government: Institutional Reforms, Institute of Defence and Strategic Analyses, 19 May 2014.
295. Vandana Asthana: Cross-Border Terrorism in India–Counterterrorism Strategies and Challenges; University of Illinois at Urbana-Champaign, June 2010, p. 14.
296. Nasir Iqbal: Military courts get Supreme Court nod, *Dawn*, 5 August 2015, http://www.dawn.com/news/1198533. The Parliament passed the 21st Amendment and the Pakistan Army Act, 1952, to establish the special courts after the massacre in the Army Public School, Peshawar, last year. Incidentally, Pakistan has already hanged six of the planners of the massacre.
297. There are six departments and 20 divisions as per the organizational chart of the MHA. Of these, three departments can form a new ministry for internal security with border management, and J and K affairs under it. The remaining three departments–Home, Official Languages and States—can be restructured as a Ministry of Home Affairs. The Intelligence Bureau, Central Bureau of Investigations as well as the National Investigation Agency along with the NTRO and NCTC should come directly under the Prime Minister with a Minister of State (Independent Charge) reporting directly to the Prime Minister. Also see http://mha.nic.in/department_mha and http://mha.nic.in/divisions.
298. KPMG and ASSOCHAM Paper: Homeland Security in India–An Overview, 2010, pp. 10-17.
299. *FICCI Task Force on National Security And Terrorism*, vol. 1, pp. 9-17.
300. CBI: Extradition Treaties and Arrangements; http://cbi.nic.in/interpol/extradition.php
301. Ashley Tellis: The Merits of De-hyphenation: Explaining U.S. Success in Engaging India and Pakistan ; *The Washington Quarterly*, Autumn 2008, pp. 21-23.
302. Fair: op.cit., p. 1.
303. Eric Rosand and others: Countering Terrorism in South Asia: Strengthening Multilateral Engagement, International Peace Institute, Washington, 2009, pp. 6-7.
304. UN General Assembly Resolution 60/288 (September 8, 2006): UN Doc. A/RES/60/288.
305. Ibid.
306. Ibid.
307. *The New York Times*: Transcript of Obama's 2016 State of the Union Address, 12 January 2016, http://www.nytimes.com/2016/01/13/us/politics/obama-2016-sotu-transcript.html?_r=0
308. Background, Objectives and Principles BIMSTEC: http://bimstec.org/index.php?page=overview

309. Bipul Chatterjee and Surendar Singh: Time to Energize BIMSTEC, 7 January 2015, http://thediplomat.com/2015/01/time-to-energize-bimstec/
310. Fair: op.cit., pp. 64-69.
311. Aasim Sajjad Akhtar: Who runs Pakistan?, *Dawn*, Islamabad, 20 November 2015, http://www.dawn.com/news/1220924
312. Fair: op. cit., 277-279.
313. Kenneth N. Luongo: Roadmap for Success of the Nuclear Security Summits and Beyond; *Strategic Analysis*, 2014, vol. 38, no. 2, pp. 190.
314. Matthew King and Benjamin Sturtewagen: Making the Most of Afghanistan's River Basins–Opportunities for Regional Cooperation, The East West Institute, New York,, February 2010, pp. 8-9.
315. Discussions with former Defence Attache in Afghanistan, 15 December 2015.
316. Shahbaz Rana: Millennium Development: Goals Funds worth Rs. 12.5 billion diverted to other schemes, *The Tribune*, 14 February 2015,. http://tribune.com.pk/story/837989/millennium-development-goals-funds-worth-rs12-5-billion-diverted-to-other-schemes/
317. http://www.state.gov/secretary/remarks/2015/12/250388.htm, Brookings Institution's 2015 Saban Forum Keynote Address, 5 December 2015.
318. Vappala Balachandran: Why it is Not Easy For the United Nations to Define Terrorism, *The Quint*, 30 September 2015, http://www.thequint.com/opinion/2015/09/30/why-it-is-not-easy-for-the-united-nations-to-define-terrorism
319. Lauren Boyer: Former U.S. Military Official Says George W. Bush Created ISIS, US News and World Report. 1 December 2015. Lt. General Michael Flynn, former head of the Defence Intelligence Agency, says the Bush Administration played a large part in the creation of the Islamic State. http://www.usnews.com/news/articles/2015/12/01/former-military-official-says-george-w-bush-created-isis.
320. Nick Robins-Early: Was The 2011 Libya Intervention A Mistake? *The Huffington Post*, 7 March 2015, Interview with Ivo Daalder, the U.S. Ambassador to NATO during the 2011 Libyan revolution.
321. Mahin Karim: Mapping Pakistan's Internal Dynamics: Implications for State Stability and Regional Security, NBR special report, no. 55, February 2016, pp. 3-4.
322. Gurmeet Kanwal: Fighting Terrorism, Pakistan's New Policy, CLAWS Focus, October 2013, vol. VIII, pp. 9-10. Pakistan's new CT Policy titled National Counter-Terrorism and Extremism Policy 2013, focuses on eliminating terrorist networks through counter insurgency operations based on Intelligence, coordination with police and prosecution. The policy calls for building police capacity and follow up on military action in extremists' bastions with a strategy focused on development work and economic revival.
323. Tarik Parvez and Mehwish Rani: An Appraisal of Pakistan's Anti–Terror Act, United States Institute of Peace, Special Report August 2015. The authors contend that despite the law's passage, the criminal justice system has seen low conviction rates and delayed cases, and it offers a very weak deterrence against terrorism. The lengthy delays and high number of acquittals in terrorism cases are due to factors like - The definition of terrorism under the Act is too

broad; Procedural issues, among law enforcement officers and among police and intelligence agencies, also contribute to the law's ineffectiveness. Unless urgent measures are taken, public confidence in the law is likely to further erode, opening up the possibility of greater reliance on the military instead of civilian institutions to control terrorism. A holistic approach is needed to improve the ATA, based on four equally important dimensions: amending the language of the law, streamlining its application, sensitizing the courts to the provisions of the law, and strengthening the infrastructure responsible for its implementation. These two examples are cited to bring into focus that Pakistan faces a long haul in its CT efforts, which seems selective in any way–omitting focus away from the principal state-sponsored groups, i.e., LeT and Haqqani factions.

324. Smruti S. Pattanaik and Ashok K. Behuria: India's Regional Strategy: Balancing Geopolitics with Geo-economics in South Asia; India's Approach to Asia: Strategy, Geopolitics and Responsibility, Institute for Defence Studies and Analyses, New Delhi, pp. 397.
325. Eric Rosand and others: Countering Terrorism in South Asia: Strengthening Multilateral Engagement,International Peace Institute, May 2009, pp. 9-12.
326. UN Security Council: Mandate–Counter Terrorism Committee, http://www.un.org/en/sc/ctc/aboutus.html. The mandate of this committee includes monitoring implementation of UN Resolution 1373 (2001) (also see http://www.un.org/en/sc/ctc/docs/2011/comparative-table-2012-11.pdf), which requested countries to implement a number of measures intended to enhance their legal and institutional ability to counter terrorist activities at home, in their regions and around the world, including taking steps to: Criminalize the financing of terrorism; Freeze without delay any funds related to persons involved in acts of terrorism; Deny all forms of financial support for terrorist groups; Suppress the provision of safe havens, sustenance or support for terrorists; Share information with other governments on any groups practising or planning terrorist acts; Cooperate with other governments in the investigation, detection, arrest, extradition and prosecution of those involved in such acts; and Criminalize active and passive assistance for terrorism in domestic law and bring violators to justice.
327. Overview: The Colombo Plan for Cooperative Economic and Social Development in Asia and the Pacific: http://www.colombo-plan.org/index.php/about-cps/overview/. The Colombo Plan for Cooperative Economic and Social Development in Asia and the Pacific was first conceived to enhance economic and social development of the countries of the region and was established on 1 July 1951 by Australia, Canada, India, Pakistan, New Zealand, Sri Lanka and the United Kingdom and currently has expanded to include 26 member-countries including non-Commonwealth countries and countries belonging to regional groupings such as ASEAN (Association of South-East Asian Nations) and SAARC (South Asian Association for Regional Cooperation). The Colombo Plan is a partnership concept of self-help and mutual-help in development aimed at socio-economic progress of its member countries. The objectives of the Colombo Plan: to promote interest in and

support for the economic and social development of Asia and the Pacific; to promote technical cooperation and assist in the sharing and transfer of technology among member-countries; to keep under review relevant information on technical cooperation between the member governments, multilateral and other agencies with a view to accelerating development through cooperative effort; to facilitate the transfer and sharing of the developmental experiences among member countries within the region with emphasis on the concept of South-south cooperation. The Colombo Plan has four permanent programmes: Drug Advisory Programme (DAP); Programme for Public Administration & Environment (PPA & ENV); Programme for Private Sector Development (PPSD) and Long-Term Scholarships Programme (LTSP).

328. Peace Corps Today: http://www.peacecorps.gov/today/.
329. United Nations General Assembly: The United Nations Global Counter-Terrorism Strategy Review; A/68/L.50 dated 10 June 2014.
330. Eric Rosand and others. Op.cit., pp. 23-27. The authors contend that such a mechanism should be designed to address the particular needs of the region and could draw upon the experiences of mechanisms in other regions, e.g., the Jakarta Centre for Law Enforcement Cooperation in Indonesia and other counter-terrorism training centres that have been established in Southeast Asia, in cooperation with countries from outside the region, to provide training to a range of counter-terrorism practitioners. Another example quoted is the Intergovernmental Authority on Development's Capacity Building Programme against Terrorism, which is funded entirely by partner countries and where a non-governmental organization serves as the secretariat. Active assistance and cooperation of UN agencies is advocated.
331. United Nations Security Council: Resolution 1373 (2001), adopted by the Security Council at its 4385th meeting, on 28 September 2001; S/RES/1373 (2001). This resolution was adopted immediately post the 11 September 2001 attacks on the USA. http://www.un.org/en/sc/ctc/specialmeetings/2012/docs/United%20Nations%20Security%20Council%20Resolution%201373%20%282001 %29. pdf
332. United Nations Security Council: Resolution 1624 (2005) adopted by the Security Council at its 5261st meeting, on 14 September 2005, S/RES/1624 (2005). The Council called on all states to co-operate in order to strengthen the security of their international borders by enhancing terrorist screening and passenger security procedures. Resolution 1624, along with Resolution 1625 (2005), was adopted at a meeting of heads of state or government.
333. Eric Rosand and others: op.cit.
334. N.N. Vohra: Management of National Policy; *USI Journal*, July-September 2014, pp. 372-379. Governor Vohra laments the absence of a National Security Policy and the opposition by States for the establishment of new security management agencies with pan-India jurisdiction. The absence of a National Security Management Policy with clear delineations of respective roles and responsibility of the Central and State governments, also affects the management of progressively increasing security threats.
335. George K. Tanham: Indian Strategic Thought: An Interpretive Essay, RAND

1992. Even though Tanham, in this essay, decried the absence of articulation and pursuance of its goals in a coherent, disciplined fashion, former Prime Minister Manmohan Singh bemoans its absence and was often heard complaining, "We must develop a strategic culture in this country. "He joins a large number of Indian intellectuals who decry our apparent lack of ability to plot out India's "strategic thought" or even plan a "grand strategy". Indrani Bagchi in *Economic Times*, Why India does not have a vibrant strategic culture? 21 October 2012.

336. S. Kalyanaraman: Grand Strategy for India 2020 and Beyond: Thinking about Counter Terrorism in India's National Strategy, Institute for Defence Studies and Analyses, New Delhi, 2012, pp. 107-110.
337. KPMG and ASSOCHAM Report: Homeland Security in India, an Overview, New Delhi 2012, p. 12.
338. Prem Mahadevan: *The Politics of Counter terrorism in India*; I. B. Tauris, 2012, pp. 123-124.
339. Vandana Asthana: Cross-Border Terrorism in India–Counterterrorism Strategies and Challenges; Arms Control, Disarmament, and International Security, University of Illinois at Urbana–Champaign, June 2010, pp. 5-6.
340. Author's discussions with former senior R&AW official, 12 December 2015.
341. Andrew MacAskill and Sanjeev Miglani: Insight: Indian intelligence agency on the cheap hampers war on militants, Reuters, 7 November 2014.
342. James Glanz and others: Lashkar tech expert who hid in plain sight, *New York Times*, 24 December 2014. About the attack, the then National Security Adviser, Shivshankar Menon, said that a lesson that emerged from the tragedy in Mumbai was that "computer traffic only tells you so much. It's only a thin slice." The key is the analysis, he said, and "we didn't have it". http://indianexpress.com/article/india/india-others/lashkar-tech-expert-who-hid-in-plain-sight/#sthash.01QG7j8V.dpuf.
343. South Asia Terror Portal: Police-Population Ratio (per 100,000 population), http://www.satp.org/satporgtp/countries/india/database/Police-population ratio.htm.
344. Neeraj Chauhan: Techies, MBAs, doctors join IB to become 'spies'; *Times of India*, 22 June 2015.
345. Ministry of Home Affairs website: http://mha.nic.in/, accessed on 23 October 2014 and subsequently on 20 November 2015.
346. Recommendations on Border Management, paras 5.14 to 5.50 of the Group of Ministers Report on National Security, set up by the Prime Minister to review the National Security System in its entirety and in particular, to consider the recommendations of the KRC; pages 61 to 70, accessed on 17 January 2013. The recommendations bring out the necessity for harmonization of agencies towards National Security. However there is a requirement to review existing arrangements periodically to upgrade capabilities and bring about congruence in missions. http://www.vifindia.org/sites/default/files/GoM%20Report%20on%20National%20Security.pdf.
347. Purulia Arms dropping case: http://cbi.nic.in/dop/judgements/padc.pdf, (Arising out of Jhalda P.S. Case No. 152 of 1995 dated 18.12.95), downloaded

on 12 December 2012. In this landmark event where not only did the offending aircraft deviate from the laid down route, nor was its cargo even cursorily checked at the first Indian airport, Varanasi, but drop a sizeable quantity of arms and ammunition meant for a banned terror group, the Anand Marg, overflew its intended destination, on the specious plea of bad weather and almost got away, until it was force landed on its return trip, post recovery of the incriminating evidence.

348. The Lessons of Mumbai: RAND Corporation Occasional Papers by Angel Rabasa and others, Published 2009 by the RAND Corporation, 1776 Main Street, P.O. Box 2138, Santa Monica, CA 90407-2138. Downloaded on 15 December 2012. http://www.rand.or g/content/dam/rand/pubs/occasional_papers/2009/RAND_OP249.pdf.
During this audacious attack, planned and sponsored by Pakistan, 10 Lashkar-e-Tayyaba terrorists landed by a captured Indian fishing trawler, on the shores of India's commercial capital, Mumbai, and proceeded to hold the city to ransom striking at three key establishments, killing 166 people and injuring hundreds of others. Initial disjointed and graduated responses were responsible for the terrorists spreading mayhem which lasted three days.
349. Report of the High Level Enquiry Committee (HLEC) on 26/11, appointed by the Maharashtra Government vide GAD GR No. Raasua. 2008/C.R.34/29-A, 30 Dec2008, Para 67(ii) Other Miscellaneous Recommendations, accessed on 12 December 2012, http://www.scribd.com/doc/179156650/Pradhan-Committee-Report-about-26-11-pdf#scribd
350. Office of the Director of National Intelligence: National Counter-Terrorism Centre: Who we are; http://www.nctc.gov/whoweare.html
351. V Balachandran: NATGRID will prove to be a security nightmare, *The Sunday Guardian*, 5 March 2016.
352. Editorial: Revive NATGRID with safeguards, *The Hindu*, 2 January 2016.
353. Task Force Report on National Security and Terrorism, FICCI, 2009, pp. 14-15.
354. Government of India, National Investigation Agency: NIA Cases. http://www.nia.gov.in/nia-cases.htm
355. http://www.satp.org/satporgtp/countries/india/index.html
356. National Investigation Agency. op.cit. Cases relating to 'flag hoisting 'by PLA/RPF and murder of a Manipuri couple, both of 2012, are still under investigation.
357. Bharti Jain: NIA gets no support from West Bengal police in Burdwan blast probe, *Times of India*, New Delhi, 25 October 2014.
358. Vohra: loc. cit. 379.
359. Government of India: Second Administrative Reforms Commission, Eighth Report, Combating Terrorism Protecting By Righteousness, June 2008, pp. 42-44.
360. Ibid.
361. Vohra: loc. cit. 371.
362. Debabrata Mohanty: Draft CAG report on coastal security finds Odisha's marine police stations foundering; *Indian Express*, 20 October 2015. The audit done during June to August 2015, found that the marine police stations could

not work effectively as the State Government did not procure surveillance equipment, digital cameras, office furniture and computers, despite central assistance. Even the equipment that was purchased, articles worth Rs. 83.02 lakh was kept gathering dust at the central store instead of being issued to marine police stations. In the Aravalli marine police station, a computer with printer was found to be in its original packed condition since September 2013. The staff recruited for the marine police stations also did not receive standardised training. Of the 360 police personnel who received training in marine policing at the Indian Coast Guard Centre at Paradip until March this year, only 15 were marine police staff. "Poor percentage of cases indicated sub-optimal use of interceptor boats and absence of sea patrolling. It seems these stations were set up to utilise the central assistance and without any positive effort to guard the coastline," the report said. http://indianexpress.com/article/india/india-news-india/draft-cag-report-on-coastal-security-finds-odishas-marine-police-stations-foundering/#sthash.hkmI8Xsn.dpuf

363. KPMG and ASSOCHAM: Homeland Security in India–An Overview, 2010.
364. U. Anand Kumar: India has just one doctor for every 1,700 people, *Indian Express*, 22 September 2013. The article states that India would need about four lakh more doctors by 2020—50,000 for PHCs, 0.8 lakh for community health centres (CHC); 1.1 lakh for 5,642 sub-centres and another 0.5 lakh for medical college hospitals.
365. TNN: CAG audit report points to irregularities in implementation of MGNREGA; *TNN*, April 23, 2013; http://timesofindia.indiatimes.com/india/CAG-audit-report-points-to-irregularities-in-implementation-of-MGNREGA/articleshow/19692420.cms. The report points at financial bungling, and incomplete works even five years after sanction. In another report according to CNN-IBN, in 14 states there were 129 lakh projects worth over Rs. 1.26 lakh crore that were approved. Of this, only 30 per cent had been completed.
366. National Intelligence Council: Global Trends 2030, Alternative Worlds; Washington, December 2012, p. 68.
367. Rajiv Kumar: SAARC–Changing realities, opportunities and challenges, German Development Institute, Bonn, Discussion Paper 11/2009, p. 12.
368. Vishal Chandra, (ed.): India and South Asia–Exploring Regional Perceptions; The Way Forward, Key Recommendations, Institute for Defence Studies and Analyses, New Delhi, p. 216.
369. Rohit Karki: Trilateral Security Cooperation: Nepal's New Foreign Policy, *Strategic Analysis*, 2013, vol. 37, no. 4, pp. 405-409.
370. Maddison, Angus: World Economy: World GDP, 20 Countries and Regional Totals, 0–1998 A.D. In 1700, India's GDP was estimated at $ 90,750 million (at 1990 prices) – world GDP was assessed at $ 371,369 million. http://www.theworldeconomy.org/MaddisonTables/MaddisontableB-18.pdf
371. Bharat Karnad: *Why India is Not a Great Power (Yet)*, Oxford, New Delhi, 2015, p. 1.
372. United Nations General Assembly: Resolution adopted by the General Assembly on 25 September 2015; Seventieth session, Agenda items 15 and 116.

A/RES/70/1. http://www.un.org/ga/search/view_doc.asp?symbol=A/RES/70/1&Lang=E.

373. The Declaration mentions "The Heads of State or Government strongly condemned all forms of terrorist violence and expressed deep concern over the serious threat posed by terrorism to the peace, stability and security of the region.... They emphasized the need for the strongest possible cooperation in the fight against terrorism and transnational organized crime amongst the relevant agencies of the Member States especially in the area of information exchange". Source: Fifteenth SAARC Summit, Colombo, 2-3 August 2008, Declaration: Partnership for Growth for Our People. http://www.saarc-sec.org/userfiles/Summit%20Declarations/15%20-%20Colombo,%2015th%20Summit%202-3%20August%202008%20.pdf
374. General Richard Dannatt: 'A Perspective on the Nature of Future Conflict', CGS speech to Chatham House, 15 May 2009.
375. Article 51 of the UN Charter states "Nothing in the present Charter shall impair the inherent right of individual or collective self-defence if an armed attack occurs against a Member of the United Nations, until the Security Council has taken measures necessary to maintain international peace and security. Measures taken by Members in the exercise of this right of self-defence shall be immediately reported to the Security Council and shall not in any way affect the authority and responsibility of the Security Council under the present Charter to take at any time such action as it deems necessary in order to maintain or restore international peace and security." www.un.org/en/sc/repertoire/actions.shtml
376. Associated Press: ISIS courts white-collar recruits in Pakistan, 2 March 2016, http://www.cbsnews.com/news/isis-recruiting-karachi-competition-taliban-al-qaeda/
377. Ibid.
378. Ibid.
379. *Dawn*: IS recruiting trained professionals from Pakistan, 3 March 2016, http://www.dawn.com/news/1243094/islamic-state-recruiting-trained-professionals-from-pakistan
380. K.M. Panikkar: *India and the Indian Ocean: An Essay on the Influence of Sea Power on Indian History*; George Allen & Unwin, London, 1945, pp. 82-84.

Select Bibliography

PRIMARY SOURCES

Board of Direct Taxes, New Delhi, May 2012.

Defence. -Executive Record Sheet Generator: IAS Officers-Border Management.

Indian Navy. Freedom To Use The Seas: India's Maritime Military Strategy. May 2007.

Ministry of Home Affairs Annual Report (India) 2011-2012.

Ministry of Home Affairs Annual Report (India) 2012-2013.

Ministry of Home Affairs Annual Report (India) 2013-2014.

Ministry of Home Affairs Annual Report (India) 2014 -2015.

Ministry of Finance. White Paper on Black Money. Department of Revenue, Central.

Report of an Expert Group to Planning Commission. Development Challenges in Extremist-Affected Areas. 2008.

Reforming National Security (Group of Ministers' Report on National Security, 2001) http://pib.nic.in/archieve/lreleng/lyr2001/rmay2001/23052001/r2305200110.html.

U.S. Congressional Record. Vol. 146, Part 2: Proceedings and Debates of the 106th Congress, Second Session, 24 February 2000 to 20 March 2000 (Secretary Albright's statement on the Indian subcontinent).

U.S. Hearing before the Sub Committee on Technology, Terrorism and Government Information. Serial number J–105–75. 24 February 1998.

U.S. Department of Homeland Security. The 2014 Quadrennial Homeland Security Review.

U.S. Department of Defence. Quadrennial Defence Review 2014.

——. Progress towards Security and Stability in Afghanistan,October 2014.

——Sustaining U.S. Global Leadership Priorities for 21st Century, Defence, January 2012.

——Asia-Pacific: Maritime Security Strategy, 2014.

——Sustaining U.S. Global Leadership: Priorities for 21st Century, Defence.

——Cyber Strategy, April 2015.

U.S. Department of the Navy. Maritime Strategy: A Cooperative Strategy for 21st Century Sea Power, March 2015.

U.S. Department of State, Bureau of Counterterrorism, Country Reports on Terrorism 2014, Released in June 2015.

——Country Reports on Terrorism 2015, Released in June 2016.

—— & USAID. Joint Strategy on Countering Violent Extremism, May 2016.

Joint Chiefs of Staff: The National Military Strategy of the United States, 2015.

H.M. Government. Contest: The United Kingdom's Strategy for Countering Terrorism, Annual Report, 2014.

——The United Kingdom's Strategy for Countering Terrorism, July 2014.

U.K. Government Financial Statutes. https://www.fincen.gov/statutes_regs/patriot

——Terrorism Act 2006. https://www.gov.uk/government/publications/the-terrorism-act-2006

——House of Commons, Home Affairs Committee: Roots of violent radicalization. Nineteenth Report of Session 2010–12.

United Nations Global Counter-Terrorism Strategy. 8 September 2006.

United Nations Office on Drugs and Crime. The Global Afghan Opium Trade, A Threat Assessment, July 2011.

——World Drug Report, 2014.

SECONDARY SOURCES

Books

Akbar, M. J. *India: The Siege Within: Challenges to a Nation's Unity*, Penguin, Hammondsworth, 1985.

Asthana, Vandana. Cross-Border Terrorism in India–Counterterrorism Strategies and Challenges, University of Illinois at Urbana-Champaign, June 2010.

Bammi, Y.N. *War against Insurgency and Terrorism in Kashmir*, Dehra Dun, Natraj Publishers, 2007.

Brar, K.S. *Operation Blue Star: The True Story*, UBSPD, New Delhi, 1993.

C. Christine Fair. *Fighting to the End–The Pakistan Army's Way of War*, Oxford University Press, New York, 2014.

Chadha, Vivek. *Low Intensity Conflicts in India: An Analysis*, United Services Institution and Sage Publications, New Delhi, 2005.

Cohen, Stephen. *The Indian Army: It's contribution to the development of a nation*, OUP, New Delhi, 1990.

——*The Security of South Asia: American and Asian Perspectives*, Vistaar Publications, New Delhi, 1987.

Das, Gurcharan. *India Grows At Night: A Liberal Case for a Strong State*. Penguin Books, New Delhi, 2012.

Denyer, Simon. *Rogue Elephant: Harnessing the Power of Democracy in the New India*. Bloomsbury, London, 2015.

Dhar, M. K. *Fulcrum of Evil, ISI–CIA–AL QAEDA* Nexus. Manas, New Delhi, 2006.

Dullat , A. S. with Aditya Sinha. *Kashmir–The Vajpayee Years*. Harper Collins, India, 2015.

Friedman, Thomas L. *The Lexus and The Olive Tree*. Harper Collins, London 2000.

——. *The World Is Flat: The Globalized version in the Twenty First Century*. Penguin Books, London, 2006.

Gall, Carlotta. *The Wrong Enemy, America in Afghanistan 2001–2014*. Penguin, Gurgaon, 2014.

Galula, David. *Counter Insurgency Warfare: Theory and Practice*. Pall Mall, London, 1964.

Gupta, Shishir. Indian Mujahideen: *The Enemy Within*. Hachette, India 2011; India 2014.

Hluna J. V. and Tochhawng Rini. *The Mizo Uprising*. Cambridge Scholars Publishing, Newcastle, 2012.

Haqqani, Husain. *Pakistan: Between Mosque and Military*. Carnegie Endowment for International Peace, Washington D.C., 2005.

——*Magnificent Delusions*, Public Affairs, New York, 2013.

Hobsbawm, Eric. *Globalisation, Democracy and Terrorism*. Abacus, London, 2007.

Huntington, Samuel P. *The Clash of Civilizations and the Remaking of World Order*, Simon & Schuster, New York, 1996.

India Risk Survey 2015. Report prepared by Pinkerton and Federation of Indian Chambers of Commerce and Industry (FICCI), New Delhi, 2015.

Institute for Defence Studies and Analyses, New Delhi: Grand Strategy for India 2020 and Beyond, 2012.

Jagmohan. *My Frozen Turbulence in Kashmir*. Allied Publishers, New Delhi, 1991.

James Dobbins and others. *Choices for America in a Turbulent World*, Published by the RAND Corporation, Santa Monica, Calif., 2015, RAND Corporation.

Jeffrey, Robin; Sen, Ronojoy and Singh Pratima. *More than Maoism: Politics, Policies and Insurgencies in South Asia*. Manohar, India, 2012.

Karim, Afsir. *Counter Terrorism: The Pakistan Factor*, Lancers, New Delhi, 1991.

Kaplan, Robert D. *Balkan Ghosts: Journey through History*. Picador, New York, 2005.

——. *Monsoon: The Indian Ocean and the Future of American Power*. Random House, New York, 2011.

——. *Soldiers Of God, With Islamic Warriors in Afghanistan and Pakistan*. Vintage Books, New York, 2001.

——. *The Revenge of Geography: What the Map tells us about Coming Conflicts and the Battle against Fate*. Random House, USA, 2012.

Keay, John. *China: A History*. Harper Press, London, 2008.

——. *India: A History, From the Earliest Civilisations to the Boom of the Twenty First Century*. Harper Press, London 2010.

Kissinger, Henry. *World Order: Reflections on the Character of Nations and the Course of History*. Penguin Press, USA, 2014.

Levy, Adrian and Scott-Clark, Cathy. *The Siege: The Attack on the Taj*. Penguin, India 2013.

Mackinder, Sir H. J. *Democratic Ideals and Reality: A Study in the Politics of Reconstruction*. Henry Holt and Co, New York, 1919.

Mahadevan, Prem. *The Politics of Counterterrorism in India, Strategic Intelligence and National Security in South Asia*. I. B. Tauris, London, 2012.

Majumdar, R. C. *Ancient India*, M. Banarsidas, Delhi, 2013.

Malik, V. P.. *India's Military Conflicts and Diplomacy: An Inside View of Decision Making*. Harper Collins, India, 2013.

Malviya, Gopalji et al. *Security Dimensions of Peninsular India*. Centre for Security Analysis, Chennai, 2005.

Mohammad Yousaf and Mark Adkin. *The Bear Trap: Afghanistan's Untold Story—The Defeat of a Superpower*, Casemate, Havertown PA, 1992.

Musharraf, Pervez. *In The Line Of Fire: A Memoir*. Simon and Schuster, London, 2006.

Muthaiah, S. *The Indo–Lankans: Their 200 Year Saga*. Indian Heritage Foundation, Colombo, Sri Lanka, 2003.

Nandini Sundar. *Insurgency, Counter Insurgency and Democracy in Central India*, Manohar, New Delhi, 2013.

Nilekani, Nandan. *Imagining India*. Penguin, New Delhi, 2008.

Narahari, N. S. *Security Threats to North East India: The Socio-Ethnic Tensions*, Manas Publications, New Delhi, 2002.

Narcotics Control Bureau. Annual Report 2014.

Nayar, V. K. *Threat from Within: India's Internal Security Environment*, Lancers, New Delhi, 1992.

Nayar, Kuldip and Khushwant Singh. *Tragedy of Punjab: Operation Blue Star and After*. Vision Books, New Delhi, 1984.

Nayak, Sharada. *The Raj Agent in Ceylon 1936–1940*. Education Centre Resources Trust, New Delhi, 2014.

National Intelligence Council. *Global Trends 2030*, Alternative Worlds, Washington, 2012.

Nibedon, Nirmal. *Nagaland: The Night of the Guerrillas*, Lancer, New Delhi, 1978.

——*Mizoram: The Dagger Brigade*, Lancer, New Delhi, 1979.

Pakistan Economic Survey 2013 -2014. M/o Finance, M/o Interior, M/o Foreign Affairs, Joint Ministerial Group.

Pannikar, K. M. *he Future of South East Asia–An Indian View*. The MacMillan Co, New York, 1943.

Peters, Gretchen. *Seeds of Terror: The Taliban, the ISI and the New Opium Wars.*

Powell, Jonathan. *Talking to Terrorists: How to End Armed Conflicts*. The Bodley Head, London, 2014. Hachette, India, 2009.

Raghavan, V. R. and others. *Internal Conflicts: Military Perspectives*. Vij Books, India, 2012.

Raman, B. *Terrorism–Yesterday, Today & Tomorrow*, Lancer Publications, New Delhi, 2013.

——*Intelligence: Past, Present and Future*, Lancer, New Delhi, 2002.

——*The Kao Boys of R & AW: Down Memory Lane*. Lancer, New Delhi, 2007.

Rangarajan, L. N. (ed). *Kautilya: The Arthashastra*, Penguin Books, 1992.

Rao, K.V. Krishna. *Prepare or Perish: A Study of National Security*, Lancers, New Delhi, 1991.

Rustomji, N.F. *Imperilled Frontiers: India's North Eastern Borderlands*, OUP, New Delhi, 1983.

Sangwan, Sukhdeep. *Integrated Force Projection by India*, CENJOWS Publication, New Delhi, 2011.

Sardeshpande, S.C. *Assignment Jaffna*, Lancers Publishers, New Delhi, 1992.

Shelton, Hugh. *Without Hesitation, The Odyssey of an American Warrior*. St. Martin's Press, New York, 2010.

Singh, Depinder. *IPKF in Sri Lanka*, Trishul Publications, New Delhi, 1990.

Singh, Jaswant. *India at Risk: Mistakes, Misconceptions and Misadventures of Security Policy*, Rupa, India, 2013.

Smith, Rupert. *The Utility of Force: The Art of War in the Modern World*, Vintage Books, New York, 2008.

Spykman, Nicholas. *America's Strategy in World Politics: The United States and the Balance of Power*, Harcourt, Brace and Company, New York, 1942.

——*The Geography of the Peace*, Harcourt, Brace and Company, New York, 1944.

Sundarji, K. *Blind Men of Hindoostan: Indo-Pakistan Nuclear War*, BSPD, New Delhi, 1993.

Sun Tzu. *The Art of War*, Translated by Thomas Cleary, Shambala, South Asia Editions, USA, 1999.

Swami, Praveen. *India, Pakistan and the Secret Jihad: The Covert War in Kashmir 1947–2004*, Routledge, New York, 2007.

Tanham, George K. *Indian Strategic Thought: An Interpretive Essay*. RAND, Santa Monica, 1992.

Tore Bjørgo (ed). *Root Causes of Terrorism; Myths, Reality and Ways Forward*, Routledge, New York, 2005.

United Nations Office on Drugs and Crime. World Drug Report 2012, Vienna.

World Bank. Annual Report 2015.

Journal Articles

Asian Development Bank, *Asia 2050: Realizing the Asian Century*, Philippines, 2011.

Admiral R. K. Dhowan. Indian Ocean Region: Emerging Strategic Cooperation, Competition and Conflict Scenarios, *USI Journal*, October-December 2014.

Adhikari, Monalisa. Politics and Perceptions of Indian Aid to Nepal, *Strategic Analysis*, Vol. 38, No 3, May-June 2014.

Alok Bansal. Maldives: End of Uncertainty ;CLAWS Vol. IX, November 2013.

A Summary of the Findings of the Defence Advisory Committee. Sponsored by the Peter G. Peterson Foundation, Prepared by Stimson, November 2012.

Background, Objectives and Principles BIMSTEC. http://bimstec.org/index.php?page=overview.

Bangladesh GDP Growth Rate 1994-2016.

http://www.tradingeconomics.com/bangladesh/gdp-growth

Bhaduri, Shankar and Karim Afsir. *The Sri Lankan Crisis*, Lancers Paper 1, Lancers International, New Delhi, 1990.

Carnegie Endowment. Arab Renaissance for Democracy and Development, The Arab Spring's Refugee Crisis, 22 December 2011.

Centre for Disease Control and Prevention. *Bioterrorism Overview*, Atlanta, USA, 12 February 2007.

Chellaney, Brahma. Securing India in the New Millennium, New Delhi, Centre for Policy Research, 1999.

Cordesman, Anthony H. *The Uncertain Trends and Metrics of Terrorism in 2016*, CSIS Publication (Working Draft), Washington, 2016.

—— and others, *The Indian Ocean Region, A Strategic Assessment*, CSIS Publication Washington, 2014.

Daaman Thadi. Nepal Fast Becoming the Dragon's Lair, *CLAWS Focus* No. 9, 2013.

Dasgupta, S. Al Qaeda in India: Why we should pay attention. ISN, Centre for Security Studies (CSS), ETH Zurich, Switzerland, January 2015.

Desert Storm, the Last Classic War. Richard Haas. *The Wall Street Journal*. Updated 31 July 2015.

E.N. Rammohan. Spring Thunder in Bangladesh. *USI Journal*, April–June 2013.

Eric Ros and others. Countering Terrorism in South Asia: Strengthening Multilateral Engagement. International Peace Institute, Washington, 2009.

Gambhir, Harleen. ISIS's Global Strategy: A Wargame, Institute for the Study of War, Washington, 2015.

Galeotti and Octavian Manea. Hybrid War as a War on Governance, *Small Wars Journal*, Bethesda, MD, August 2015.

Ghosh, P.K. Maritime Security Trilateralism: India, Sri Lanka and the Maldives, *Strategic Analysis*, Vol. 38, No. 3, IDSA, May-June 2014.

Gill, K.P.S. *The Danger Within: Internal Security Threats, Future Imperilled*, Viking, New Delhi,1994.

Global Financial Integrity. Illicit Financial Flows from Developing Countries: 2004-2013, http://www.gfintegrity.org/report/illicit-financial-flows-from-developing-countries-2004-2013.

Hekmatullah Azamy. Afghanistan-India-Pakistan Trilateral Cooperation: Islamist Proxies a Challenge, Centre for Conflict and Peace Studies, Afghanistan, 2014.

Galeotti M, and Octavian Manea. Hybrid War as a War on Governance. *Small Wars Journal*, 19 August 2015.

India Economic Forecasts 2016-2020, *Outlook*. http://www.trading economics.com/india/forecast.

Institute for Economics and Peace (IEP). Global Peace Index 2015, Sydney.

Kumar, A. (ed). The Terror Challenge in South Asia and Prospect of Regional Cooperation,

Institute for Defence Studies and Analyses, New Delhi, 2012.

Laskar, Rezaul H. Pakistanis say time for tough questions instead of blaming India, *Hindustan Times*, New Delhi, 21 January 2016.

Margherita Stancati and Habib Khan Totakhil. Afghan President Blames Pakistan for Series of Bombings, *Wall Street Journal*, August 2015.

Mazumdar, Arijit. Left Wing Extremism and Counter Insurgency in India: 'The Andhra Model', *Strategic Analysis*, Vol. 37, No. 4, July-August 2013.

McKinsey Global Institute. India's urban awakening: Building inclusive cities, sustaining economic growth, April 2010.

Milevski, Lukas. Asymmetry is Strategy, Strategy is Asymmetry, National Defence University Press, Washington. 2014, 4th quarter edition of *Joint Force Quarterly*.

Navhat Nuraniyah. Online Extremism: Challenges and Counter-Measures, S. Rajaratnam School of International Studies (RSIS), Nanyang Technological University, No. 218, 6 November 2014 http://www.rsis.edu.sg/

Overview, Afghanistan and Russia. http://www.understandingwar.org/russia-and-afghanistan

Pakistan's Baloch Insurgency. http://www.iar-gwu.org/sites/default/files/articlepdfs/Pakistan's%20Baloch%20Insurgency

Pattanaik, Smruti S. Making Sense of Regional Cooperation: SAARC at Twenty, *Strategic Analysis*, Vol. 30, No. 1, Jan-Mar 2006.

Patil, Sameer. Combating terror financing through SAARC, 25 November 2014, http://www.gatewayhouse.in/combating-terror-financing-through-saarc

Shah, Apoorva. The Most Dangerous Place: Pakistan's Past, Pakistan's Future, *World Affairs Journal*, Washington, May/June 2011.

Tankel, Stephen. The Indian Jihadist Movement: Evolution and Dynamics, *Strategic Perspectives*, No. 17, originally published by National Defence University (NDU) Press for the Institute for National Strategic Studies (INSS), Zurich, July 2014.

Tata, S. An Unintended Consequence of US Strategic Ambiguity: A Russia, China and Iran Troika, ISN, Zurich, July 2015.

Zhao Kejin. China's National Security Commission, ISN ETH, Zurich, July 2015.

Ziad, Mohamed. *Countering Terrorism–The Maldivian Perspective: The Terror Challenge in South Asia and Prospect of Regional Cooperation* , IDSA Publication, 2012.

United Service Institute of India Articles

Agarwal, A. K. The Sri Lankan Experience in the Use of Air Power against LTTE in subduing the Maoists Insurgency. April-June 2013

Arya, Shailender. Myanmar: Simmering Insurgencies–Search for solutions. January-March 2014.

Chandan, Tejal. Sri Lanka: Prospects for Reconciliation. April–June 2014.

Chauhan, Sanjeev. Social Media: A Tool to Incite Ethno-Religious and Civil Society unrest in India. October-December 2013.

Davar, K. India's North West: The New Great Game. April-June 2013.

Dhowan, Adm R.K. Indian Ocean Region: Emerging Strategic Cooperation, Competition and Conflict Scenarios–Keynote address. October–December 2014.

Katoch, P.C. Countering Terrorism. July-September 2012.

Kundra, Swati. The Afghan National Solidarity Programme: A Grassroots Development and Governance Model. July-September 2013.

Mahadevan, Prem. National Counter Terrorism Centre: Critique and Recommendations. July-September 2012

Menon, M.S. The Indus Water Treaty-Changed Ground Realities Necessitate a Review. July–September 2014.

Rammohan, E.N. Spring Thunder in Bangladesh. April-June 2013.

Rammohan, E.N. Burma–In Retrospect and Prospect. April–June 2014.

Rammohan, E.N. The role of Pakistan in the Taliban Insurgency in Afghanistan. July–September 2014.

Rammohan, E.N. The Rise of the Islamic State of Iraq and Syria in the 21st Century. October–December 2014.

Sharma, J.C. Diaspora, Foreign Policy and National Security. July-September 2013.

Singh, K.R. Coastal security and Coastal states. July–September 2014.

Subbu, B.R. Geostrategic Importance of India's Island Territories and Implications for National Security. July-September 2013.

Institute for Defence Studies and Analyses (India)

Strategic Analysis, Volume 37, Number 2, March–April 2013

Bhat, R.K. Strategic Importance of Radio Kashmir in Countering Pakistan's War of Words against India.

Shah, Riddhi. Bangladesh-Myanmar ITLOS verdict: Precedence for India.

Shehzad, Mohammad. The state of Islamic radicalism in Pakistan.

Ogden, Chris. Beyond Succession: China's Internal Security Challenges.

Volume 37, Number 3, May–June 2013

Huda, Mirza. Can robust Bilateral Cooperation on Common Rivers Between Bangladesh and India Enhance Multilateral Cooperation on Water Security in South Asia?

Kumar, Anand. Impact of West Bengal Politics on India-Bangladesh relations.

Narula, Kapil. Energy Strategy for the Indian Navy: Need, Scope and a Roadmap.

Volume 37, Number 4, July–August 2013

Dasgupta, Sunil. How will India respond to Civil War in Pakistan?

Mazumdar, Arijit. Left Wing Extremism and Counterinsurgency in India: Andhra Model.

Volume 37, Number 6, November–December 2013

Mukherjee, Kunal. Prospects and challenges of ASEAN.

Ramana, P. V. Taming India's Maoists: Surrender and Rehabilitation.

Volume 38, Number 1, January–February 2014

Ngaihte, Thangkhanlal. Beyond the Indo-Naga Talks: Some Reflections.

Sen, Rabindra. India's South Asian Dilemma and Regional Cooperation: Relevance of cultural diplomacy.

Volume 38, Number 2, March–April 2014

Namboodri, P. K. S. Nuclear Terrorism.

Salik, Naeem. Nuclear Terrorism: Assessing the Danger.

Volume 38, Number 3, May–June 2014

Das, Pushpita. Issues in the Management of the India-Pakistan International Border.

Ghosh, P.K. Maritime Security Trilateralism: India, Sri Lanka and the Maldives.
Pattanaik, Smruti S. Northern Provincial Council: What does it mean for Tamil Political Aspirations in the Post-War context?
Volume 38, Number 4, July–August 2014
Chandra, Satish and Gupta, Arvind. India-Pakistan Human Rights Imbroglio in Geneva.
Heickero, Roland. Cyber Terrorism: Electronic Jihad.
Miklian, Jason. The Past, Present and Future of the 'Liberal Peace'.
Roberts, Adam. Addressing violent extremism: Lessons from Sri Lanka.
Volume 38, Number 5, September–October 2014
Pattanaik, Smruti S. The Tamil Nadu factor in post-War Sri Lanka: Perspectives of
Singh, Swaran and Krupakar, Jayanna. Indo–US Cooperation in Countering Cyber Terrorism: Challenges and Limitations.
Sinha, U.K. Water issues in the Near East and South Asia Region: Risks and Solutions;Tamils and Muslims.
Asian Strategic Review 2016. Terrorism: Emerging Trends, Editors: S.D. Muni & Vivek Chadha.

Indian Defence Review
Vol. 29 (3) July–September 2014
Sinha, Deepak. Employing Special Forces.
——Rightsizing the Military: The Need for a Comprehensive Examination, Net Edition, May 2016.
Special Correspondent. Modernising India's security sector for Homeland security.
Thapliyal, Sheru. The Challenges of Global Terrorism.

Centre for Land Warfare Studies (CLAWS)
Maneckshaw Papers
No. 35. Peoples Liberation Guerrilla Army of CPI (Maoists), 2012.
No. 38. The Kautilya Arthashastra: a Military Perspective, 2013.
No. 41. Circle of Treason: Bangladesh Beyond the Threat of Illegal Migration, 2013.
No. 44. Quest for Peace in Assam: A Study of the Bodoland Movement, 2014.
No. 59. Afghanistan: A Tale of Pakistan's Lies and Deceit, 2016.
Journal Summer 2012
Bahadur, Kalim. Pakistan as an Islamic state.
Bansal, Alok. Pakistan's Nationalism and Ethnic Pulls.
Katoch, Dhruv. Indus Waters and Pakistan: Seeds of Future Conflicts?
Spring 2012
Bansal, Alok. India and the new Myanmar.

Mukerjee , Udipan. On Counterinsurgency: Evaluating the role of civil militias.

Sering, Senge. Gilgit-Baltistan: An Overview.

Srivastava, Manoj. Intelligence mechanisms in our neighbourhood: An Indian perspective.

Summer 2013

Gokhale, Nitin. Higher Defence Management in India: Need for Urgent Reappraisal.

Kanwal, Gurmeet. Defence Reforms: Managing Threats and Challenges to National Security.

Singh, Jasjit. Higher Defence Management: Principles and Practice in India.

Autumn 2013

Hariharan, R. China's Strategic Presence in Sri Lanka.

Kanwal, Gurmeet. Pakistan–Afghan Relations: Challenging Prospects.

Lal, Avantika. Indian footprints in Afghanistan.

Winter 2013

Chaudhury, Rajeev. Violent Non-State Actors: Contours, Challenges and Consequences.

Dabas, Amit. Endgame in Afghanistan: Debating the Kashmir Connection.

Katoch, Dhruv. Combating Cross-border Terrorism: Need for a Doctrinal Approach.

Katoch, Prakash. Strategic Options against State Sponsored Terrorism.

Singh, R. S. N. Nepal on the edge.

Autumn 2014

Transition in Afghanistan: Future Scenarios.

Arya, Shailender. Xinjiang: China's Restive Northwest.

Bansal, Alok. Pakistan: Operations in North Waziristan Agency.

Bansal, Alok. War in Iraq and Implications for India.

CLAWS Research Team. Emerging situation in Pakistan.

Hariharan, R. Revival of Tamil Tigers in Sri Lanka.

Possible Scenarios.

Sareen, Sushant. Pakistan's Faults Worsen its Faultlines: Unfolding Situations.

Venkataraman, Arjun. Cyber War: An Emerging Threat in an Increasingly Connected World.

Summer 2014

Balasubramaniyan, V. Counter–Terrorism Approaches post -9/11: Challenges and Conflict Resolution.

Katoch, Dhruv. Tackling Left Wing Extremism: Current Trends and Road Map.

Kumar, Narender. Border Management with Myanmar: A Strategic Imperative. Responses.

South Asia Terrorism Portal

Mahadevan, Prem. The Gill Doctrine: A Model for 21st Century Counter-Terrorism?

Bangladesh Assessment: 2010-2016.

Bhutan Backgrounder

Nepal, Terrorist Groups.

Pakistan Assessment 2010-2016.

Balochistan Assessment 2016.

FATA Assessment 2015.

Khyber Pakhtunkhwa Assessment 2015.

Punjab Assessment 2015.

Sindh Assessment 2015.

Terrorist Groups

Sri Lanka Assessment 2016.

Faultlines: Volume 19, April 2008.

National Bureau of Asian Research

NBR Special Report #55. Mapping Pakistan's Internal Dynamics: Implications for State Stability and Regional Security, Washington, 2016.

Rand Corporation

Madden, Dan et al. Special Warfare: The Missing Middle in U.S. Coercive Options. Research Report, 2014.

Fair, Christine C. Urban Battle Fields of South Asia: Lessons Learned from Sri Lanka, India and Pakistan. Research Report, 2004.

Jones, Seth G. Counterterrorism and the Role of Special Operations Forces. Testimony before the Committee on Foreign Affairs Subcommittee on Terrorism, Non-Proliferation, and Trade, United States House of Representatives, April 8, 2014.

Dobbins, James et al. Choices for America in a Turbulent World. Research Report 2015.

Ayalon, Amichay and Jenkins, Brian. War by what means, according to whose rules? The Challenge for Democracies Facing Asymmetric Conflicts: Proceedings of a RAND–Israel Democracy Institute Workshop, December 3–4, 2014.

Blank, Jonah. Lashkar-e Taiba and the Threat to the United States of a Mumbai-Style attack. Testimony presented before the House Homeland Security Committee, Subcommittee on Counterterrorism and Intelligence on June 12, 2013.

Jenkins, Brian Michael. The Threat of a Mumbai-Style Terrorist Attack in the United States. Testimony submitted before the House Homeland Security Committee, Subcommittee on Counterterrorism and Intelligence on June 12, 2013.

Madden, Dan et al. Special Warfare: The Missing Middle in U.S. Coercive Options, 2014.

Libicki, Martin, C. Cyber Deterrence and Cyber War, 2009.

Chalk, Peter et al. The Evolving Terrorist Threat to Southeast Asia: A Net Assessment.2009.

Web Sources

http://www.vifindia.org/document/2011/the-unlawful-activities-prevention-amendment-bill

http://www.vifindia.org/document/2010/the-anti-hijacking-amendment-bill.

http://www.vifindia.org/document/2008/the-national-investigation-agency-act.

http://www.vifindia.org/document/2007/asean-convention-on-counter-terrorism.

http://www.vifindia.org/document/2004/the-prevention-of-terrorism-repeal-ordinance.

http://www.vifindia.org/document/2002/the-prevention-of-terrorism-act.

http://www.vifindia.org/document/2009/bimstec-convention-on-cooperation-in-combating-international-terrorism-transnational-organised-crime-and-illicit.

INDEX

*